Tolkien and Modernity
2

edited by
Thomas Honegger & Frank Weinreich

2006

Cormarë Series

No 10

Series Editors
Peter Buchs • Thomas Honegger • Andrew Moglestue

Library of Congress Cataloging-in-Publication Data

Honegger, Thomas and Frank Weinreich (editors)

Tolkien and Modernity 2

ISBN 978-3-905703-03-0

Subject headings:

Tolkien, J. R. R. (John Ronald Reuel), 1892-1973 – Criticism and interpretation
Tolkien, J. R. R. (John Ronald Reuel), 1892-1973 – Language
Fantasy fiction, English – History and criticism
Middle-earth (Imaginary place)
Literature, Comparative.
Modernism

All rights reserved. No portion of this book may be reproduced, by any process or technique, without the express written consent of the publisher.

for Jana (T.H.)

for my mother (1920-2006) (F.W.)

Table of Contents

Thomas Honegger & Frank Weinreich
Introduction   i

Patrick Brückner
Tolkien on Love
Concepts of 'Love' in *The Silmarillion*
and in *The Lord of the Rings*   1

Margaret Hiley
The Lord of the Rings and 'Late Style':
Tolkien, Adorno and Said   53

Martin Simonson
An Introduction to the Dynamics of
the Intertraditional Dialogue in *The Lord of the Rings*:
Aragorn's Heroic Evolution   75

Anna Slack
Slow-Kindled Courage. A Study of
Heroes in the Works of J.R.R. Tolkien   115

Judith Klinger
Hidden Paths of Time:
March 13th and the Riddles of Shelob's Lair   143

Thomas Honegger
The Passing of the Elves
and the Arrival of Modernity:
Tolkien's 'Mythical Method'   211

Heidi Krueger
The Shaping of 'Reality' in Tolkien's Works.
An Aspect of Tolkien and Modernity   233

Index   273

Introduction

Tom Shippey's *J.R.R. Tolkien: Author of the Century* was not the first, but certainly the most prominent study to claim Tolkien and his literary work for the 20th century. It does not lack a certain irony that the impetus to such an approach had come, once again (*pace* Rosebury), from a philologist. The arguments brought forward by Professor Shippey, Dr. Rosebury and other scholars have since then been taken up, modified, elaborated, criticized, emulated, and developed by various critics. As a consequence, an increasing number of literary scholars who are not primarily (or even secondarily) 'Tolkienists' have begun to treat Tolkien's works as 'mentionables'. Hard-core Tolkienists have to get used to the fact that a critic may not know the difference between light-elves and dark-elves or between Westernesse and Eriador, but that s/he, nevertheless, is able to contribute relevant points to the understanding of the literary quality of Tolkien's work. Books like *Reading The Lord of the Rings*, edited by Robert Eaglestone, illustrate the strengths (and minor weaknesses) of such a development.

The present volume(s) grew out of the wish to further the exploration of Tolkien as a 'contemporary writer', i.e. an author whose literary creations can be seen as a response to the challenges of the modern world. This does not mean that we should disregard or even consider obsolete the other, hitherto dominant approaches, such as the exploration of Tolkien's 'roots' in the medieval and philological traditions, his Victorian/Edwardian background, his Catholicism, etc. The shift of focus from Tolkien as 'the Other' towards Tolkien as a contemporary character has been overdue for a long time and complements these earlier approaches. Such a development is profitable for all involved since, if we want to see and appreciate the 'tree' in its entirety, it is necessary to look at it from as many points of view as possible.

The current volume, being the second of two dedicated to 'Tolkien and Modernity', comprises papers that focus on four broad themes: love, time, heroism, and style. Although one could argue that these topics have been present since the beginning of literature, though sometimes temporarily submerged, it is with the cataclysm of World War I and the entry of Einstein's Theory of Relativity into the public consciousness – two events that shook the very foundations of pre-modern society – that they gained a new and immediate relevance.

The trial of the trenches re-defined, the meaning of heroism. Many officers, who had carried *The Illiad* in their packs to the front, became painfully aware of the contrast between (literary) Homeric battles and the reality of modern warfare. Heroism no longer meant shining arms and trumpets, clashing of swords and red blood on white sand, but became rather the ability to endure the intellectually deadening monotony of the deadlock and the squalor of dirt, mud, and lice. It is against this background that Anna Slack analyses the heroism of the hobbits.

Furthermore, the circumstances often forced the fighting men into close-knit groups of mutual dependence and trust that, though based on older models, developed an emotional quality that is in many points similar to love. This development finds its literary epitome in the figures of Frodo and Sam, whom Patrick Brückner, in his contribution, compares to and contrasts with other typical lovers such as Beren and Lúthien or Arwen and Aragorn. His analysis goes beyond the superficial characterisations of (heterosexual) love and does not stop at the categorisation of Frodo and Sam as 'officer and batman', but provides a deeper understanding of their relationship by means of an analysis within the framework of the modern sociology of love.

The scientific proof that time is no uniform and linear phenomenon links earlier, pre-modern observations of 'Other Time' – such as found predominantly in fairy and folk tales – with the scholarly discourse. Verlyn Flieger, in her monograph *A Question of Time*, has discussed the relevant contemporary theories and publications on the subject and related them to Tolkien's concept of Time as found in his literary works. Her findings provide the starting point for Judith Klinger's analysis of the events of 13th March 2020 T.A. that, in a skilful combination of close reading and textual archaeology, relates the seeming discrepancies in Tolkien's chronology of events to the concept of Other Time.

In literature, modernity saw the rise of Modernism as a reaction to the loss of security and the failure of the 'canonical' tradition to provide adequate models for coming to terms with contemporary experiences. *The Lord of the Rings*, with its emphasis on loss and its dominant elegiac mood, reflects this. Tolkien's 'mythical method', as Thomas Honegger outlines in his paper, does not rely on irony or playfulness, but aims at smoothing the break without glossing over the feeling of loss and sorrow. Tolkien endeavours to come to terms with 'modernity' by means of providing the lost context(s) to the fragments of modern existence so that he – and his readers – arrive in modernity not via ironic disenchantment but by commemorating of what has been lost.

The concept of 'late style', which is about 'lost totality', melancholy, and death, is used by Margaret Hiley to point out essentially modern elements in Tolkien's work, placing him within a modern(ist) context.

Tolkien's narrative technique and his presentation of 'reality' are discussed in Heidi Krueger's essay. She demonstrates how Tolkien's creation of reality not only follows progressive literary programmes of earlier authors but also leads to new territory by means of his narrative technique – despite a superficially conventional narrative approach.

A few remarks on the editorial principles. Although we did not take lightly the responsibility of editing the two volumes, we opted for a 'light editorial hand' approach. This means that we strove to unify, as far as possible, (bibliographical) references, that we proofread the papers and suggested alterations and emendations to the authors, and that we kept an eye on the papers on similar topics in order to prevent too much of an overlap. Yet we decided against too strong an intervention in matters of style and culture-specific scholarly traditions. Many of the papers therefore still show (as is intended by the editors) their 'cultural' roots in their selection of themes and in the way they approach a topic – and give a wider audience the opportunity to gain a glimpse of the multiple traditions of international Tolkien scholarship.

Thomas Honegger & Frank Weinreich
Jena & Bochum, Summer 2006

Tolkien on Love
Concepts of 'Love' in
The Silmarillion and *The Lord of the Rings*

PATRICK BRUECKNER

Abstract

With Beren/Lúthien, Arwen/Aragorn and Sam/Frodo Tolkien has created three literary couples that have more in common than scholarship is often willing to acknowledge. Beren/Lúthien are generally read as the paradigmatic couple of lovers in *The Silmarillion* – validated by Tolkien's own marriage – and used as a foil for Arwen/Aragorn in *The Lord of the Rings*. Frodo/Sam, however, are constantly interpreted as exponents of friendship – another concept of forming couples. Yet when Luhmann's model that conceptualises love as communication, not emotion, is applied to all three couples, one finds that Sam/Frodo may be read as a variant of the Beren/Lúthien model even more easily than Arwen/Aragorn. The essay concludes that, notwithstanding all differences, these three couples must be understood as 'lovers'.

1 TOLKIEN ON LOVE

When talking about love, one thinks of grand emotions, internalisation, intimacy and not least of marriage. One knows what love is, what its symptoms are, that love makes a 'good marriage', but first and foremost one knows that one cannot force love (cf. Theweleit 1994:2). This knowledge, however, clashes with the fact that the notion of an intimate (hetero-normative) relationship of two individuals – marriage based on love – is an invention of modernity (cf. Luhmann 1986:32). In modern, functionally differentiated societies, love and its representations function as 'generalized symbolic media of communication'. This implies, too, that less differentiated societies will exhibit strategies for the formation of couples other than 'love'. The medium of love renders improbable events (two individuals – amongst many – meet and form a stable relationship) thinkable and, in fact, likely. Love, just like money or the law, is a regulatory medium that increases the possibility of improbable events (cf. Luhmann 1986:9ff.). Love most certainly is an emotion; if one were to call it simply a natural given, one would, however, have to turn a blind eye to some rather important aspects of 'love'.

As Western culture places love firmly within the realm of words – "Love was first and foremost a concern of literature" (Theweleit 1994:3) – it appears worthwhile to analyse the function and logic of love and loving relationships in Tolkien's texts. What does 'love' mean in Tolkien's works?

Pondering Tolkien's concepts of love and modes of marriage, one swiftly comes across something resembling a dogma in the critical reception of his work: Beren and Lúthien are generally identified as the dominant couple on which all other romantic couples are modelled. Structural similarities facilitate the identification of the most prominent heterosexual couple in *The Lord of the Rings*, namely Arwen/Aragorn, as a variation of Beren/Lúthien. Yet another couple whose story could be read as analogous to Beren/Lúthien meets far greater critical restraint. The relationship of Sam and Frodo is generally classified as a friendship that forever increases in intensity.[1] Friendship, as opposed to 'love', is then described as a fundamentally different concept of how couples relate. This essay intends to prove that an analysis focusing on the similarities between the relationships Beren/Lúthien, Arwen/Aragorn and Frodo/Sam could be worthwhile.

---

[1] Original: "[...] zunehmende[r] intensiver Freundschaft" (Döffinger 1997:101). All quotes in languages other than English were translated by Siobhán Groitl.

It is a curious fact that studies interpreting Tolkien's notions of love inexorably interweave seemingly fictional textuality with reality. In academic writing, Tolkien's own marriage to Edith takes on a paradigmatic role for all analyses of the constellation of Beren and Lúthien (and thus in turn of Arwen and Aragorn). It seems a given that "[t]he myth [of Beren and Lúthien] is a stylized version of Tolkien's own courtship" (Fredrick/McBride 2001:120) and that "the story of Beren and Lúthien remained deeply personal to Tolkien till he died: he had the names 'Beren' and 'Lúthien' carved on his and his wife's shared tombstone, a striking identification" (Shippey 2002:247).

How is one to approach this equivocation of a fictional relationship and a real-life marriage? Where is one to situate the couples Arwen/Aragorn and Frodo/Sam in relation to this paradigmatic relationship? This paper will not treat or explain love (especially not Tolkien's marriage) as part of a romantic writing but intends to analyse the function that 'love' performs in the texts themselves.

Niklas Luhmann states: "love will not be treated [...] as a feeling (or at least only secondarily so), but rather in terms of its constituting a symbolic code which shows how to communicate effectively in situations where this would otherwise appear improbable. The code thus encourages one to have the appropriate feelings" (Luhmann 1986:8ff.). Building on this insight, I will analyse how love is constructed and which discourses feed into its creation in Tolkien's texts, and, also, question whether the ongoing inscription of Tolkien's marriage into his literary œuvre is just another product of these discourses.

2 BEREN AND LÚTHIEN – A 'PRIVATE' KIND OF LOVE

> Ever since the world began it's been that way
> For man and woman were created to make love their destiny
> Then why should true love be so complicated?
> (*Tell him*, The Exciters)

What renders the love of the Elven princess Lúthien and the human Beren so obviously romantic? At first sight Tolkien's story does not even appear to be a 'real' love story: werewolves, vampires and monsters inhabit the pages, wolves gobble up limbs and it is death – not only of the couple – that ends it all. On the other hand, it is very much a story about 'love unto death'. In a letter from 1972, Tolkien himself calls the story a "romance" (Tolkien 2000:417); twenty years earlier, in another letter from 1951, he places the emphasis quite differently when he calls it: "the first example of the motive (to become dominant in Hobbits) that the great policies of world history [...], are often turned not by the Lords and Governors, even gods, but by the seemingly unknown and weak [...]" (Tolkien 2000:149).

Great restraint should be exercised when using Tolkien's letters as an interpretative tool for his stories;[2] both quotes, however, prove how differently this story can be read.

2.1 Falling in Love

What, then, makes this story a love story? Luhmann holds that love is "a symbolic code which shows how to communicate effectively in situations where this would otherwise appear improbable" (Luhmann 1986:8). Beren and Lúthien, however, do not seem to be in need of communication. (Doubtless, their encounter is just such an 'improbable' event. The

---

[2] Why Tolkien's remarks on Beren and Lúthien, and on his œuvre in general, can only be read as interpretations in their own right, cf. Foucault (2001).

general, symbolic code 'love' thus lends itself rather easily as the communicative medium of choice.) Lúthien's appearance and song suffice for Beren to lose himself in love for her. The woman's beauty is all it takes to trigger the man's desire, and this might explain why beauty is Lúthien's only signifier initially:

> Lúthien was the most beautiful of all the Children of Ilúvatar. Blue was her raiment as the unclouded heaven, but her eyes were grey as the starlit evening; her mantle was sewn with golden flowers, but her hair was dark as the shadows of twilight. As the light upon the leaves of trees, as the voice of clear waters, as the stars above the mists of the world, such was her glory and her loveliness; and in her face was a shining light. (Tolkien 2001:194)

It is this beauty that tumbles Beren "into an enchantment" (Tolkien 2001:194). Beren's gaze, however, is not sufficient to bind her to him. Both remain on their own, and it is only when Lúthien sings that Beren becomes an active agent. He calls out to her and gives her a new name: a name of his own creation. With this, all distance is overcome, and he may approach her. It is her song that performs the trick of turning a wilderness into an artificial location that allows for the emergence of love.[3] But it remains unclear what triggers Lúthien's desire. One is tempted to assume that she only desires Beren because he desires her. In this context, Luhmann talks about the "possibility of anticipation: one can orientate oneself towards the inner experience of the other person" (Luhmann 1986: 23); an altogether romantic notion of silent collusion. However, one needs to take into account the fact that the text adopts the male – Beren's – perspective: "In his [Beren's] fate Lúthien was caught" (Tolkien 2001:195).

---

[3] Cf. Eilmann (2006:108ff.).

We do not, in fact, observe the merging of two fates, but watch Beren's fate becoming Lúthien's. Up to this point, we may safely say that this story describes a man taking possession of a woman:[4] an altogether less romantic notion. The beautiful woman, i.e. Lúthien, has only one *raison d'être*: saving a man. Beauty has the power to do so: "The idea of beauty's perfection is so compelling because it disproves the idea of disintegration, fragmentation and insufficiency" (Bronfen 1992:62). Only as 'lover' may the utterly bereft Beren be rendered a subject again. For this, he depends on Lúthien. (Lúthien, in turn, receives her subject status only upon becoming a 'lover'.)[5]

One aspect becomes clearer now. Even before meeting Lúthien, Beren has a story of his own that is firmly based in the realm of the political. It involves the loss of a country, indeed of a whole people. Beren's social ties and their subsequent loss have to be taken into account to better understand his turning to Lúthien. Beren undoubtedly is a hero; his political agency, however, has been increasingly curtailed by the passing of his father and all remaining allies.

All alone in the world, he reverts to something resembling a 'state of nature': "he became the friend of birds and beasts, and they aided him" (Tolkien 2001:192). The help of these creatures, however, does not strengthen his agency, but rather undermines it: "Beren was pressed so hard that at last he was forced to flee" (Tolkien 2001:193). It is in exile that he encounters Lúthien and transforms his 'political' persona

---

[4] It might be worthwhile to interpret "and she loved him; yet she slipped from his arms and vanished from his sight even as the day was breaking" (Tolkien 2001:194) as indicative of a sexual encounter, in analogy to the Middle High German genre *Tagelied* (cf. Dronke 1968:182ff.). We would thus be faced with a physical encounter that is not the effect of an 'emotion', but the very reason for it. "The tragedy is not longer that the lovers fail to find each other, but rather in the fact that sexual relationships produce love and that one can neither live in keeping with it nor free oneself of it" (Luhmann 1986:160). Sexuality as such could thus take on a rather negative connotation.

[5] On the subject status cf. Althusser (1970:90ff.).

into a private one. Beren wants to be strong again, whole and integrated; Lúthien functions as the means to that end. His 'enchantment' can thus be identified as Beren's desire for identity; to be precise, he is not looking for Lúthien but for an identity restored by Lúthien: "in his fate Lúthien was caught" (Tolkien 2001:195). Lúthien so far has no fate of her own, as Beren is already in possession of hers and will eventually bestow it on her. Her fate is to share his and to (re-)construct his and, consequently, her own identity.

Lúthien 'anticipates'.[6] As they can only communicate on the basis of the code of 'love', Lúthien may interpret Beren's call only in relation to this code (and not, for instance, as indicative of 'danger'). Thus she can act as 'lover' instantaneously, with no need for further communicative effort on Beren's part. She can do so as their relationship is an absolutely private matter, so that she need not position herself in relation to a third party (cf. Luhmann 1986:23). The relationship, at this stage, is absolutely self-reflexive and asocial. It is the *site* where it occurs that renders it possible and safe. The forest is among those places "which are something like counter-sites [heterotopias], a kind of effectively enacted utopia in which the real sites, all the other real sites that can be found within the culture, are simultaneously represented, contested, and inverted" (Foucault 1986:24).[7] Heterotopias differ from utopias in that they do not proffer virtual counter-models to, or improvements of, existing social conditions, but can be described as "real

---

[6] "In other words, the lover does not need to be turned in by action, question or requests on the part of the beloved: the latter's inner experience is supposed to immediately trigger the lover's action" (Luhmann 1986:25). Lúthien is turning into the bearer of 'love' by anticipating Beren's symbolic actions and thus rendering them unnecessary for the time being. In this instance it is the woman who initiates and performs 'love' by acting on the assumption that the man is 'capable of love'. (It is appropriate that Beren is interpellated as such as he is by then unfit for all other forms of socialisation.)

[7] Original: "[...] lieux qui s'opposent à tous les autres, qui sont destinés en quelque sorte à les effacer, à les compenser, à les neutraliser ou à les purifier. Ce sont en quelque sorte des contre-espaces" (Foucault 2005:40).

places – places that do exist and that are formed in the very founding of society [...]. Places of this kind are outside of all places, even though it may be possible to indicate their location in reality" (Foucault 1986:24).

Beren's and Lúthien's subjectivisation depends on this counter-site. It is the pre-requisite for their self-referentiality and subjectivisation as 'lovers' as well. Their love is something supremely private.

2.2 Conditions

Love, however, is more than a simple private matter. Beren and Lúthien are discovered and their love in its 'political' manifestation turns into a problem for society. After a short respite in the sylvan idyll, their relationship is made public. As a consequence, Lúthien cannot freely 'anticipate' any longer: The relationship enters a new phase.

That Lúthien has her father swear an oath to leave Beren unharmed, and presents him to her father, the King "as if he were a honoured guest" (Tolkien 2001:195), only superficially serves to protect Beren's life. In a far more encompassing sense, these measures serve to ensure Beren's continued ability to interact successfully.

Now the heart of the matter is no longer how the couple's private relationship may be characterised, but rather how the lovers may be integrated into the existing societal structure. The story is no longer about Lúthien. The need to render Beren – the unknown outsider – socially intelligible is paramount. Thingol's question, "Who are you, [...] that come hither as a thief, and unbidden dare to approach my throne?" (Tolkien 2001:195), is highly significant. It is essential to establish the identity of whoever approaches the throne. The love of a King's daughter always comes with (at least) half a kingdom.

Thingol's questions do not focus on love as a 'private matter' but negotiate its political dimensions when he inquires about the suitor's genealogy ("baseborn mortal") and allegiance ("who in the realm of Morgoth has learnt to creep") (Tolkien 2001:196). It is no coincidence that neither love nor beauty (both signifiers without political relevance) lead to the crucial insight that "it [Beren's fate] is wound with yours [Thingol's]" (Tolkien 2001:196), but Beren's bloodline and heroic deeds, as symbolised by Felagund's (Barahir's) ring.

A strange paradox arises: the seemingly 'private' (love) and the 'political' (governance) intersect. Lúthien's love has already so successfully incorporated Beren into the social organism that he cannot be removed without significantly harming its integrity. The fulcrum of Thingol's politics is squarely placed within the centre of his private existence: it is Lúthien. Within the economy of an exchange of daughters and goods,[8] Lúthien is thus rendered an object; she turns into a "treasure" (Tolkien 2001:197), just like the Silmarils, one of which Beren is supposed to hand over in exchange for taking possession of Lúthien.

This task seems impossible: a venture that must end in certain death. There is precious little logic in Beren's acceptance of Thingol's offer. Theweleit, however, points out that "[c]ombining love & marriage transgresses the socio-economic rules, one could also say, economic reason. For this [...] a certain state is required, a state [...] of exquisite madness" (Theweleit 1994:6). This is not (only) about the economy (of exchange), but also about love and its secondary function of bestowing identity on the implicated lovers. The private aspect leads Beren to dismiss all calculation: The code of 'love' functions "to secure an adequate degree of probability for the reception of improbable expectations" (Luhmann 1986:55). Beren is incapable of calmly calculating the risks and benefits of the venture ahead, because if he were, 'love' would already have been replaced by economic reasoning pure and sim-

---

[8] "In these types of marriage, the 'woman' (a daughter) is either part of the paternal economy bringing money or taking some of it away, creating coalitions and power and business ties; or is part and parcel of her husband's economic needs; she must restore his energies for work, help him get by or climb the ranks." (Theweleit 1994:4f.)

ple; Beren would have lost his status as lover and, as a consequence, his subjectivity. The logic of the private that initially rendered him a political subject, now forces him to act politically against all odds. Love forces him to act, against all reason.

2.3 Being in Love

The crux of the code of 'love' lies in the fact that it absolutely demands the voluntary and unconstrained nature of all decisions made within this context (cf. Luhmann 1986:50ff.). Despite a strong economic imperative, Thingol insists: "if she will, Lúthien may set her hand in yours" (Tolkien 2001:197). The flipside of 'love's' voluntary nature, however, rests in the fact that one can never be certain of one's 'lover's love' and thus forever depends on proofs of love.

This "double contingency – the freedom each partner has to decide whether or not to become involved in a love relationship" (Luhmann 1986:50) – constantly requires signs that confirm and thus renew the existence of the loving relationship. Separation will always constitute a great danger to any such relationship,[9] but will paradoxically provide the very possibility for proofs of love.

Beren and Lúthien must separate. Initially, both behave according to the clichés of established gender roles: "Lúthien was silent, and from that hour she sang not again" (Tolkien 2001:198). She is left quite passive and ceases her only activity, singing. The one for whom her song constructs the world is absent. These 'lovers' mean the world to each other! Beren, on the other hand, actively enters the 'political' realm. He renews old treaties, always lovingly recalling Lúthien: "he [Beren] wept, recalling Lúthien and their joy together" (Tolkien 2001:199). Both suffer from and for love and thus keep it alive. The lovers' tor-

---

[9] As beauty is neither a universal nor constant notion (cf. Wolf 1990:13), and it is Lúthien's beauty that renders her Beren's love object, it is she that must suffer most from uncertainty.

ment constitutes the very first step in shifting their relationship from the heterotopia of the forest – a location not accessible by society – towards an acceptable socio-political framework whilst staying 'lovers'. Luhmann points out: "Love inevitably ends [...]. The essence of love itself, excessiveness, is the very reason for its end" (Luhmann 1986:70).

Separation and the pain it causes thus produce the emotion: "Love, however, only existed as the 'not yet'; the moment of happiness and the eternity of suffering mutually determine each other, are identical" (Luhmann 1986:71). But the commingling of the political agenda and that of 'love' harbours great risks, as the forging of political alliances does not necessarily win or confirm 'love'. Quite the reverse: the private threatens the public realm. Felagund is aware of that: "it seems that this doom goes beyond his purpose" (Tolkien 2001:199). Oaths, vows and political will collide with Beren's private amorous desires and eventually threaten – as will be shown later – the social order in its entirety. Ostensibly political means are discounted as a feasible method of generating 'love' relationships. The traditional economic-political model, aimed at forming alliances, can no longer encompass Beren's private agenda and now requires a new element: 'love'. This new factor does not simply emulate the economic logic of an exchange of goods but requires its active production by both 'lovers'. An explanation for Beren's and Felagund's respective failures could then be that the wrong agents are using incorrect means.

Their attempt at proving their valour and worth by committing heroic deeds (reflecting a medieval logic of adventure) is no longer apt. They must prove their mettle in their role as 'lovers'. The 'couple', and thus also Lúthien, must actively work at love. Lewis and Currie are certainly correct when they comment that Lúthien "is active, not passive; she has her own creative powers; she knows her own will and is prepared to act on it" (Lewis/Currie 2002:196).

This, however, does not solve the riddle of what Lúthien's 'own will' desires, as she is most certainly not the 'girly-type' that Lewis/Currie make her out to be. She is not "any father's nightmare" (Lewis/Currie 2002:196), it is just that she knows that 'love' for her now means "activities and events [...] judged in terms of what they may possibly imply for the future" (Luhmann 1986:71). The experience shared with Beren thus forges a bond that may be identified as an expression of love, hereby constituting the exceptional, singular status of the loved one.

When Lúthien encounters Celegorm and Curufin during her flight, a scene takes place that may be read as a parallel to her very first meeting with Beren. Lúthien makes herself known and "so great was her sudden beauty revealed beneath the sun that Celegorm became enamoured of her" (Tolkien 2001:204). She does not reciprocate his feelings – for a very simple reason: Celegorm and Curufin are exponents of the father-husband economic discourse. They intend "to keep Lúthien" (Tolkien 2001:204) in order to eventually accrue "all the might of the Elf-kingdoms under their hands" (Tolkien 2001:204).

Lúthien has risen above this concept as she "spoke often [...] in her loneliness, telling of Beren" (Tolkien 2001:204). It is of paramount importance for 'love', as Roland Barthes states, that memory within the discourse of love create an imperfect (past) tense (cf. Barthes 1990:216), thus simultaneously imagining a future centred on the loved object. (The significance of this discursive mechanism will become apparent later.)

First, we need to understand the role that the dog Huan plays for Lúthien when she remembers Beren. Two attributes distinguish his character: "[he] was true of heart, and the love of Lúthien had fallen upon him [...] and [he] understood all that was said" (Tolkien 2001:204). Huan not only understands the words spoken but he comprehends their symbolic dimension, as he grasps their meaning with his heart. As a consequence, his love for Lúthien renders him the only one in the story capable of understanding the 'love' that Beren and Lúthien feel, apart from the lovers themselves. We thus observe a quasi-naturalisation of the discourse of love.[10] Love (the text seems to say) does not depend on social interaction, but is firmly placed within the 'interior' – of the heart. Any (albeit noble) creature may testify to this fact.

The importance of remembering the loved one is highlighted by the manner in which Lúthien frees Beren. Their second encounter directly alludes to the scene in the forest of Neldoreth:

> [S]he [Lúthien] sang a song that no walls of stone could hinder. Beren heard, and he thought that he dreamed; for the stars shone above him, and in the trees nightingales were singing. And in the answer he sang a song of challenge that he had made in praise of the Seven Stars, the Sickle of the Valar that Varda hung above the North as a sign for the fall of Morgoth. Then all strength left him and he fell down into darkness. (Tolkien 2001:205)

Once again Lúthien appears right at the moment when Beren is all alone, bereft of political allies, facing his death; and once again she sings, prompting Beren to recall a whole panoply of images. Against the reality of the present world, this song creates an 'other space', a heterotopia, that cancels out the reality of the dungeon. The forest reappears and Beren is no longer a stranger to it. The song of the nightingales reveals the exclusive character of this site.

Only Beren and Lúthien ('Tinúviel') may enter here. Because they are part of this place, Beren is able to answer. The distinctly 'political' character of the lyrics indicates that their 'love' is about to leave the private sphere, turning into an impulse to act in public. Not only Sauron

---

[10] Huan also represents the 'divine' nature of 'love' as he is a creature of the Valar.

is defeated in the name of 'love'; this 'love' continues to do good even after Huan (whose role will be explored later on) has chased Sauron away. "Then Lúthien [...] declared her Power: and the spell was loosed that bound stone to stone, and the gates were thrown down, and the walls opened, and the pits laid bare; and many thralls and captives came forth in wonder" (Tolkien 2001:207).

Lúthien's power is the power of 'love', an 'enchantment' protecting her against the terrible world, which, for the very first time, becomes visible for all *within* this same world. When Beren and Lúthien reunite, a temporary paradise bursts forth around them: "flowers lingered where Lúthien went, and the birds sang beneath the snowclad hills" (Tolkien 2001:207). The 'imperfect (past) tense' is taken up again. Love is renewed in the couple's serial action, but this love is also a throwback to a privacy that completely turns its back on society. Its exponent is (still) only the woman; Beren, on the other hand, "took thought his vow" (Tolkien 2001:208).

It seems as if Beren has not yet grasped the logic of 'coupling' within the conceptual framework of 'love'. He intends to return Lúthien to her father in order to then re-exchange her for the object her father demands. Lúthien has good reason to disagree. Luhmann expounds on the character of intimate love relationships: "[they do not] depend on qualities [...]; what is important is the other person in my environment who bestows meaning upon my world, but can only do so if I accept him and his environment as my own" (Luhmann 1986:174).

Meaning is thus not generated through outside confirmation, but by the other 'lover' and the couple's ensuing joint (confirming) experiences. Beren's oath has become irrelevant for Lúthien; she only cares that their "doom shall be alike" (Tolkien 2001:209). She defines her status as a subject in relation to the lover alone. For Beren, his love and his oath remain two distinctly separate matters (cf. Tolkien 2001:210).

Beren still privileges his existence as a 'political subject',[11] yet this lasts for only a short while. When he sings in memory of Lúthien on the border of enemy territory, another heterotopia is called forth. With the arrival of Lúthien and her active willingness to weave Beren's fate into her own, this imaginary space turns into a site in the 'real' world.

Only after Huan's instruction does Beren finally understand "that Lúthien could not be divided from the doom that lay upon them both" (cf. Tolkien 2001:211). So Beren – it seems – has finally grasped in its entirety the concept of love. We know that Beren has indeed internalised this concept when, on turning into a monster, he manages to keep his inner self unaffected: "Beren became in all things like a werewolf to look upon, save that in his eyes there shone a spirit grim indeed but clean" (Tolkien 2001:212).

However, the concept that Beren only manages to grasp eventually has been lived by Huan for quite some time in the text. Huan can, in fact, be read as a counter-model to the male hero. The initial bellicose logic of Beren, the warrior, is juxtaposed with Huan's empathy as a 'Schöne Seele' [beautiful, i.e. sensitive, soul]. For there is more involved than the mere conquest of a woman. Huan actually demonstrates that beneath the exterior of the 'animal' man, there is someone who "is not only generous, patient, free of anger and uncontrolled emotions" (Oesterle 2002:187),[12] but also "capable of sympathetically meeting a woman's wishes up to the point of complete self sacrifice" (Oesterle 2002:187).[13]

---

[11] The attack by Curufin/Celegorm supports Lúthien's logic, as the reciprocity of their saving each other's life proves that the world of one can (physically) only continue with the other.

[12] Original: "[...] nicht nur großzügig, geduldig, frei von Zorn und Affektausbrüchen."

[13] Original: "[...] bis zur Selbstaufgabe fähig, auf die Wünsche einer Frau sympathetisch einzugehen."

The couple may now turn to their joint task; initially, they are quite successful at it. The guards at the gate are overcome and Morgoth's court is sung to sleep by Lúthien (cf. Tolkien 2001:212ff.). But why does Morgoth fall asleep? Within this text, Lúthien's song has the power to bring forth the heterotopia of a *locus amoenus* (a paradisical place). If, as Foucault claims, heterotopias are capable of neutralising their counter-sites, we could argue that the political realm of Morgoth is neutralised by Lúthien's song.[14]

The sphere of the political, and Morgoth within it, are temporarily suspended. Read thus, the text constructs 'love' as the only way of fulfilling a task that has been created for this very purpose. Love can bestow the power to create heterotopias and to potentially improve on the existing father-husband economy.

The heterotopia collapses at the very moment when Beren sets out to do more than his love-task requires. The text remains silent on the reasons for his attempts to acquire all Silmarils, but we may safely assume that he wants to better his social status. As his task has to be fulfilled solely because of 'love', this action that is not primarily caused by love must destroy the *locus amoenus*. Morgoth awakes.

Beren has to leave behind the Silmaril – now the token of his merely half-hearted love – in the innards of the wolf Carcharoth. Eagles save the lovers (cf. Tolkien 2001:214ff.), but Beren continues to languish at the threshold of death: "Long Beren lay, and his spirit wandered upon the dark borders of death, knowing ever an anguish that pursued him" (Tolkien 2001:216).

How may one interpret Beren's torment? The 'merging' that Beren and Lúthien have undergone has a counter-model in what Luhmann calls the "concept of interpersonal interpenetration"

---

[14] As Morgoth is incapable of accessing this space, we understand why he is the only one who, on beholding Lúthien's beauty, does not fall in love but into "evil lust" (Tolkien 2001:213).

(Luhmann 1986:174). All actions of one lover may be judged by the other with regard to whether they signal or exclude love. Beren must fear that Lúthien will judge him thus. His double failure (as 'lover' and within the husband-father economy) might render him unfit as an adequate 'lover'. Therein lies his torment. It is no coincidence that only Lúthien's song, reflecting her recollection of him, can relieve him of his suffering. And she sings, indeed. Once merged, the text does not allow for any "interpersonal interpenetration" between these lovers. 'Love', the text states, is absolute.

This renewal of their love (cf. Tolkien 2001:216ff.) once again is not meant to last: "but he [Beren] could not for long forget his oath [...]. For he held by the law of Men, deeming it perilous to set at naught the will of the father" (Tolkien 2001:216). It is the conflict between the political and the private sphere that forces Beren to return to Menegroth, even though Lúthien suggests a joint exile in the forests. He must refuse. Lúthien, the woman, bases her identity on a 'love' that is firmly located in the private realm. For Beren, who set out to fulfil his side of a father-husband transaction and finds himself enclosed in the privacy of a love story, this state cannot suffice.

Concern for Lúthien is not the reason why Beren appears before Thingol. This becomes apparent the very moment he states his intention: "I am come now to claim my own" (Tolkien 2001:218). He resorts to the language of the father-husband economy. This sentence is just as equivocal as the proof for fulfilling his task that he offers Thingol. Lúthien is his own because he has performed something that surpasses the father-husband economy: "And it seemed to Thingol that [...] the love of Lúthien [was] a thing new and strange" (Tolkien 2001:218). Beren and Lúthien have succeeded in adding something to the transactions of the marriage economy. They have developed empathy; they have developed feelings for each other. They marry. That is love!

If the story of Beren and Lúthien ended here, its fairytale aspects would dominate. The world would have been made a better place. The numerous monsters, werewolves and vampires would simply have put the lovers to the test; a test that needed to be passed to "sanction an anarchistic morale that finally the world works the way it should" (Brittnacher 1994:14).[15] The lovers would have lived happily ever after.

The story, however, ends in death. Brittnacher points out that elements of horror can be read as symptoms of a conflict of social order. Beren's and Lúthien's new concept of love threatens the political sphere and the common welfare is in danger. Even though they are implicated in the father-husband economy, they remain first and foremost self-centred and 'strange'. The victory of 'love' is followed by Carcharoth's destruction of Doriath. The egotistic quest to 'love each other' has upset the social order of the world of which they are a part; the price paid for this love is the destruction that now threatens everybody. It is significant that Carcharoth is motivated as much by self-centred pain as the lovers are motivated by self-centred torment. It is self-centredness – their private motives – that lie at the root of the ensuing destruction.

The permanent transformation of the heterotopia into the social-political realm has failed. To compound the problem, the logic of the father-husband economy also threatens the social order. Beren and Lúthien have set loose the destructive force that is now threatening Doriath, yet Thingol and his mode of marriage politics have triggered this fatal sequence of events in the first place. It is no coincidence that Thingol's politico-economically motivated actions result in dire political fallout: the monstrous wolf, after all, is a creature of his political enemy Morgoth.

---

[15] Original: "[...] eine anarchistische Moral zu sanktionieren, nach der es endlich einmal in der Welt zugeht, wie es dort eigentlich zugehen sollte."

The competition of different orders of forming couples causes a catastrophe. In order to prevent this, ('private') man has to recall his political responsibilities: "Beren [...] understood, that the Quest was not yet fulfilled" (Tolkien 2001:219). This time the oath is adhered to, the 'political' asserts its dominance and simultaneously generates the question about the authenticity of 'love'. At this point, it is impossible to establish whether Beren loves Lúthien of his own accord, or whether he desires her as part of the economy of exchange. Beren has successfully turned into a rational, political subject, whether he has succeeded in becoming an empathic lover as well remains unclear. He dies as an agent in the political realm.

Beren's passing also affects Lúthien's status as a (love-)subject. The question that remains concerns the unique nature of her relationship with Beren. It is conceivable that she would 'anticipate' another man, which would once again render her an object of exchange within the father-husband economy. As we have tried to show, Luhmann's notion of 'interpersonal interpenetration' remains alien to the text. Lúthien's love always remains in the imperative. She renews her love for Beren, suffering and remembering him, as her song actually calls forth a final heterotopia that firmly excludes all things political and public. True love, after all, usually ends in death!

2.4 The Structure of Love I

Building on the analysis of Beren's and Lúthien's 'love', we will attempt to feed the specific findings into a more general structure.

This story is less about 'love' than it is about the correct strategy of turning into a couple. The text is not so interested in describing how 'love' comes about, but focuses on its specific character, its social positioning and general effects on society. With regards to the latter, 'love' seems to compete with an apparently older model of the father-husband economy.[16] Both strategies are represented in the text. Obviously, Thingol represents the economy of exchange, whereas Huan and Lúthien represent the concept of 'love'. This may seem odd, but, as mentioned before, Huan can be interpreted as a representative of the 'sympathetic', a constituent of 'love' in this text.[17] Beren gets entangled in both models. 'Love' in this text is first and foremost kindled by the perception of a body. The strong emphasis on Lúthien's extraordinary beauty and the early 'erotic' encounter might be taken as evidence for my argument. However, her looks seem not to suffice (any longer).

Speaking about Romanticism, Luhmann postulates: "The man loved loving, the woman loved the man; [...] the woman was the primary lover and enabled him to love" (Luhmann 1986:136). This description shifts into focus the disjunction at the very heart of the text. It is more than obvious that Lúthien loves Beren so much that she is willing to sacrifice herself for him. (It is highly significant that she saves his life all of five times in this rather short story.) It is the primary function of her love to render the man 'capable of love'. The text points out the means to effect this transformation: selfless sacrifice, renewal of love in 'memory', interiorisation and 'merging'. These are the cause and aim of Lúthien's "own will".

To be able to compete with and within the established model of the father-husband economy, 'love' requires an active and decisive woman. Lúthien is anything but a "young thing, wild or merely bright [and] always mobile" (Rowbotham 1999:120) that Sheila Rowbotham identifies as symptomatic of English society in the 1920s and '30s. These "young thing[s]" only ever affected the public sphere.

---

[16] One could also inquire whether on introducing the new notion of 'love', the concept of 'privacy' is grafted onto the text simultaneously.

[17] The fact that Huan's 'love' is of an entirely moral character not tainted by economic considerations, is proven by his leaving Celegorm once he starts behaving in an amoral fashion.

All of Lúthien's activities are focussed on Beren. It is she who keeps providing all the ingredients to concoct 'romantic love'. Beren cannot fully participate in this endeavour, as 'romantic love' is a most private matter, and he only seems capable of fully supporting the notion of 'romantic love' enclosed within a heterotopic space. That music generates this perfect heterotopic space corresponds with a well-developed romantic concept. Music in the romantic period is perceived as "a perfect, *qua* unfettered (absolute) form of expression, that has shed all aporias inherent to language as it is rid off the basic tension between ›nature‹ and ›sign‹. [It] has no representational function; it points to nothing [...] and thus is of an utmost autonomy" (Lubkoll 1994:342).[18]

It is the very unboundedness and lack of referentiality of this heterotopia that prevent Beren from fully immersing himself in 'romantic love'. Neither 'love' nor 'marriage' may ever be a completely private matter. Butler points out that "[t]he state receives its army from the family, and the family meets its dissolution in the state" (Butler 2000:36). The political will always dominate the private. Beren and Lúthien, and the concept of love that is bound up with them, attempt to reverse this constellation and so dissolve the political through the private. This is no ethical mode of conduct. But, as some aspects to the subject Beren are too firmly entrenched within the political, the only recourse left for him is to attempt a balancing act that can only fail. (Huan, on the other hand, is capable of acting thus, but he 'loves' no specific other.)

Love thus needs a special space of its own, or else it is condemned to fail. It is death that finally bestows this space on the lovers. It is only there and then that Beren can 'love' to the exclusion of everything else.

---

[18] Original: "[...] eine vollkommene, weil ›losgelöste‹ (ab-solute) Ausdrucksform, die sich der Aporien der Sprache, der grundlegenden Spannung zwischen ›Natur‹ und ›Zeichen‹, entledigt. [Sie hat] keine Abbildfunktion, sie verweist auf nichts [...] und folgt daher einer größtmöglichen Autonomie."

In order for this to come about, both lovers have to actively engage with the tasks that their respective spheres allot to them: both sacrifice themselves for their cause. Beren does so for politics, for the state and honour; Lúthien for the realm of the private, for 'love'. At the very end, both conduct themselves in accordance with a moral code and accept the separation of both spheres by embracing their respective 'correct' deaths. Then, and only then, can their relationship be transported into a final lasting heterotopia – a love that outlives death.

3 ARWEN AND ARAGORN – GOOD COUPLE, BAD LOVE

> you'll have bad times
> and he'll have good times
> (*Stand by your man*, Tammy Wynette)

Before any attempt can be made to interpret the story of Arwen and Aragorn, one peculiar difficulty must be acknowledged: there is, strictly speaking, no such story in *The Lord of the Rings*. At first, the narrator comment introduces Arwen: "So it was that Frodo saw her whom few mortals had yet seen; Arwen" (Tolkien 1995:221). Then, towards the end of the novel, the wedding of Arwen and Aragorn comes about as a rather unexpected event (cf. Tolkien 1995:951), while the actual story may be found only in the shadowy realm of Appendix A. Cathy Akers-Jordan states that "[c]asual readers [...] might see Arwen Undómiel as either a fairy princess (a prize for Aragorn's successful completion of his quest) or a tragic heroine (who dies in despair after the death of her beloved)" (Akers-Jordan 2004:195).

Tolkien himself does not seem to have been particularly interested in their relationship. In a letter draft he mentions their story, but attributes little significance to it: "When she [Arwen] weds Aragorn (whose love-story elsewhere recounted is not here central and only occasionally referred to) [...]" (Tolkien 2000:192).[19] Why is their story not a love-story? Because love plays no part in its rendering within the main text? If one focussed exclusively on *The Lord of the Rings,* such a conclusion might be valid, but the story in Appendix A raises some complex issues.

3.1 Falling in Love

If Theweleit is correct in stating that 'love' is, first and foremost, a problem of literature, and if we follow Luhmann in his claim that "personal elements began to enter into literature, and literature was in turn interpreted with reference to the personal element" (Luhman 1986:135), then some aspects of the factors that turn Arwen/Aragorn into a couple may become clearer. When Aragorn sets eyes on Arwen for the very first time, "[he] had been singing a part of the Lay of Lúthien which tells of the meeting of Lúthien and Beren in the forest of Neldoreth" (Tolkien 1995:1033). He sings, sees Arwen and "yet from that hour he loved Arwen" (Tolkien 1995:1033).

It is the same story. The correct text (the Lay of Lúthien), sung in the correct location (the forest), in the presence of the correct person (Arwen) generates an emotion. Sometimes 'love' can be as easy as that![20] At least, at first sight ... Only the day before, Aragorn discovered *his story*; he, who had been raised fatherless in exile, finds himself heir to Barahir's ring and the broken sword, Narsil. His kinship ties (with Beren amongst others) and his fate (a long and difficult quest) have been revealed to him (cf. Tolkien 1995:1032).

---

[19] The fact that Tolkien in yet another letter calls it "the highest love-story" (Tolkien 2000:160) just goes to show how little we may trust the interpretations that he proffers.

[20] 'Love' here is rendered visible (lisible) by referring to the (literary) paradigmatic couple Beren/Lúthien.

When – on the very next day! – Aragorn encounters Arwen, under the circumstances mentioned above, he also 'anticipates' – himself. He relates the prophecy of his fate to what is happening there and then, and draws the correct conclusion: He recognizes 'Tinúviel'. Aragorn is an exponent of "object-choice according to the social climbing strategy model: loving or marrying the object which helps one become what one wishes to be or wishes to be in future" (Theweleit 1994:39). However, his love is not (yet) reciprocated.

3.2 Conditions

There are several reasons to identify Aragorn's 'love' as a "social climbing strategy" put into action. At the end of *The Lord of the Rings* Arwen is handed over alongside the Sceptre of Annúminas (cf. Tolkien 1995:951). Also, Aragorn's mother herself points out the insurmountable nature of the difference in social status: "My son [...] your aim is high, even for the descendant of many kings. For this lady is the noblest and fairest that now walks the earth. And it is not fit that mortal should wed with the Elf-kin" (Tolkien 1995:1034).

Another indicator for the enormous potential residing in a relationship with Arwen can be found in Aragorn's conversation with Elrond. They seem to be going through the motions within the structure of a father-husband economy, negotiating the deeds Aragorn has to perform in order to attain Arwen. However, the main concern is that Aragorn must guarantee her a minimum of social status, once they are married (cf. Tolkien 1995:1036).

3.3 Love

It seems that Aragorn is set to emulate Beren's fate. But Aragorn has one advantage: he is capable – from the very beginning – to 'empathise' with his love(d) object. He can relate to her in a way that transcends the merely physical: "yet even in the saying he [Aragorn] felt that this high lineage, in which his heart had rejoiced, was now of little worth, and as nothing compared to her dignity and loveliness" (Tolkien 1995:1033).

Are we to assume that this sentiment runs counter to a social climbing strategy? Theweleit points out the curious set of conditions required to successfully engender a 'social climbing object-choice'; it is

> a very special mixture of affects, one that is triggered at the moment a particular female object enters the man's strategic plans as a 'suitable lover' [...]: the curious ability to enter (in one's own eyes and in those of the woman who is being courted) an 'extreme state of infatuation' which actually manages to appear to be 'love'. (Theweleit 1994:40)

Aragorn really does love Arwen. He not only develops feelings, he can also put them to good strategic use. Aragorn's love is anything but a sham. On gazing into Aragorn's heart (established by now as the supreme seat of emotion), Elrond immediately perceives this love (cf. Tolkien 1995:1034). He, however, also knows of the disruptive force self-centred love can unleash on society as a whole. It is Aragorn's age that is the problem.[21] Therefore Elrond advises: "You shall neither have wife, nor bind any woman to you in troth, until your time comes and you are found worthy of it" (Tolkien 1995:1034).

---

[21] It can be assumed that this a significant discursive shift from a dynastic marriage model to one based on economic reasons as the prologue still advocates a speedy union of Arathorn and Gilraen (cf. Tolkien 1995:1032).

Not only Arwen, but women in general, pose a danger for the still youthful Aragorn; he is in danger of drifting off into a 'private' kind of marriage. The focus of this particular 'love' now seems to lie in the arrangement of a marriage that will support governance. That is why Arwen cannot yet reciprocate his feelings: He is just too young and not yet suitable husband material.[22]

Aragorn's long absence thus serves not the renewal of his love but his political valorisation. Arwen is far more than "the love interest of Aragorn" (Fredrick/McBride 2001:110) – she is the primal impulse for his political career. Paradoxically, her very presence in the story is rendered secondary. It is Aragorn who roams the land, proves his mettle in dangerous battles (thus forging important political alliances), and cultivates his body and mind, eventually turning "elven-wise" (cf. Tolkien 1995:1035). Arwen and his love for her are absent; he does not think of her in thirty years. These years, however, render him marriageable: "Aragorn was grown to full stature of body and mind" (Tolkien 1995:1035) and "[Arwen's] choice was made" (Tolkien 1995:1035). She falls in love with him and his marriageability.

There is another aspect that needs to be considered here. Even though all protagonists are related to each other, the resulting kinship bonds are slight, a phenomenon Luhmann describes for the 19th century: "What were now called 'relations' in a somewhat pallid sense of the word, were regarded rather more as potentially disruptive, and certainly not as something which facilitated getting married and making a marriage work" (Luhmann 1998:147).

Elrond primarily cares not about dynastic gain, but about the loss of his daughter (cf. Tolkien 1995:1036), as Arwen is irrevocably isolated from her kin after the wedding (cf. Tolkien 1995:1037). This couples

---

[22] Aragorn's inappropriate – because obsolete – choice of terms from the father-daughter economy shows that he has not yet grasped the cause and aim of 'love' (cf. Tolkien 1995:1034).

generates no further horizontal kinship ties or alliances typical of dynastic marriages.[23] The 'love' of Arwen and Aragorn seems to point towards the replacement of the alliance type model of family by a kind of 'nuclear family'.[24] Only the 'nuclear family' seems to permit a happy synthesis of the 'private' and the 'political'. The destructive potential still found in the separation of Beren and Lúthien is mitigated by a separation of spheres: Arwen is designated to represent the 'private' and Aragorn acts out the 'political'. Aragorn's 'social climbing strategy' is no simple 'marrying up'; it is, in fact, the woman who provides the trigger for his political activities. The 'private' drives the 'political' and the 'political' refers to the (seemingly merely) 'private'.

It is Arwen's banner that flies over Aragorn's victory. Arwen and the Sceptre of Annúminas are transferred simultaneously into his hands. A responsible statesman makes a good husband and is worthy of love. Physical attributes and social rank as triggers for 'love' have been replaced by a moral code of conduct – something eminently political.

Only now can we make sense of Aragorn's odd death. His decision to die of his own will is a moral one. His question, "Ask whether you [Arwen] would indeed have me wait until I wither and fall from my high seat unmanned and witless" (Tolkien 1995:1037), does not pertain to his physical integrity but to the endurance of his political clout.

Arwen does not understand: "for all her wisdom and lineage she could not forbear to plead with him to stay yet" (Tolkien 1995:1037). For her, the political is only secondary, therefore Aragorn's death, for her, comes "before [his] time" (Tolkien 1995:2001). She cannot understand her 'error', as she is bound to another sphere. This response suddenly calls into question the very purpose of their marriage and 'love':

---

[23] As evidenced by the fact that only close family members are present at Aragorn's death (cf. Tolkien 1995: 1037).

[24] Defined for the purposes of this paper as the concept that puts the family at the centre of society.

"But let us not be overthrown at the final test [...]. In sorrow we must go, but not in despair" (Tolkien 1995:1038). Arwen's pleading for Aragorn to enter her sphere not only negates him as a subject, but also the whole point of their union. A man's triumph – it seems – is greatest when he prevails not over an enemy but over himself – with the help, and at the expense, of a woman. The death that he chooses prevents her meddling in life. He also takes care to prevent an enforced privacy of post-mortem love when he casts loving 'remembrance' in a rather negative light: "The uttermost choice is before you [Arwen]: to repent and [...] bear away into the West the memory of our days together [...] but never more than memory; or else to abide the Doom of Men" (Tolkien 1995:1037). When he demands that Arwen accept her own death, he does not transfer their relationship into an absolutely 'private realm', as Beren and Lúthien did,[25] but turns her decision into a final proof of the success of a 'love' not based on passive suffering but action. This is politics. This is 'love'!

3.4 Structure of Love II

At first sight, the marriage of Arwen and Aragorn resembles the love experienced by Beren and Lúthien. The protagonists share similar backgrounds, the place of their very first encounter is alike, separation defines both relationships, the couples' bond vanquishes an all-powerful enemy and, finally, both (erstwhile immortal) women follow their loved ones into death.

We hope to have pointed out some of the structural and discursive shifts in the construction of both relationships and their distinct concepts of 'love', however. 'Love' in these texts is generated not only by mere generic physicality, but by more complex patterns of behaviour

---

[25] Even in death Arwen and Aragorn cannot relinquish their assigned spheres: He turns into "an image of the splendour of the Kings of Men in glory". She ends up in a "green grave [...] forgotten" (Tolkien 1995:1038).

such as intimacy, betterment of self and a 'moral' code of conduct. Arwen and Aragorn do anything but simply 'fall' in love – they have to work at their relationship. The result is that Aragorn "presumes that she [Arwen] must have a full and rich life simply remaining dedicated to him" (Fredrick/McBride 2001:111), because that is what he had, by remaining dedicated to her. 'Remembering' the loved one is thus no longer aimed at renewing 'love' but has turned into a impulse for any kind of betterment of self. The successful bestowal of emotions onto the man results in a discursive shift away from the large dynastic alliance towards the nuclear family (with all it concomitant structures) (cf. Foucault 1990:104ff.).

Furthermore we are able to observe a change in the choice of the love object. Strategic behaviour is rendered possible as long as it falls under the premise of 'a moral code of conduct'. Moral failure now threatens love. Here it is only the man who sacrifices himself for the good of the state; the woman must sacrifice herself for 'nothing' (cf. Zižek 2004), but do so of her own free will.[26] 'Interpersonal interpenetration' now reigns supreme. The text has managed to construct a love that is defined by a man's "ability to achieve the aim on which he has set his sights" (Theweleit 1994:40), all based – needless to say – on the selfless support of the woman. Not the most romantic of reasons to love – rather patriarchal, one might add – and thus probably the reason why Tolkien and the 'casual readers' do not consider this the most riveting of love stories. Yet this couple can claim one advantage over Beren and Lúthien: It does not depend absolutely on a heterotopia and can in fact exist within the world. Finally, and maybe most importantly, this couple can put literary text to good use to further their aims within the world.

---

[26] Phrased differently: "men are [now] moral, while only women are properly ethical" (Zižek 2004).

4 SAM AND FRODO – NO LOVE, BUT ONE?

> When I go out yeah I know I'm gonna be
> I'm gonna be the man who goes along with you
> (*500 miles*, The Proclaimers)

In studying the couple Sam and Frodo, one encounters a strange phenomenon: The story of a couple[27] that makes up the bulk of *The Lord of the Rings* is simply overlooked and interpreted as friendship; a friendship, however, whose character can assume various forms, such as that of master and servant, or officer and batman, to name only the most frequently quoted models (cf. Smol 2004:965). The reading of Sam as a loyal but rather simple person, who, even though he does not understand Frodo's actions, will follow him faithfully, is widely accepted.[28] Lewis/Currie state: "The 'majority view' [of 'Victorian Values'] regarded friendships between people of the same sex as being very important. It also drew a sharp line between the sort of emotional ties that come from shared interest […], and those that have sexual roots" (Lewis/Currie 2002:184).

This chapter will examine the validity of this distinction with regards to the similarities between the couples Beren/Lúthien (whose erotic roots are a visible part of their relationship), Arwen/Aragorn (who at least engender offspring) and Frodo/Sam. In view of the sheer size of the textual corpus, I will focus on the scenes of leave-taking from the Shire, the events in Rivendell and during the Breaking of the Fellowship, in addition to the events in Lothlórien, on the Stairs and in the Tower of Cirith Ungol, as well as the scenes at Mount Doom and the Grey Havens.

---

[27] The very couple, among those analysed here, that most often talks of 'love'.
[28] It is probably Tolkien himself who is responsible for this reading (cf. Tolkien 2000:392).

4.1 Falling in Love

When the relationship of Sam and Frodo is first portrayed, soon after Gandalf has told Frodo about the Ring, its dangers and the necessity of Frodo's exile (cf. Tolkien:1995:41ff.), we already know a great deal about Frodo: He is an orphan and a 'foreigner' from Buckland, but was raised by Bilbo as a member of the Hobbit 'aristocracy' (cf. Tolkien 1995:21ff.). Clearly, Bilbo has taught Frodo how to read and write, making him part of the 'educated elite' of the Shire. "There have been times when I thought the inhabitants [of the Shire] too stupid and dull for words" (Tolkien 1995:61), Frodo once tells Gandalf.

About Sam the reader learns only three facts: He is a gardener (which is highly significant), he belongs to the "ordinary hobbits" (Tolkien 1995:43), but has "more on his mind than gardening" (Tolkien 1995:44).[29] Sam knows the same stories as Frodo, but "didn't rightly understand" (Tolkien 1995:62). Journeying with Frodo will enable him to change all that. Taking Sam along on the journey does not succeed in keeping him silent about it (he tells Merry and Pippin); Sam's company, however, turns the journey into an endeavour that will refine and cultivate both hobbits in more ways than one. It is neither friendship (Frodo's "closest friends were [...] Pippin, and Merry") (Tolkien 1995:41) nor a master's order that impels Sam to leave. He wants to see elves and on succeeding sheds tears of joy (cf. Tolkien 1995:62ff.). He might not set out on his journey for love of Frodo, but his actions distinctly resemble Aragorn's in the forest of Rivendell. He 'anticipates' himself.

Sam's character changes quickly, once the hobbits have set out: for the very first time, he sings a song he has composed himself.[30] He may call it "a bit of nonsense", but it is striking that he (not the 'aristo-

---

[29] The fact that Sam's wish comes true when gardening points to his ability (albeit rudimentary) to create a heterotopia even then.

[30] First evidence of Sam's role as 'author'.

cratic' hobbits Merry and Pippin) is the most prominent singer in the group, besides Frodo. His song links and relates disparate locations and events: After Frodo's wounding at Weathertop this is the first time that the memory of Bilbo's adventures and the location the travellers find themselves in merge to create a safe space. Sam's song, sung to an "old tune" but "out of his own head" (cf. Tolkien 1995:201ff.), interlaces with the faint spectre of 'an other space'. But something else has happened before the travellers reach Rivendell (to be of significance later): For the first time, Sam has heard the story of Beren and Lúthien from Aragorn.

It is in Rivendell that Sam and Frodo are first separated from each other. Frodo (as Ring-bearer an eminently political subject) is invited to the Council; Sam is not. We hardly notice this separation, however, as Sam cancels it out immediately (cf. Tolkien 1995:233ff.). Still, his presence at the Council amounts to a transgression, as Pippin rightly remarks (cf. Tolkien 1995:264), and it is Elrond who perceives at this early stage, "It is hardly possible to separate you from him" (Tolkien 1995:264). Lúthien follows Beren against the will of her father. We have identified that as a sign of love; what does Sam's transgression signify here? It must also be noted that Sam alone is apparently immune to the negative heterotopia that the Ring can trigger (cf. Tolkien 1995:263).[31]

In Lórien, the change in Sam continues, and here Frodo proves to be affected, too. Their joint experiences, culminating in the events related to Gandalf's death, transform the character of their relationship for Frodo as well. The perfect heterotopia of Lórien bears witness to their joint singing. Whereas Sam's song of the trolls had still been less than perfect, now Sam seems to turn into someone that Frodo is 'able to love' when he asks Sam to complete his unfinished song for Gandalf:

---

[31] This will become an issue when interpreting Gollum's role.

"No, I'll leave that to you, Sam. Or perhaps to Bilbo" (Tolkien 1995:351). Sam has proven once and for all that he harbours a 'Schöne Seele'.[32] Only a little later, he emulates Arwen's choice. Galadriel's mirror shows him "[his] poor old gaffer going down the Hill with his bits of things on a barrow" (Tolkien 1995:353). Initially, this vision draws Sam back to the Shire, but then he makes his choice: "I'll go home by the long road with Mr. Frodo, or not at all" (Tolkien 1995:354). Just like Arwen, he decides against his kin (even though kinship is of paramount importance in the Shire) in order to follow Frodo. In Arwen's case, this choice signified love!

That it could carry the same significance for Sam we may glean from an incident that took place shortly before. "What did you blush for, Sam?" (Tolkien 1995:348), Pippins asks, after Sam has been exposed to Galadriel's glance. Her glance triggers the same effect in all the members of the Fellowship: "each had felt that he was offered a choice between a shadow full of fear that lay ahead, and something that he greatly desired" (Tolkien 1995:348). But it is only Sam who blushes – as his desire and the 'shadow' are inextricably intertwined. Thus he is in "no mood for jest" (Tolkien 1995:348). His heart's desire is bound to Frodo's suffering and 'shadow'; a motive that we have encountered in the story of Beren and Lúthien as well. At first reading, Sam's greatest wish, "a nice little hole with – with a bit of garden of my own" (Tolkien 1995:348), may be easily overlooked, but in this context the hyphen is no coincidence. The elision harbours Sam's private 'desire': a nice little hole with – Frodo. Only Frodo can fill the hole in Sam's desire.[33] In the end, we know, he will succeed.

---

[32] His 'Schöne Seele' already shows in the way he treats the pony Bill.

[33] In this, we already grasp the reason why the Ring is unable to affect Sam. His greatest desire is for 'a bit of garden' – with Frodo, not the monstrously expanded garden that the Ring offers (cf. Tolkien 1995:880). Furthermore, the One Ring's promise is aimed at an isolated recipient, whereas Sam's desire, the garden heterotopia, necessarily requires the presence of an other: Frodo. Therefore the Ring's

Once Boromir's actions have caused the Fellowship to break up, Frodo wants to set off to Mordor on his own. This again resembles Beren's last attempt to leave for Morgoth all alone. Just like Beren, Frodo wants to slip away unnoticed, so that his fate won't be imposed on the others: "those I can trust are too dear to me" (Tolkien 1995:392). But, just like Lúthien, Sam will not accept that. It is rather telling that it is – according to Tolkien (cf. Tolkien 2000:83) – 'simple' Sam who can put himself in Frodo's position. Sam is the 'Schöne Seele', he can empathise and draw conclusions in a way that Aragorn and the others cannot. Only Sam can foresee what Frodo is about to do (cf. Tolkien 1995:396), and it is Sam alone who can act appropriately. This development transcends any kind of master/servant or officer/batman relationship: their bond takes on a distinct new quality. For the third time, Sam is offered a chance to leave Frodo, and still continue to cultivate his body and mind (as Merry and Pippin will on their journeys), but he decides to stay with Frodo instead. Frodo, on the other hand, wants to protect him, even though this seems to be of strategic harm to the Quest.

> 'Coming, Mr. Frodo! Coming!' called Sam, and flung himself from the bank, clutching at the departing boat. He missed it by a yard. With a cry and a splash he fell face downward into deep swift water. [...] An exclamation of dismay came from the empty boat. [...] 'Up you come, Sam my lad!' said Frodo. 'Now take my hand!' 'Save me, Mr. Frodo,' gasped Sam. 'I'm drownded. I can't see your hand.' 'Here it is.' (Tolkien 1995:396)

---

proposal is instantly identified as "only a trick" (Tolkien 1995:881), and the Ring can offer nothing more than this 'trick' to Sam.

Huan tells Beren: "if you will not deny your doom, then either Lúthien, being forsaken, must assuredly die alone, or she must with you challenge the fate that lies before you" (Tolkien 2001:211). Sam is threatened by something far worse than mere death by drowning. Missing the boat indicates that his efforts alone do not suffice; according to the logic of 'interpersonal interpenetration', he must find out how Frodo relates to him. His inability to see Frodo's hand may be read as prompting Frodo's decision, now that Sam has made his. Furthermore this interaction reveals that, for Sam, being left behind equals death, just as it did for Lúthien. Frodo in turn understands two things: He grasps that his very existence would be threatened, if Sam were to die because of him: "'It would be the death of you to come with me, Sam,' said Frodo, 'and I could not have borne that'" (Tolkien 1995:397). Frodo also understands that he has to respect Sam's voluntary decision to stay with him. Frodo saves Sam. Their fates merge for good. If this motive signifies love for Beren and Lúthien, it must signify love for Sam and Frodo. As opposed to Beren/Lúthien, however, it is not 'doom' that effects their merging but a successful 'interpersonal interpenetration'.

4.2 Love

On the Stairs of Cirith Ungol, this couple achieves something that eludes all others and once and for all proves that, if one applies the logic of the two other couples to the hobbits relationship, it can only be called love. It is Sam who raises the question "I wonder what sort of a tale we've fallen into?" (Tolkien 1995:696). A short while later he answers it himself: It is – the tale of Beren and Lúthien. Sam employs the tale as told by Aragorn to explain Frodo's fate.[34] He interprets their bond by drawing on literature: A love story is used to make sense of the relationship

---

[34] It proves that quite early on Sam identifies the Story of Beren and Lúthien as a foil that can help him make sense of his own relationship with Frodo.

Frodo/Sam. Here it becomes evident that their relationship should be read as a love story in its own right. This passage also illustrates that Frodo/Sam – very much like Aragorn on meeting Arwen – will refer to literary texts to interpret their entanglement and to express emotions for their respective counterparts.

Peter von Matt points out that it is the topic of love (marriage) in literature that effects "a continual switching from the past to the present, from the textually archaic to what takes our breath away right here and now and thus in turn [...] has the past shine as a second present" (Matt 1991:29).[35]

Sam begins to transform Frodo into a text and Frodo "laughed, a long clear laugh from his heart" (Tolkien 1995:697). Just like Lúthien's song, Frodo's very laughter calls forth a heterotopia: "the stones were listening and the tall rocks leaning over them" (Tolkien 1995:697). Frodo in turn weaves Sam into the story, imagining him as 'Samwise the stouthearted'. Sam and Frodo have transported the story of Beren and Lúthien from the past into the present, thereby perpetuating their own. If someone were to say, "Shut the book now" (Tolkien 1995:697), others could still relate their 'love' to the story of Sam and Frodo.[36]

The triple layers of text ("Still, I wonder if we shall ever be put into songs or tales. We're in one, of course; but I mean: put into words [...] read out of a great big book [...] years and years afterwards." [Tolkien 1995:697]) all point to one thing only: Sam and Frodo loved each other in the past (they relate to the past story of Beren and Lúthien), they love each other in the present (while they are conversing), and they will love each other in the future (as there will be a story telling of their love).

---

[35] Original: "[...] dauernde Umschaltung vom Historischen ins Aktuelle, vom Altertümlichen eines Textes in das, was uns hier die Sprache verschlägt und was dann auch rückwirkend, [...] das Historische aufleuchten lässt als eine zweite Gegenwart."

[36] As 'love' is a literary topic, always.

The heterotopia thus generated is so powerful that even Gollum can be integrated into their 'love' – albeit only for a moment, it seems (cf. Tolkien 1995:699). Tolkien himself was the first (and Peter Jackson the last so far) who incorrectly accused Sam of interrupting Gollum's catharsis, thereby prompting him to carry out his betrayal (cf. Tolkien 2000:329). *The Lord of the Rings* tells a very different story, however: "But at that [Gollum's] touch Frodo stirred and cried out" (Tolkien 1995:699). Gollum disturbs the hobbits' heterotopia as he has just returned from Shelob's lair (cf. Tolkien 1995:721). Contaminated by this place of darkness[37] (a supremely negative heterotopia), his touch disrupts Sam's and Frodo's 'merging' into their 'other space'. Frodo's cry marks Gollum as forever lost to 'love'.

The scene on the Stairs of Cirith Ungol holds importance for another reason. In Lubkoll's definition, the bourgeois subject constitutes itself in the ambition to create a genealogy by projecting economic (legacy) and biological capital (offspring) into the future (cf. Lubkoll 1994:349). Sam (underclass) and Frodo (his inheritance lost) engender a new concept: the usurpation of history by means of story, replacing music as the main means to create heterotopias. It is striking that we are observing a reciprocal process. Sam initially denies himself entry into the story and thus into history; Frodo, however, insists on it. The following scene will present us with the exact opposite.

The events in Shelob's Lair can only be described as the catastrophe in the relationship of Sam and Frodo; it is a disaster of such magnitude that it leaves no "remainder" (cf. Barthes 1990:49). Both Sam and Frodo constitute their identities with regards to each other, to the extent that one without the other "sees himself doomed to total destruction" (cf. Barthes 1990:48).[38] Sam has to choose between politically responsi-

---

[37] Cf. Judith Klinger's essay in this volume.

[38] Lúthien dies because her 'doom' is inexorably interwoven with Beren's fate. Arwen must die so that her 'interpersonal interpenetration' with Aragorn may not be ques-

ble action and his private love for Frodo and decides to observe his political duty, all the while aware: "I'll be sure to go wrong" (Tolkien 1995:715).

He has to betray his love in order to save the world. Like Arwen, he has to face the question, "Did I come all this way with him for nothing?" (Tolkien 1995:714). He has to sacrifice his private happiness in order to save Middle-earth, just as Arwen had to sacrifice her private existence to politics. Yet Sam is incapable of doing so; his "place is by Mr. Frodo" (Tolkien 1995:718). It might be this very statement that brings Roger Sale to the conclusion: "Sam serves Frodo and Sméagol serves the Ring, but only Frodo serves the heroic idea of the Ring's destruction" (Sale 2000:83). But that observation is incorrect. Gollum does indeed bring the Ring closer to Sauron, but he wants it for himself.[39] Although he sets the events of Cirith Ungol in motion, they unfold counter to his plan. (And at the very end he will destroy the Ring.) Sam, however, chooses to stay with Frodo and this decision (even though Sam himself does not believe it) is the right one. He saves Frodo and the Ring. The private here is political indeed.[40] By making Sam a Ringbearer and having him return it to Frodo, the text points out the advantages of merging ethical and moral acts. "In that hour of trial it was the love of his master that helped most to hold him firm; but also deep down in him lived still unconquered his plain hobbit-sense [...]. The one small garden of a free gardener was all his need and due" (Tolkien 1995:881).

---

[39] tioned. It is evident that Sam, whose tie with Frodo is based on both principles, cannot leave him.
I can touch upon Gollum only briefly. He can be read as the antithesis to Huan. His desire is the Ring and the Ring only, a veritable counter-image of the 'Schöne Seele'. Gollum represents the economy of the political in its pure form; a will that acts and feels only for itself. Sméagol und Gollum are the same person, who loves only itself, i.e. the 'power' of the Ring.

[40] The 'political' is triggered by 'happiness' or 'doom' so that it may follow 'love'.

As Tolkien's heterotopias have a marked affinity to nature, Sam's trade – he is a gardener – is probably the most prosaic way of creating one. The Ring can only offer him something that will simultaneously exclude the Ring from it: the heterotopia as a space for and of 'love'.[41] Sam is capable of acting politically without the danger (experienced by Galadriel and Gandalf) of losing himself to it (as did Gollum). It is striking that, structurally, we find parallels not only with Beren and Lúthien's story (Sam's fight with Shelob, the assault on the fortress against all odds, the couple's reunion) but also a reiteration of the scene on the Stairs.

The story of Beren and Lúthien (the older text) is transformed by Sam's decision against the political in his own present (i.e. at the time of the *The Lord of the Rings*); upon Frodo's rescue, it is re-projected into the story and thus turned into history. Like the scene on the Stairs, the sequence concludes with an image of 'merging' (cf. Tolkien 1995:877ff.).[42]

Storytelling does not seem necessary any longer. Sam renounces his chance to ever hear the complete tale when he decides to stay with Frodo (cf. Tolkien 1995:718), and when he says "There's no time for

---

[41] The image of the garden as a heterotopia of 'love' supports the reading of the lacuna in Sam's wish, "a nice little hole with – with a bit of garden of my own" (Tolkien 1995:348), which may only by filled by Frodo.

[42] There is no denying the significance of the physical side to Sam's and Frodo's relationship. One can distinguish two strategies of making sense of this. Either all sexual implications are denied with recourse to the 'friendship model' (this is the etablished position), or, on the contrary, the couple could be read as homosexual. The text does not support either reading. Certainly there is a strong physical bond between Sam and Frodo – they kiss and embrace and lie naked in each other's arms. (Beren/Lúthien and Arwen/Aragorn are a great deal less affectionate in that respect.) Michel Foucault points out that the 'bourgeois couple' grounds sexuality in reproduction and thus renders the legitimate, reproductive couple the norm (cf. Foucault 1990:1). Frodo and Sam, however, have devised a method that guarantees a genealogy of their own, depriving sexuality of its privileged status. As a consequence, sexuality is relieved of reproduction. The 'sexuality dispositif' (cf. Foucault 1990:103ff.) is cancelled and physicality nothing more (and nothing less) than what Sam and Frodo make it: the most obvious sign of their 'merging'.

tales" (Tolkien 1995:889) on reuniting with Frodo: A 'literary theoretical' model of 'merging' has been transposed into a practical one, it seems.

Without consciously relating to a literary model, Sam emulates one (the story of Beren and Lúthien). He acts as a 'lover'. Thus he may create his own, albeit fragile 'other space' even in a very dark place (the negative heterotopia). He sings in the Tower of Cirith Ungol (and Frodo can answer, as he also acts as a 'lover') and retrieves Frodo – and thus himself – for the story and history. The literary model as a means of 'merging' has prevailed.

This becomes apparent on their continued journey to Mount Doom, as a kind of congruency of body and 'soul' seems to ensue. Sam, who had not been capable of becoming Frodo for political reasons (he may take up Frodo's insignia: his sword, the mithril coat, the Phial of Galadriel and the Ring, but he cannot leave Frodo) (cf. Tolkien 1995:711ff.), slowly assumes the functions of Frodo's body and 'soul'. He carries him, holds his hand when Frodo loses control over it and guards his memories of a shared past, but also of their political task, once Frodo's strength wanes. He is the bearer of the 'heroic idea' of the destruction of the Ring, as Frodo sporadically forgets where they are heading (cf. Tolkien 1995:895ff.).

At Mount Doom Frodo cannot let go of the Ring. Shippey pursues the question whether Frodo finally succumbs to the Ring, or whether the Ring at Mount Doom is so overpowering that Frodo has no more room to manoeuvre (cf. Shippey 2002:112ff.). His analysis leaves out one important factor: Frodo is alone when he fails!

A reading of the scene at Mount Doom may profit from comparison with Beren/Lúthien as well, especially when one focuses on the deviations from the model they provide. Beren fails because he lapses into a politico-economic pattern of behaviour. Frodo fails because that very pattern (represented here by Gollum) separates him from Sam: "I have come" (Tolkien 1995:924): Frodo's words exclude Sam, who is no longer in any position to act: he "gasped, but he had no chance to cry-out" (Tolkien 1995:924).[43]

Frodo's statement seems to stem from the same political logic that Beren adhered to. The latter wanted more than just the one Silmaril necessary to claim Lúthien. Had Frodo acted according to this logic, he would indeed have succumbed to the Ring. But Sam's inability to speak points to the power of the strongest of all the negative heterotopias in the text. At Mount Doom, both Sam and Frodo lose the ability on which their 'love' is based: language itself, the possibility of relating to the 'story', and any opportunity of communicating with each other. This is the place where all stories end.

The question remains why it is Gollum who destroys the Ring. Events now seem to call for a political will, a will necessarily rendered naught by the ethic of a love that calls for self-sacrifice. It is Gollum who, in the presence of the strongest of all negative heterotopias, can still act selfishly. His story is only interwoven with himself and that is why he can act and die for desire – for himself (and the Ring). It is the very same desire that distracted Morgoth from Lúthien that can destroy the Ring as well. And Gollum is the one who loves himself to the exclusion of all others. This is a death out of love, too – albeit in the form of a savage caricature – and Gollum dies happily.

Frodo pays for his 'betrayal' with only one finger, whereas Beren lost a hand; evidence that Frodo's 'betrayal of love' is sanctioned less harshly, because his deeds cannot be attributed to his will to the same extent. At the end, we witness the merging of Sam and Frodo. Significantly, Frodo, unlike Beren, is not at death's door. He is "himself again" (Tolkien 1995:926).[44] The symmetry of the relationship remains intact

---

[43] It is evident that it is the 'us' enabling Sam and Frodo to actually reach Mount Doom. It is their separation (by Gollum) that is problematic.
[44] Evidence that Frodo was not corrupted by the Ring.

because, just as Frodo did not want to surrender the Ring, so did Sam once want to take it. The principle 'we' is temporarily disrupted by Frodo's "I have come" as well as Sam's (passing) decision to take up the Ring and to leave Frodo (whom he believes to be dead). However, since these disturbances of the united 'we' are caused by the compelling interference of external forces (Sam has to follow 'political' duties, Gollum violently separates the two hobbits, and the Ring overwhelms Frodo's will) they do not amount to a disruption of love. "I am glad you are here with me [says Frodo]. Here at the end of all things, Sam" (Tolkien 1995:926). Whereas Beren and Lúthien are never absolved of their anxiety, the journey of Sam and Frodo ends like it began. The flames of Mount Doom's explosion point back to the fireworks at Bilbo's birthday party. They act according to Barthes' dictum: "The amorous subject experiences every meeting with the loved being as a festival." (Barthes 1990:119)

4.3 Conditions

After the Ring is destroyed, the story of Beren and Lúthien is evoked again. As the eagles rescue Sam and Frodo, their actions are validated politically, and they return to a home that has suffered destruction in the meantime – a side-effect of their actions. This time, however, neither of the couple has to die to restore the old order (cf. Tolkien 1995:930ff.). Rather, the old order needs to be modified in a way that only Sam and Frodo can effect. After Sam has put Galadriel's gift to good use and turned the Shire into a heterotopia (thus completing a primarily political task, while simultaneously creating a heterotopia for himself and Frodo), is seems only natural that Frodo asks Sam: "When are you going to move in and join me, Sam?" (Tolkien 1995:1001)

But Sam is wiser than Frodo. He knows that a bourgeois genealogy is defined by the transmission of economic and biological capital into the future. Once the Sackville-Bagginses have left, Frodo's precarious economic situation (caused by his adventure) is resolved. The model that governs the transmission of wealth and genealogy in a relationship such as the one of Bilbo/Frodo seems to have lost its validity. To the people of the Shire "Bilbo was [...] very peculiar" (Tolkien 1995:21). In order to ensure that the place of Sam and Frodo in 'story' and 'history' alike remains without blemish (the gossip common to the 'Ivy Bush' threatens to wreak havoc[45]), it seems safer to resort to the model of family (which in turn is subsumed into the heterotopia of Frodo/Sam). Frodo grasps Sam's point immediately: "'I see,' said Frodo: 'you want to get married, and yet you want to live with me in Bag End too? But my dear Sam, how easy! Get married as soon as you can, and then move in with Rose. There's room enough [...] for as big a family as you could wish for.'" (Tolkien 1995:1001)

The relationship Sam/Rose, one could argue, cancels out the love-based relationship of Sam and Frodo. However, Frodo spells it out: it is all (just) about family, i.e. genealogy based on reproduction. One glance at the names given to the children that are born to Sam and Rose reveals whose genealogy this truly is: they are called Elanor, Frodo, Merry, Pippin, Bilbo (cf. Tolkien 1995:1077). Rose serves as a vehicle to transmit the genealogy of Sam and Frodo.[46]

The naming of Sam's firstborn supports this argument. As a girl, she cannot be called Frodo (since she is to carry on Frodo's genealogy, this would be the first and most logical choice; Sam's second child is eventually named Frodo). Frodo and Sam therefore decide to call her

---

[45] There is the very real danger that their story, just like Bilbo's, turns into the object of untrammelled speculation and becomes distorted and fragmented in the process. It is with good reason that "Sam was pained to notice how little honour he [Frodo] had in his own country" (Tolkien 1995:1002).

[46] It is inappropriate to read Sam/Rose as exponents of 'love'. Neither the narrator nor any of the protagonists ever refer to their relationship this way, whereas the relationship Frodo/Sam is often labelled 'love', especially by others in the text (cf. Smol 2004:949ff.).

Elanor, a name that sounds traditional at first, but relates intimately to Sam's and Frodo's relationship (and not to Sam's and Rose's). Elanor bloomed in Lothlórien where they sang together for the very first time (cf. Tolkien 1995:1003). The union with Rose is a pragmatic (and sufficient) one; 'love' plays no part in it.

Frodo, however, holds an important position in relation to Rose, which simultaneously furthers his relationship with Sam. Nowhere in the text do we find an allusion to Sam/Rose without a mention of Frodo in the immediate vicinity. On the one hand, he provides the necessary economic means to transmit his genealogy and thereby replace the clan-based system of the Bagginses by a nuclear family, the type of family, that is, on which the larger society depends. On the other hand, Frodo successfully achieves the transition from an oral tradition of transmitting history to historiography (which is of relevance for Sam only). At the very beginning of the *The Lord of the Rings*, Gandalf can still tell Bilbo: "nobody will read the book, however it ends" (Tolkien 1995:32). When Frodo finishes the record of his (and Sam's) story and hands the book to Sam, both of them together take charge of history (cf. Tolkien 1995:1004). Sam is obliged to continue the genealogy and so has to stay "to be one and whole, for many years" (Tolkien 1995:1006). He has to take care of his (their) family, after all.

Sam, who at the outset of the story resembled Aragorn, seems to end up like Arwen: "I thought you were going to enjoy the Shire, too, for years and years," he tells Frodo (Tolkien 1995:1006). While Arwen has to die in order to ensure the genealogy of a monarchy, Sam has to model his life on Aragorn in memory of Frodo. He is elected Mayor seven times, forges and strengthens the political alliances that the Ring-war has brought about. He acts politically and morally,[47] but only (and in

---

[47] As 'moral' I define the sum of social norms that regulate social interaction and are accepted as binding by society. The 'ethical' is solely bound to the individual's intentions.

this he differs from Aragorn) to preserve the memory of Frodo. His motivation may therefore be called ethical as well. Consequently, it is not death that brings about the reunion of Sam and Frodo, but, resembling Beren and Lúthien, they are allowed to 'merge' completely in the heterotopia of Valinor: "Samwise [...] went to the Grey Havens, and passed over the Sea" (Tolkien 1995:1072).[48]

4.4 Structure of Love III or Who is Edith Tolkien?

Theweleit (1994:3) states: "Love was first and foremost a concern of literature." As a literary model, Beren/Lúthien provide the matrix for the relationships of Arwen/Aragorn and Frodo/Sam. The (literary) markers of their 'love' are: making sense of and overcoming separation, fulfilling a task that is bound up with the couple and, in fact, relates the 'lovers' to each other in the first place. The creation of a heterotopia can be identified as the means to 'realizing their love'. Its ultimate aim is the creation of a genealogy and the final 'merging' of the couple in an everlasting heterotopia. So far, we are not able to discern any differences between Beren/Lúthien and Frodo/Sam.

Luhmann argues that 'love' is not an end in itself but primarily an instrument to ensure the reproduction of humankind within marriage (cf. Luhmann 1986:149). Once again all three couples meet these definitions of 'love', albeit in a broader sense. One cannot deny, however, that certain structural ruptures and shifts may be observed. With Beren/Lúthien, we can identify two distinct and separate spheres, wherein both lovers must actively conduct themselves morally in order to ensure their genealogy. With Arwen/Aragorn one partner (the woman) shifts towards the ethical (the passive and 'private') which in turn implies an even

---

[48] This again proves that Sam's and Rose's marriage is supremely pragmatic. He chooses not to lie with her in death, but to live with Frodo in the Immortal Realm where they may freely choose the time of their passing from Arda (cf. Tolkien 2002:341).

stronger affinity with the moral code of conduct (the political) for the other. With Sam/Frodo we find this separation suspended: both may act morally and ethically simultaneously. Their 'posterity' is guaranteed by their appropriation of history. Reproductive sexuality is 'outsourced', as it is of no consequence to the concept of love as played out in the text. 'Love' for Tolkien is in no way related to the number of children born. (Beren's/Lúthien's and Arwen's/Aragorn's offspring are indicative not of 'love' but simply of an act of procreation. We find no mention of the birth or even the conception of these children.)

It is remarkable that the physical aspect of 'love' is hardly ever mentioned in the stories about the heteronormative couples, quite in contrast to Frodo/Sam.[49] Why then should their relationship not be called 'love'?

Halperin (2000:100) points out: "The friendship of virtuous men is characterized by a disinterested love that leads to a merging of individual identities and hence to an unwillingness to live without the other, a readiness to die with or for the other." This definition clearly covers the relationship of Frodo and Sam but leaves out Beren/Lúthien and Arwen/Aragorn. Are we to assume, then, that it is friendship after all that binds Sam and Frodo? How are we to make sense of the emotionality and physicality that characterises this couple's interactions? Halperin (2000:100) continues: "The language used to convey such passionate male unions often appears to modern sensibilities suspiciously overheated, if not downright erotic." But where exactly does one draw the line when comparing this union to those of the heteronormative couples? Lewis and Currie postulate that the dividing line between 'shared interest' and sexuality accounts for the fundamental difference.

---

[49] To quote only one passage of many from the events at Cirith Ungol: "He [Frodo] was naked, lying as if in a swoon on a heap of filthy rags [...] 'Frodo! Mr. Frodo, my dear!' cried Sam [...] He half lifted his master and hugged him to his breast. [...] and he [Frodo] lay back in Sam's gentle arms, closing his eyes" (Tolkien 1995:889).

Frodo and Sam, however, are at pains to ensure offspring within history. The dividing line grows blurred.

Michel Foucault describes how, on transitioning into modernity with its specific 'sexuality dispositif', the family was rendered the mandatory site for emotion, sentiment and love (cf. Foucault 1990:108). He also points out that, at the very centre of the 'sexuality dispositif', one finds the married couple engaged in reproduction (cf. Foucault 1990:103). It can therefore be argued that reproductive sexuality defines the crucial difference between friendship and love. Luhmann states that the inclusion of sexuality into intimate relationships, starting in the 18th century, was particularly apt "to foster a neutralization of class differences" (Luhmann 1986:116), which is of relevance for all couples analysed here. Luhmann also puts forward the hypothesis that it is that very inclusion of sexuality that prises 'love' and 'friendship' apart.

With a view to reproductive sexuality, it is obvious that only the heteronormative couples may be called 'lovers', but there is no textual evidence that Tolkien's adheres to this concept of love. Paramount for the Tolkienian concept of 'love' is the 'other space', the heterotopia called forth by songs that refer to 'love stories' and join new couples of lovers, modelled on existent literary patterns. 'Love' for Tolkien does not serve to first and foremost produce offspring (children), but to reproduce story and history. The logic of the text itself (that constructs this model without a 'sexuality dispositif') provides no reason to read Frodo/Sam any differently from Beren/Lúthien and Arwen/Aragorn. As shown, Tolkien's concept of 'love' allows for no text-based differentiation between 'heterosexual' and 'homosexual' couples.

But why are they hardly ever identified as lovers, and what does Edith Tolkien have to do with it? Peter von Matt points out the role literature plays in creating a second present. Erll et al. (2003:iv) state:

> Literature relates to and is prestructured by reality that precedes and exists outside of it. [...] Secondly,

> literary texts may represent memory and identity. [...] Such literary performances of memory and identity may retroactively influence extra-literary reality.[50]

While reading a text that s/he can relate to, any reader will access existent culturally constructed knowledge. When reading about 'love', the 'sexuality dispositif' that constitutes the identity of any modern *lecteur* (cf. Foucault 1990:75ff.) will come into play. Any perception of 'love' will thus invariably be bound up with one's own sexuality. The text may, however, try out and shape non-sanctioned and excluded identities. Suspending 'sexuality' within the concept of 'love' might be a case in point. The supremely successful model of Frodo/Sam could lead any reader to re-evaluate their self-perception. This could seriously affect heteronormativity as we know it.

The question could be raised, for example, whether Tolkien's marriage to Edith was based on 'love'. (A reader might also wonder whether Beren/Lúthien and Arwen/Aragorn are exponents of a successful 'love-model'.) Another literary text relieves us of such pondering: Tolkien had the name 'Lúthien' engraved on Edith's tombstone, thus paradoxically rendering the real relationship fictional and literary:[51] real marriage becomes the site of ideal (literary) 'love'. In the recipients' view, the 'sexuality dispositif' is buttressed by this identification, and heteronormative identity is reinforced. The real marriage corroborates the authenticity of the literary, fictional model. The reader's cultural

---

[50] Original: "Literatur ist bezogen auf und präformiert durch eine vorgängige, außerliterarische Wirklichkeit. [...] Zweitens können literarische Texte Erinnerung und Identitäten darstellen. [...] Solche literarischen Inszenierungen von Erinnerung und Identität vermögen drittens auf die außerliterarische Wirklichkeit zurückzuwirken."

[51] At the 'Tolkien 2005' conference in Birmingham, Priscilla Tolkien was asked how her mother responded to being compared with Lúthien. In response, Priscilla said that she did not think her mother had ever been aware of it: evidence, perhaps, for a veritable literary manoeuvre by Tolkien.

identities are confirmed: Beren und Lúthien are selected as the couple that validates the 'majority view' and merges 'love', marriage and reproduction (bearing the consequences). The relevance of their model is thus rendered incontestable by Tolkien's own marriage. Tolkien and his marriage, however, have little bearing on this reading of the text. It is the readers (not to forget the majority of Tolkien scholars) who bow to the totalitarian, all-pervasive heteronormativity of the 20th century and separate Sam/Frodo from Beren/Lúthien and Arwen/Aragorn. The reading of Tolkien's marriage as the 'real' story of Beren and Lúthien in no way legitimises such an approach – it only accommodates it!

Literature and 'love' determine each other. Thus the reader may decide: someone who subscribes to the 'sexuality dispositif' will doubtless label Sam and Frodo friends. Yet someone who follows the text alone will find that only one aspect distinguishes their story from those of Beren/Lúthien and Arwen/Aragorn: it is the most emotional and 'romantic' of all love stories in Tolkien's œuvre.[52]

PATRICK BRUECKNER is a student of German Medieval Literature, Women's Studies and Sociology at the University of Potsdam. He is working on aspects of gender in the works of J.R.R. Tolkien. He held joint seminars with Judith Klinger on 'Tolkien and the Middle Ages' at the University of Potsdam. His publications include: 'Zur Konstruktion 'richtiger' Weiblichkeit in J.R.R. Tolkiens *Lord of the Rings*' (Masquerade and Essence, Death and Desire. The construction of 'correct' femininity in J.R.R. Tolkien's *The Lord of the Rings*) in *Hither Shore* 2 (Yearbook of the German Tolkien Society).

---

[52] I am most grateful to Siobhan Groitl for her translation and to Judith Klinger and Sandra Schramm for their support.

Bibliography

Althusser, Louis, 1970, 'Ideology and ideological state apparatus (Notes towards an investigation)', in Louis Althusser, 2001, *Lenin and Philosophy and Other Essays*, New York: Monthly Review Press, pp. 85-126.

Akers-Jordan, Cathy, 2004, 'Fairy Princess or Tragic Heroine? The Metamorphosis of Arwen Undómiel in Peter Jackson's *The Lord of the Rings*', in Janet Brennan Croft, 2004, *Tolkien on Film: Essays on Peter Jackson's The Lord of the Rings*, Altadena, CA: The Mythopoeic Press, pp. 195-214.

Barthes, Roland, 1990, *A Lover's Discourse. Fragments*, (translated from French by Richard Howard. Original title: *Fragments d'un discours amoureux*, 1977), Harmondsworth: Penguin Books.

Brittnacher, Hans Richard, 1994, *Ästhetik des Horrors. Gespenster, Vampire, Monster, Teufel und künstliche Menschen in der phantastischen Literatur*, Frankfurt: Suhrkamp.

Bronfen, Elisabeth, 1992, *Over Her Dead Body: Death, Femininity and the Aesthetic*, Manchester: Manchester University Press.

Butler, Judith, 2000, *Antigone's Claim. Kinship Between Life & Death*, New York: Columbia University Press.

Döffinger, Birgit, 1997, *Das Ende des Dritten Zeitalters. Tolkiens »Herr der Ringe« zwischen Hochliteratur und populärem Fantasy-Roman*, (Schriftenreihe und Materialien der Phantastischen Bibliothek Wetzlar 23), Wetzlar: Förderkreis Phantastik.

Dronke, Peter, 1968, *The Medieval Lyric*, London: Hutchinson University Library.

Eilmann, Julian, 2006, 'Das Lied bin ich: Lieder, Poesie und Musik in J.R.R. Tolkiens Mittelerde-Mythologie', in Thomas Fornet-Ponse et al. (eds.), 2005, *Hither Shore, Interdisciplinary Journal on Modern Fantasy Literature. Tolkiens Weltbild(er)*, (Jahrbuch der Deutschen Tolkien Gesellschaft 2), Düsseldorf: Scriptorium Oxoniae, pp. 105-136.

Erll, Astrid et al., 2003, 'Literatur als Medium der Repräsentation und Konstruktion von Erinnerung und Identität', in Astrid Errl et al., 2003, *Literatur-Erinnerung-Identität: Theoriekonzeptionen und Fallstudien*, Trier: WVT, pp. iii-ix.

Foucault, Michel, 1986, 'Of Other Spaces', (translated by Jay Miskowiec), *Diacritics* 16, Spring 1986, pp. 22-27.

---, 1990, *The History of Sexuality. Vol. I. An Introduction*, (translated from French by Robert Hurley. Original title: *Histoire de la sexualité. 1: La volonté de savoir*, 1976), London: Penguin Books.

---, 2001, 'Qu'est-ce qu'un auteur', in Michel Foucault, 2001, *Dits et écrits I, 1954-1975*, Paris: Gallimard, pp. 838-862.

---, 2005, 'Les hétérotopies', in Michel Foucault, 2005, *Die Heterotopien. Les hétérotopies, Der utopische Körper, Les corps utopique, Zwei Radiovorträge, Zweisprachige Ausgabe*, Frankfurt: Suhrkamp, pp. 37-52.

Fredrick, Candice and Sam McBride, 2001, *Woman Among the Inklings. Gender, C.S. Lewis, J.R.R. Tolkien, and Charles Williams*, (Contributions in Woman's Studies 191), Westport, Connecticut and London: Greenwood Press.

Halperin, David M., 2000, '"How to Do the History of Male Homosexuality"', *GLQ, A Journal of Lesbian and Gay Studies* 6/1, 2000, pp. 87-123.

Kern, Stephen, 1992, *The Culture of Love. Victorians to Moderns*, Cambridge, Massachusetts and London: Harvard University Press.

Lewis, Alex and Elizabeth Currie, 2002, *The Uncharted Realms of Tolkien. A Critical Study of Text, Context and Subtext in the Works of J.R.R. Tolkien*, Weston Rhyn, Oswestry: Medea Publishing.

Lubkoll, Christine, 1994, 'Die heilige Musik oder Die Gewalt der Zeichen. Zur musikalischen Poetik in Heinrich von Kleists *Cäcilien*-Novelle', in Gerhard Neumann (ed.), 1994, *Heinrich von Kleist: Kriegsfall-Rechtsfall-Sündenfall*, Freiburg i.Br.: Rombach, pp. 337-364.

Luhmann, Niklas, 1986, *Love as Passion. The Codification of Intimacy*, (translated from German by Jeremy Gaines and Doris L. Jones. Original title: *Liebe als Passion. Zur Codierung von Intimität*, 1982), Cambridge: Polity Press.

Matt, Peter von, 1991, *Liebesverrat. Die Treulosen in der Literatur*, München: DTV.

Oesterle, Günter, 2002, 'Grenzerfahrung oder Härtetest. Das Verhältnis der Geschlechter in den französischen Feenmärchen: Charles Perrault *Griseldis* und Gabrielle-Suzanne de Villeneuve *Die Schöne und das Tier*', in Harlinda Lox et al. (eds.), 2002, *Mann und Frau im Märchen. Forschungsberichte aus der Welt der Märchen*, (Veröffentlichung der Europäischen Märchengesellschaft 27), München: Diederichs, pp. 175-189.

Sale, Roger, 2000, 'Modern Ideas of Heroism Are a Cornerstone of *The Lord of the Rings*', in Katie de Koster, (ed.), *Readings on J.R.R. Tolkien*, San Diego, CA: Greenhaven Press, pp. 80-85.

Shippey, Tom, 2002, *J.R.R. Tolkien. Author of the Century*, (paperback edition), New York: Houghton Mifflin.

Smol, Anna, 2004, '"Oh ...Oh ... Frodo!": Readings of Male Intimacy in *The Lord of the Rings*', *Modern fiction Studies (MfS). J.R.R. Tolkien* 50.4, Winter 2004, pp. 949-979.

Theweleit, Klaus, 1994, *Object-Choice. (All you need is love ...). On Mating Strategies & a Fragment of a Freud Biography*, (translated from German by Malcolm Green. Original title: *Objektwahl. (All you need is love ...). Über*

Paarbildungsstrategien & Bruchstücke einer Freudbiographie, 1990), London and New York: Verso.

Tolkien, J.R.R., 1995, *The Lord of the Rings*, (one volume paperback edition), London: HarperCollins.

---, 2000, *The Letters of J.R.R. Tolkien,* (edited by Humphrey Carpenter with assistance of Christopher Tolkien), (first edition 1981; paperback edition), New York: Houghton Mifflin.

---, 2001, *The Silmarillion,* (second edition, first edition 1977), (edited by Christopher Tolkien), New York: Ballantine Books DelRey.

---, 2002, *Morgoth's Ring*, (The History of Middle-earth volume 10, edited by Christopher Tolkien), (paperpack edition, first publication 1993), London: HarperCollins.

Rowbotham, Sheila, 1999, *A Century of Women. The History of Women in Britain and the United States*, (second edition with new material, first edition 1997), London: Penguin Books.

Wolf, Naomi, 1990, *The Beauty Myth*, London: Chatto & Windus.

Žižek, Slavoj, 2004, 'Death's Merciless Love', http://www.lacan.com/zizek-love.htm, 02-27-06.

The Lord of the Rings and 'Late Style': Tolkien, Adorno and Said

MARGARET HILEY

Abstract

This paper aims to relate *The Lord of the Rings* to the concept of 'late style' used by Theodor Adorno and Edward Said. This theory can be used to point out essentially modern elements in Tolkien's work, placing him within a modern(ist) context. Late style is about 'lost totality', melancholy, and death. Both Adorno and Said note as its central characteristics a discarding of formal conventions, tension, and a desire to appear self-generated. Late style's fragmented utterances ultimately end in silence.

These traits can all be found in Tolkien's novel. *The Lord of the Rings* uses a highly unconventional form: it presents itself as a collection of fragmented historical documents, hiding its author, and is supposed to read as if it had not been written, just as Adorno states that late Beethoven is "supposed to sound as if it had not been composed". The predominant themes of the book are exile, cultural decline, and mortality: after the departure of the last ship, those who remain in Middle-earth must endure what Arwen calls "the Doom of Men [...]: the loss and the silence". The text itself is all that is left of Middle-earth's 'lost totality'.

This tension between the fantastic and its loss is central to Tolkien's own 'late style'; his works have the power Said states is particular to late style, namely "to render disenchantment and pleasure without resolving the contradiction between them." Thus *The Lord of the Rings* subscribes not to an outmoded literary aesthetic, but to a modern one central to the twentieth century.

INTRODUCTION

While much early criticism dismisses Tolkien because he supposedly wrote in an archaic, reactionary or out-of-date style, attempting (vainly) to "retrieve [...] the old, prepubertal moral certainties of late-Edwardian England" (Rissik), several recent books on J.R.R. Tolkien claim that that Tolkien, far from being a freak phenomenon, can be read as a representative author of the twentieth century. Tom Shippey's *J.R.R. Tolkien: Author of the Century* is foremost among these works, stating that "he needs also to be looked at and interpreted within his own time, as *an* 'author of the century', the twentieth century, responding to the issues and anxieties of that century" (Shippey 2000:xxvii). This claim is echoed in works such as Verlyn Flieger's *A Question of Time* and Patrick Curry's *Defending Middle-earth*. Shippey's pioneering study focuses on thematic elements that seem particular to the twentieth century. For example, he locates a sense of overpowering evil in Tolkien and other authors such as Vonnegut and Orwell; he also focuses upon historical events that influenced Tolkien's matter. What remains largely unaddressed however, both in Shippey and subsequent works following his lead, is what is specifically twentieth-century or modern about Tolkien's style. Does the form of Tolkien's writings betray their modern origin?

A study of the modern elements of Tolkien's form and style seems long overdue, especially in light of the claims made above. While it seems obvious at first glance to relate his works back to the Norse and Anglo-Saxon myths and sagas he loved so dearly, if Tolkien is to be taken seriously as a modern author of the twentieth century his style will have to be seen in the context of that century, not just his subject-matter. This will prevent it being both lambasted as "Winnie-the-Pooh posing as epic" (Moorcock, quoted in Timmons 2000:1) and defended anachronistically as "a twentieth century *Beowulf*" (Thomson 1967:59). Of course, as content and form are parts of one whole that cannot be entirely separated from one another, any discussion of a work's form will touch on its themes also and vice versa. But analysing the form can also reveal new dimensions to the content: perhaps trying to read Tolkien's forms as twentieth-century can show us more of what is modern about his themes.

The present article represents a rather experimental attempt to come to terms with what is particularly modern about Tolkien's style, and it should be pointed out here that it is neither its aim nor desire to provide a comprehensive study of the modernism or modernity of his forms. Instead, it will focus only on his masterpiece, *The Lord of the Rings*, and read it in the light of the – again experimental – concept of 'late style' developed by Theodor Adorno and Edward Said. Indeed, perhaps a more fitting title for this examination would be "Tolkien read experimentally through Adorno's experimental theory of 'late style' as used experimentally by Said"! Nonetheless, it is to be hoped that this concept of 'lateness' can illuminate at least some of the specifically modern characteristics of Tolkien's writing.

'LATE STYLE': ADORNO AND SAID

'Late Style' is a concept developed by the philosopher and critic Theodor Adorno in his writings on the composer Ludwig van Beethoven. Two essays on late style survive: one is complete and polished, the second tentative and fragmented. It is Beethoven's late symphonies in particular that interest Adorno, for they have always posed a problem of form, breaking with the traditional conventions of the sonata form. Critics have sought to find an explanation for their structural oddity ever since their first performances: Adorno's essays represent one of the more interesting attempts to come to terms with them.

Adorno sees the difficulty of Beethoven's forms as following a pattern found in the mature works of major artists. These works break with the traditions of their time, and the new style they advance often appears inharmonious, obscure and incomprehensible:

> The maturity of the late works of important artists is not like the ripeness of fruit. As a rule, these works are not well rounded, but wrinkled, even fissured. [...] They lack all that harmony which the classicist aesthetic is accustomed to demand from the work of art, showing more traces of history than of growth.
> (Adorno 1998a:123)

This 'maturity' Adorno (1998a:125) relates to "reflection on death" or a sense of decline. While according to Adorno, it is the awareness of death that causes 'lateness', he calls it a metaphysical mistake to attempt to locate the creating subject's awareness of death in the work itself (for example, to try and interpret the late work psychologically). For Adorno states the difficult form should be attributed to the *lack* of subjectivity in late works:

> [Subjectivity], as something mortal, and in the name of death, vanishes from the work of art in reality. The force of subjectivity in late works is the irascible gesture with which it leaves them. It bursts them asunder, not in order to express itself but, expressionlessly, to cast off the illusion of art. Of the works it leaves only fragments behind [...]. Touched by death, the masterly hand sets free the matter it previously formed. [...] the work falls silent as it is deserted, turning its hollowness outwards.
> (Adorno 1998a:125)

The late work is thus characterised by a disappearance of subjectivity rather than a heightened subjectivity. In his second essay, Adorno (1998b:154) reflects further on what the disappearance of subjectivity from the work entails for it: "The late Beethoven *covers its traces*. [...]

Does he, in order to enable tonality, and so on, to emerge in this way, obliterate the traces of *composition*? Is this supposed to sound as if it had not been composed?" For him, Beethoven's late works take on a self-generated appearance. He concludes that in its strange and fragmented form, "Beethoven's polyphony [...] presents the lost totality of the alienated world" (Adorno 1998b:157).

Adorno's theory of a late style is taken up by Edward Said in an article published posthumously in the *London Review of Books*.[1] It is Said who claims that 'lateness' can be related to modernism and modernity; carrying on from Adorno's statement quoted last, Said (2004:5) concludes that "Beethoven's late style, remorselessly alienated and obscure, is the prototypical modern aesthetic form." Said states that the characteristics of late style are the same as the alienation and formal disruption typical of the early twentieth century; in this sense all modern or modernist works are 'late' (in his article, Said interprets for example works by the modernist writers Lampedusa and Cavafy as late works). This is a valid claim as Adorno relates lateness to a sense of decline and death, and much of Modernism is concerned with both individual and cultural decline and death, which it thematises in its works and expresses in its unconventional and fragmented forms.[2] Accordingly, Said (2004:5) finds in the modern works he calls late a "particular melancholy associated with senescence, loss and death" and a "sense of all-pervading mortality".

---

[1] An entire book by Said on late style is due to be published in 2006, but could of course not be taken into consideration while writing this article: Edward Said, April 2006, *Late Style: Music and Literature Against the Grain*, New York: Random House.

[2] Thus Leon Surette likens modernism's view of history to "the antique view of history as a story of decline from some pure origin" (Surette 1993:253), and Art Berman claims that "decline is often modernism's subject: there would be no modernism without it" (Berman 1994:212).

For both Adorno and Said, late style's most special characteristic is that it is capable of expressing contradictions without having to resolve them. Thus Adorno (1998a:126) describes Beethoven's music as "a process, but not as a development; its process is an ignition between extremes which no longer tolerate a safe means or a spontaneous harmony": oppositions are not reconciled, nor is it felt necessary to do so. Said (2004:7) sees this lack of a "spontaneous harmony between extremes" as "equal forces straining in opposite directions" that hold one another in tension. Tension thus becomes a further characteristic of the late work, and once again it is a characteristic typical of the modernist work of art as well.[3] Said (2004:7) sees this as the factor which above all others makes late style special and noteworthy: "This is the prerogative of late style: it has the power to render disenchantment and pleasure without resolving the contradiction between them." Late works are those that can accommodate contradictions both thematic and structural without having to resolve them.

THE RED BOOK AND THE HIDDEN AUTHOR

J.R.R. Tolkien might not at first glance seem the likeliest author to which to apply this concept of 'late style'. The characteristics enumerated above seem reminiscent for example of the mature poems of W. B. Yeats, such as *Sailing to Byzantium*, where the poet sees himself exiled from the 'new' Ireland as a result of his age ("That is no country for old men") and wishes to escape into "the artifice of eternity" only to find that even in Byzantium he must sing "Of what is past, or passing, or to come" (Yeats 1989:301-302). This is a work obsessed with decline and death, that simultaneously manages to escape and remain trapped within time; the oppositions between youth and age, time and eternity, are

---

[3] Cf. for example Rainer Emig: "the essential character of the modernist work [is] tension." (Emig 1995:241)

explicitly *not* reconciled, showing Yeats's poem to be representative of lateness. However, Said's claim that late works have a "sense of all-pervading mortality", and a "particular melancholy associated with senescence, loss and death", might remind the reader equally of *The Lord of the Rings*. For example, W. A. Senior (2000:173) claims that its "most pervasive and unifying component of atmosphere and mood [is] the sustained and grieved sense of loss." Tolkien's topics of the Escape from and the Escape to Death can also be read within the context of lateness. However, these topics of death and loss have already been covered extensively in Tolkien criticism and I here only wish to point out their possible relation to a modern(ist) late style before turning to my main point of interest: Tolkien's form and style.

Generally speaking, the form of *The Lord of the Rings* is a trilogy, one large novel made up of three smaller ones. However, surrounding the main narrative is a mass of extra material – a long prologue, explaining about hobbits, the Shire, and the Ring; and six appendices, giving extra information on the realms of Gondor and Rohan, the genealogies of the Kings of Gondor, the Dwarves of Moria, and the main hobbit families, along with notes on the various calendars and languages that occur in the story. Even the main narrative is interspersed with footnotes referring the reader to the Appendices: all in all, a highly unusual form whose strangeness is seldom commented upon as such. It is probably safe to guess that the greater part of readers do not plough their way through the Prologue and Appendices.[4] For Tolkien however, they were an integral part of his book; indeed, he took so much time compiling them that the publication of *The Return of the King* was seriously delayed. The mass of critical material, if taken seriously by the reader (as was the author's intention), disrupts the conventional reading process as it

---

[4] For example, I noted that in the newest German translation of *The Lord of the Rings* the Appendices were not even included in the three-volume edition, but sold separately (Tolkien, 2000, *Der Herr der Ringe*, Stuttgart: Klett-Cotta).

encourages him or her to interrupt reading the main story by looking up the footnotes in the Appendices; the unity of the narrative is broken up. This disruption is a first hint that the form of Tolkien's novel is, as Adorno (1998a:123) states of late works, "not well rounded", not as unified a narrative as it might appear at first glance.

With all the extra material encompassing the main story, *The Lord of the Rings* very strongly resembles an academic critical edition. And in fact this is exactly what the book pretends to be. In the Prologue, *The Hobbit* is referred to as a "selection from the Red Book of Westmarch" (Tolkien 1992:13), and it is stated that "[t]his account of the end of the Third Ages is drawn from the Red Book of Westmarch" (Tolkien 1992:26). This Red Book is referred to several times in the course of the story of *The Lord of the Rings*. It is the book in which Bilbo writes down the account of his "*Unexpected Journey*" (Tolkien 1992:1065), and which is completed by Frodo and Sam. In its complete form as "preserved at Undertowers, the home of the Fairbairns, Wardens of the Westmarch" (Tolkien 1992:26) – the descendants of Elanor, Sam's daughter – it contained Bilbo and Frodo's stories, Bilbo's poetry and translations from the Elvish, and "commentaries, genealogies, and various other matter concerning the hobbit members of the Fellowship" (Tolkien 1992:26). In the Prologue to *The Lord of the Rings*, we are given an overview of the main hobbit manuscripts and the history of their transmission. All the material in the Appendices is said to derive from these sources, such as the "Thain's Book of Minas Tirith", which is Aragorn's copy of the Red Book, or "Herblore of the Shire", written by Merry. These various sources and their copies are carefully compared and their differences listed. This is the kind of documentation one would certainly expect to find in the edition of an ancient text preserved in various manuscript forms (of course, Tolkien himself made several such editions). *The Lord of the Rings* itself thus appears as a selection of material from the fictional Red Book, presented in a scholarly edition.

Similarly, the poetry collection *The Adventures of Tom Bombadil* carries the sub-title "verses from The Red Book" (Tolkien 1962:3), and in a Preface its poems are ascribed to Bilbo and Sam, among others.

The implications of this fictitious transmission history are far-reaching. When Tolkien changed the story of *The Hobbit* for the 1947 edition to accommodate the sinister nature of the Ring, a hint of the original was preserved as the story Bilbo made up about his encounter with Gollum (that he found the Ring, and Gollum showed him the way out of the mountains). Now, in the Prologue of *The Lord of the Rings*, we are told that this false account

> still appeared in the original Red Book, as it did in several copies and abstracts. But many copies contain the true account (as an alternative), derived no doubt from notes by Frodo and Samwise, both of whom learned the truth, though they seem to have been unwilling to delete anything actually written by the old hobbit himself. (Tolkien 1992:25)

Of course, this is nothing but a disguised history of the various editions of *The Hobbit*. The original edition is thus supposedly derived from the original Red Book, while the later edition contains Frodo's emendations to Bilbo's story, which are in fact Tolkien's changes. Tolkien's desire to present the tales of Middle-earth as actual documents is so strong that he makes up a transmission history to account for his own changes to his stories! The end result is one that Adorno cites as typical of 'late works': *The Lord of the Rings* "shows more traces of history than of growth." It does not appear as an organically conceived tale, but as a history or a tale whose different stages of development can still be perceived. Though the tale according to Tolkien "grew in the telling", the impression the reader receives is not of one single story, but of many layers and fragments of stories: "a history of the Great War of the Ring [including] many glimpses of the yet more ancient history that preceded it." (Tolkien 1992:9)

The Lord of the Rings's fictitious transmission history serves several purposes. For one, the whole critical apparatus accompanying *The Lord of the Rings* actually strengthens the impression, already given in the story itself, of the reality of the secondary world and the authenticity of the tale being told: it has been preserved in historical documents, survives in several slightly different versions, but is ultimately to be traced back to the original authors (Bilbo, Sam and Frodo), tangible historical figures. However, the transmission history also neatly covers the traces of the real author – Tolkien himself. Adorno's question (1998b:154) about Beethoven's music, "Is this supposed to sound as if it had not been composed?", must thus remind one of Tolkien's strategies – for *The Lord of the Rings* is certainly supposed to read as if it had not been authored, at least not by any single person. Instead, it presents itself in a way as self-generated, as a multitude of already extant historical fragments found and collected together rather than a newly composed story. The novel's controversial form, a collection of fragmented and incomplete documents, dissociates itself from an authorial subject we usually expect to find in a conventional narrative. The pseudo-academic form commands an objective register, and the multiplicity of very different voices we encounter in the various unfinished or unpreserved fragments denies any one creative 'subjectivity' in *The Lord of the Rings*. Instead, what we have is a grouping of partially related and unfinished narratives, histories and scientific writings, loosely held together in the form of a scholarly edition. As already quoted above, Adorno (1998a:125) states that the

> force of subjectivity on late works is the irascible gesture with which it leaves them. It bursts them asunder, not in order to express itself but, expressionlessly, to

cast off the illusion of art. Of the works it leaves only fragments behind.

The Lord of the Rings also wishes to "cast off the illusion of art", it poses as reality; in order to do so, the creative subject eliminates itself from the work. This means that the disappearing authorial subject can leave behind only fragments, no complete narrative. In this sense then, too, *The Lord of the Rings* is a 'late work', and the concept of 'late style' can be used to interpret its unusual form. It is through this disappearance of the author made evident through 'late style' that the novel can also be related to modernism, for the disappearance of subjectivity and ensuing fragmentation are also typical of modernist works; to stay with the example of Yeats, this can be seen in his use of 'personae' or masks to try and purge his works of subjectivity that marks his entire oeuvre, from *The Lover* of his earlier poetry to the golden bird of *Sailing to Byzantium*. While Tolkien's editor-persona is quite different in type, the basic urge behind the adoption of masks is the same: to eliminate creative subjectivity and present the work of art as self-generated.[5]

TENSION: PRIMARY AND SECONDARY WORLD

The editor-persona used by Tolkien in *The Lord of the Rings* and *The Adventures of Tom Bombadil* (and, to a lesser degree and with different intent, in *Farmer Giles of Ham*) makes us aware of another kind of tension in his work. Several questions inevitably arise when reading the Prologue and the Appendices: Who is the 'editor' of this story, and where and when is he writing? In the Prologue, an explanation of the nature of hobbits seems to imply that readers of the text are no longer familiar with the creatures. For "[e]ven in ancient days they were, as a

---

[5] For further reading on modernism and impersonality, see Maud Ellmann (1987) and Richard Ellmann (1987).

rule, shy of 'the Big Folk', as they call us, and now they avoid us with dismay and are becoming hard to find." (Tolkien 1992:13) The use of 'us', implying identity of editor and reader, suggests that both are human, not hobbits like the original writers of the edited manuscripts. The events recorded in the hobbit manuscripts are long past, and the world is now very different: "Those days, the Third Age of Middle-earth, are now long past, and the shape of all lands has been changed." (Tolkien 1992:14) The manuscripts edited were written during the Fourth Age, and the edition presented is obviously much later still. Mythical creatures such as Elves and Dwarves no longer exist, and the hobbits themselves appear to be becoming extinct due to the destruction of their habitat by man. Obviously, this is a clear link to modern England and its increasing industrialisation. The Prologue has other hints that suggest Middle-earth is related to our world: "the regions in which Hobbits then lived were doubtless the same as those in which they still linger: the North-West of the Old World, east of the Sea." (Tolkien 1992:14) – that would imply in Europe. The editor appears to be writing in our time, discussing the changes that have taken place in the world since the recording of the events of the War of the Ring. For example, the calendar of the Shire is said to have "differed in several features from ours" (Tolkien 1992:1141). This 'ours' clearly refers to the Gregorian calendar used in England and Western Europe. The editor is thus mysteriously positioned somewhere between the Primary World and Middle-earth, and it is strongly suggested that actually our world and Middle-earth are the same.

Tolkien himself actually states this. His biography quotes him as saying "Middle-earth is *our* world" (Carpenter 1977:98), and in his letters he writes "Middle-earth is not an imaginary world" (Carpenter 1981:239). These statements, if taken seriously, place Middle-earth in an uneasy position somewhere between the imaginary and the real. The actions described in his works supposedly take place in the actual world, but Tolkien calls the time in which they take place "a purely imaginary (though not wholly impossible) period of antiquity." (Carpenter 1977:98) Is the spatial dimension therefore real while the temporal one is not? Questions of this kind quickly highlight a tension between the primary and the secondary world – again, a tension that Tolkien never resolves. We never find out what exactly is 'real' about Middle-earth; but its creator denies its 'unreality' (among other things, as shown above, by making up an elaborate transmission history of supposedly historical documents and by ridding the work of subjectivity).

Thus *The Lord of the Rings* sets up a dichotomy between the Primary World and the Secondary World of Middle-earth; the two are held in contrast and at the same time a connection between the two is posited – a connection which is never made entirely clear. Tolkien's novel holds the two 'opposites' of Primary and Secondary World, as Said says, "in tension, as equal forces straining in opposite directions", without ever resolving this tension. In fact, the entire structure of *The Lord of the Rings* is conditioned by this unresolved tension. For if it were to be resolved, then we would need either an explanation of the way Middle-earth changed into our present world – a gap which the present transmission history does not fill – or we would need a confession that Middle-earth actually does not exist, which would render the fragmented history provided totally unnecessary. Thus we can see that this unresolved tension typical of late style structures the very foundation of Tolkien's sub-creation, making it a fundamentally late work. Again, this vexed relation between a mythic, prehistorical past and the actual present, between which a temporal continuity is simultaneously implied and denied, is also evident in works by Yeats, especially in those that try to construct a coherent mythic past for a modern Ireland.[6] Tolkien's own nationalistic

---

[6] For example, Yeats's poems and plays on the Easter Rising of 1916 portray the mythic Cuchulain as the guiding spirit behind Pearse and Connolly (cf. *The Death of Cuchulain*), yet that mythic heroism (espoused by the revolutionaries them-

project of a 'mythology for England', a project at once put forward and denied, should thus be seen similarly as a modernist project full of the tension typical of late style.

THE FANTASTIC AND ITS LOSS

The tension between Primary and Secondary World is reflected in *The Lord of the Rings*'s choice of subject-matter already touched upon above: decline, melancholy and mortality. The time described in the narrative is one of fundamental change: it is the time when Middle-earth becomes disenchanted, gradually turning into the Primary World. Thus Patchen Mortimer (2005:125) states that "the subject of the novel, the true concern, is emphatically not the defeat of Sauron, but rather the passing of Middle-earth's Third Age." It is this passing that Treebeard is talking about when he says to Celeborn and Galadriel, "It is sad that we should meet only thus at the ending. For the world is changing: I feel it in the water, I feel it in the earth, and I smell it in the air. I do not think we shall meet again." (Tolkien 1992:1017) The narrative focuses on this transition from the enchanted Third to the disenchanted Fourth Age, and the fantastic reality of Middle-earth is counterbalanced with the loss of the fantastic. Thus after following the fate of the tale's protagonists for over thousand pages, in the novel's last chapter we are confronted with the departure of all its wonderful and magical creatures as well as the Baggins family on Círdan's last ship. Sam is left alone on the shores of the sea, watching only "a shadow on the waters that was soon lost in the West." (Tolkien 1992:1069) And while Sam finds comfort with Rosie and his family, the certainty remains that Middle-earth

---

selves, not just Yeats in his view of them) is questioned by the bleak historical reality of their deaths: "Was it needless death after all? [...] they dreamed and are dead" (*Easter 1916* in Yeats 1989:288). Myth and reality cannot be brought together.

has become a poorer place for that ship's sailing. Similarly, in 'The Tale of Aragorn and Arwen', Aragorn wins his elven princess only for both to succumb to mortality; after Aragorn's death "Arwen went forth from the House, and the light of her eyes was quenched, and it seemed to her people that she had become cold and grey as nightfall in winter that comes without a star." (Tolkien 1992:1100) – the enchanted Evenstar turns to dull and starless night. This shift of the fantastic to the mundane is also focused upon and expressed particularly well in Tolkien's poem 'The Last Ship' (according to the 'editor' of *The Adventures of Tom Bombadil*, "derived ultimately from Gondor" [Tolkien 1962:8]). Here a mortal girl, Fíriel, watches the last ship of the Elves pass on its way to Valinor; when first she goes down to the river, she is dancing, the sun is shining, and her gown is decked with jewels; after she has refused the call of the Elves to join them and they have departed, the world turns dull and dark:

> No jewels bright her gown bore,
> as she walked back from the meadow
> under roof and dark door,
> under the house-shadow.
> She donned her smock of russet brown,
> her long hair braided,
> and to her work came stepping down.
> Soon the sunlight faded.
> (Tolkien 1962:63-64)

The poem concludes:

> [...] never more
> westward ships have waded
> in mortal waters as before,
> and their song has faded.
> (Tolkien 1962:64)

Tolkien is particularly fond of this picture of songs fading or ending as a symbol for the end of the magical Third Age. In *The Return of the King* we encounter the passage "the Third Age was over, and the Days of the Rings were passed, and an end was come of the story and song of those times." (Tolkien 1992:1067) Similarly, the account of the Third Age from *The Silmarillion* states "an end was come for the Eldar of story and song." (Tolkien 1994:367) Even in *The Lord of the Rings* itself we constantly come across songs "that none now remember aright as [they] were told of old." (Tolkien 1992:208) The impression is one of a slow and inexorable cultural loss – an impression we also encounter in many modernist works of art; as Yeats laments: "Many ingenious lovely things are gone / That seemed sheer miracle to the crowd" (*Nineteen Hundred and Nineteen* in Yeats 1989:314). When we relate this loss, constantly thematised in *The Lord of the Rings*, back to the novel itself, we can see that it actually conditions the novel's form: Middle-earth's story and song have faded away until all that is left are the fragments that form the novel. By the time the 'edition' of the Red Book is made, all that is left of this 'period of antiquity', as Tolkien calls it, is in fact the edition itself. *The Lord of the Rings* represents all that is left of Middle-earth in our modern day and age. In this, its fragmented and incomplete form, like Beethoven's polyphony, it "presents the lost totality of the alienated world" (Adorno 1998b:157). It is all that remains of a complete world that has given way to our modern and alienated one, in which, as Tolkien scoffs in 'On Fairy-Stories' (Tolkien 1997:149), motor-cars are perceived to be more alive than dragons and more real than horses: "How real, how startlingly alive is a factory chimney compared with an elm tree!" In this, too, *The Lord of the Rings* is late: as a text, it represents all that is left of Middle-earth's 'lost totality'. One might exclaim as with the speaker of T. S. Eliot's *The Waste Land*: "These fragments I have shored against my ruins." And once again, one of Adorno's (1998a:126) statements on lateness comes to mind: "the work falls silent [...] turning its hollowness outwards." In *The Lord of the Rings*, what ultimately remains is silence as the fragmented utterances of the work fade away. The fate of the late work is the same as what Arwen terms "the Doom of Men [...]: the loss and the silence." (Tolkien 1992:1100)

Tolkien simultaneously establishes and subverts his fantastic world, as what fragments remain of it basically chronicle its ending; we have neither a complete magical Secondary World, nor a fully disenchanted Primary one. Nor is there a harmonious transition between these polar opposites, as the result of their collision is fragmentation and loss. *The Lord of the Rings* is, to my mind, the work that above all others fulfils Said's demands of a 'late work': that it have "the power to render disenchantment and pleasure without resolving the contradiction between them." (Said 2004:7) In Tolkien's work, fantasy and reality, pleasure and disenchantment stand side by side, each one holding the other in balance. The delight the reader takes in the Secondary World is not lessened by the fact that it does not last forever – perhaps the delight is the keener for it. But neither is the disappointment and disenchantment felt at the loss of the fantastic made in any way less significant. That Tolkien did not feel it necessary to resolve either one or the other makes his book a masterpiece of late style.

TOLKIEN, 'LATE STYLE' AND MODERNISM

It is to be hoped that this article has been able to show that Tolkien's *The Lord of the Rings* fulfils the criteria that both Adorno and Said set in their definition of late style. Its subject-matter is deeply concerned with an "all-pervading mortality". The novel defies convention in its form as a collection of narrative and non-narrative fragments, collected in a mock-scholarly edition. In its many layers and fragments, *The Lord of the Rings* truly shows "more traces of history than growth", an impression strengthened by the fictitious transmission history Tolkien makes up for his various narratives. The fragmented form also conditions the disappearance of the authorial subject from the work (or, the other way around, the disappearance of subjectivity fragments the work). The unresolved tension typical of late works is evident in Tolkien's balancing of the Primary and Secondary World; in its form as a critical 'edition', the novel hangs between both, as it does thematically in simultaneously establishing the fantastic and countering it with its loss.

Of course, to make this analysis of the modernism of Tolkien's 'late style' complete, one would have to compare him at length to at least one modernist writer using the criteria of 'late style' as the basis of comparison. While there is not enough space here for such an investigation,[7] the brief quotes from W. B. Yeats may give a small hint of what might be possible when taking this line of study, and how fruitful such a comparison might be. What is missing from Tolkien studies is a detailed and objective literary evaluation of Tolkien as a twentieth-century writer, comparing him to those writers against whom he is traditionally defined. As Brian Rosebury (2003:7) writes: "Tolkien belongs to the same century as Proust, Joyce and Eliot, and is read with pleasure by many of the same readers. Criticism needs to confront this fact and make sense of it." This is where studies of Tolkien to date have failed.[8] Shippey's *J.R.R. Tolkien: Author of the Century* draws a quick comparison between Tolkien and the Modernists, but relies on superficial definitions of Modernism given in *The Oxford Companion to English Literature* and the *Johns Hopkins Guide to Literary Theory and Criticism* (cf. Shippey 2000:313). This distressingly leads to a total misinterpretation of what is meant by Modernism's 'mythical method', and the naïve

---

[7] I am currently working on a longer study that aims to do this in greater detail.

[8] In the past years, Brian Rosebury's *Tolkien: A Cultural Phenomenon* (esp. chapter 4, 'Tolkien and the Twentieth Century') and an article by Patchen Mortimer (2005) have offered insightful but (of necessity) very brief re-evaluations of the relation between Tolkien and his modernist contemporaries.

accusation that the Modernists were interested in experiments with language and reality simply because these experiments were engaging intellectually, not because they took these experiments seriously. As anyone reasonably well acquainted with Modernism can tell, the very opposite was the case. Another study that tries to place Tolkien in the context of the twentieth century and frustratingly shies away from a literary comparison with the canonised Modernists and Postmodernists is Patrick Curry's *Defending Middle-earth*. Curry (1997:33) states in his introduction: "We shall also consider *The Lord of the Rings* as literature." Yet his definitions of what is modern or postmodern about Tolkien's work remain one-sidedly based on cultural phenomena and his personal ideas, with no examination of modernist or postmodernist literary techniques. If Tolkien "needs to be looked at and interpreted within his own time, as *an* 'author of the century', the twentieth century, responding to the issues and the anxieties of that century" (Shippey 2000:xxvii), an evaluation of his work in the terms of the literature of the twentieth century is surely essential.

Using this concept of a late style that is characteristic of modern and modernist works of art can perhaps help to tell us more about why *The Lord of the Rings* should be read as a representative work of the twentieth century. The late elements in it can be compared to those in other modern works, works that might resist another form of comparison. Obviously, as already stated, such a comparison falls beyond the scope of the present article. But hopefully it has shown that *The Lord of the Rings* can be read as a 'late work'. Indeed, of all the works that Edward Said cites as evincing late style, I cannot think of one that would fits this concept better than Tolkien's masterpiece.

MARGARET HILEY is a PhD student at the University of Glasgow, working on aspects of Modernism in the works of C.S. Lewis, J.R.R. Tolkien and Charles Williams. She has published several articles on the Inklings and fantasy in general. She teaches at the University of Glasgow and at the University of Regensburg, Germany. Margaret also holds an M.A. in musicology and her further research interests include Early Music (particularly lute music) and the relationship between music and literary texts.

Bibliography

Adorno, Theodor W., 1998a, 'The Late Style (I)', in Rolf Tiedemann (ed.), 1998, *Beethoven. The Philosophy of Music*, (translated by Edmund Jephcott), Cambridge: Polity Press, pp. 123-137.

---, 1998b, 'The Late Style (II)', in Rolf Tiedemann (ed.), 1998, *Beethoven. The Philosophy of Music*, (translated by Edmund Jephcott), Cambridge: Polity Press, pp. 154-161.

Berman, Art, 1994, *Preface to Modernism*, Urbana: University of Illinois Press.

Carpenter, Humphrey, 1977, *J.R.R. Tolkien: A Biography*. London: Unwin Hyman.

---, (edited with the assistance of Christopher Tolkien), 1981, *The Letters of J.R.R. Tolkien*, London: George Allen & Unwin.

Curry, Patrick, 1997, *Defending Middle-Earth*, London: HarperCollins.

Ellmann, Maud, 1987, *The Poetics of Impersonality*, Brighton: Harvester.

Ellmann, Richard, 1987, *Yeats: The Man and the Masks*, Harmondsworth: Penguin.

Emig, Rainer, 1995, *Modernism in Poetry*, London: Longman.

Flieger, Verlyn, 1997, *A Question of Time: J.R.R. Tolkien's Road to Faërie*, Kent, Ohio: The Kent State University Press.

Mortimer, Patchen, 2005, 'Tolkien and Modernism', in *Tolkien Studies* 2, 2005, pp. 113-129.

Rissik, Andrew, 2000, 'Middle Earth, middlebrow', (Review of Tom Shippey's *J.R.R. Tolkien: Author of the Century*), in *The Guardian*, 2 September 2000.

Rosebury, Brian, 2003, *Tolkien: A Cultural Phenomenon*, (revised and enlarged edition; first published 1992), Houndmills: Palgrave Macmillan.

Said, Edward, 2004, 'Thoughts on Late Style', *LRB* 26.15, (5 August 2004), pp. 3-7.

Senior, W. A., 2000, 'Loss Eternal in Tolkien's Middle-earth', in George Clark and Daniel Timmons (eds.), 2000, *J.R.R. Tolkien and His Literary Resonances*, Westport, CT: Greenwood Press, pp. 173-182.

Shippey, Tom A., 2000, *J.R.R. Tolkien: Author of the Century*, London: Harper-Collins.

Surette, Leon, 1993, *The Birth of Modernism: Ezra Pound, T.S. Eliot, W.B. Yeats and the Occult*, Montreal: McGill University Press.

Thomson, George H., 1967, '*The Lord of the Rings*: The Novel as Traditional Romance', in *Wisconsin Studies in Contemporary Literature* 8, Winter 1967, p. 59.

Tolkien, John Ronald Reuel, 1962, *The Adventures of Tom Bombadil*, London: George Allen & Unwin.

--, 1992, *The Lord of the Rings*, (one volume edition with the text of the second edition; first edition 1954-55; second edition 1966), London: HarperCollins.

---, 1997, 'On Fairy-Stories', (originally Andrew Lang Lecture given on 8 March 1939; first published in 1947), in John Ronald Reuel Tolkien, 1997, *The Monster and the Critics and Other Essays*, (edited by Christopher Tolkien), London: HarperCollins, pp. 109-161.

Yeats, William Butler, 1989, *Yeats's Poems*, (edited by A. Norman Jeffares), Basingstoke: Macmillan.

An Introduction to the Dynamics of the Intertraditional Dialogue in *The Lord of the Rings*: Aragorn's Heroic Evolution

MARTIN SIMONSON

Abstract

This paper attempts to disclose the different stages in Aragorn's evolution as a character with reference to how he internalises the narrative traditions encountered on the road to Minas Tirith. In this, the analysis is a statement on how Tolkien's approach to these traditions differs from modernist expressions of what Frye, in his theory of modes, terms "ironic myth".

INTRODUCTION: TOLKIEN AND IRONIC MYTH

In a narrative that constantly puts different narrative traditions in dialogue, like *The Lord of the Rings*, it becomes important for any critic aiming at analysing the presence of different literary genres in this work, to take into account the particular *dynamics* of this intertraditional dialogue. Quite obviously, given that *The Lord of the Rings* is not *exclusively* a novel, it would be just as misleading and absurd to read and judge it exclusively from a novel perspective, as it would be to complain about the limited psychological evolution of Ulysses in *The Odyssey*, the physical impossibility of Atlas being transformed into a mountain in the story taken from Ovid's *Metamorphoses*, the excessive emphasis on heroic feats in *Chanson de Roland*, or the lack of verisimilitude in the descriptions of physical space found in *Le Mort D'Arthur*, to mention only four examples from different narrative traditions.

The challenge of analysing literary genre in this work is further increased by the fact that the character-drawing, the descriptions of action and the treatment of different themes are not coherent from the point of view of any fixed, genre-based conventions, but seem to acquire coherence from the *dialogue* between traditions. Depending on the particular narrative characteristics of each situation, the traditions may merge or clash, adding or aborting the influence of others. This process defines a great deal of the narrative treatment of characters, physical space and action, and an important part of the narrative is dedicated to exploring the limits of the literary traditions in dialogue.

I have elsewhere concluded that, as Tolkien integrates the greater part of the narrative traditions of Northern Europe in *The Lord of the Rings*, he shares many features with several representatives of what Frye terms "ironic myth".[1] At the same time, he proposes a radically different alternative to this literary mode.

Frye's (1971) theory of modes, and the concept of ironic myth, shows that the evolution of Western literature is characterised by a displacement from the supernatural (myth) towards increasingly realistic modes, which resulted in a return towards mythic paradigms in the literature of the 20th century. There are examples of both poets of the Great War and modernists, such as Edward Thomas and T.S. Eliot, whose literary creations illustrate a return to mythic patterns, and how they, in the process, tend to incorporate references to a great part of the Western literary canon in their own works (Simonson 2005:158-163). The First World War brought about a radical break with the past that engendered an atmosphere of transition, which in turn inspired poets and writers to approach the concept of time as a cyclical phenomenon. An epoch had ended, the novel could not evolve further, and the next step in literature seems to have been not a step forward, strictly speaking, but rather a retrospective, encyclopaedic approach, which involved a compilation of

---

[1] For a more extensive comparison between the ironic myth in modernism and in Tolkien, see Simonson (2005).

the narrative traditions of the past, presented on a simultaneous temporal level set in the modern, post-war world.

Tolkien, however, was not particularly inclined to accept the conditions of modern life, which seemed to him abominable in many ways, and instead of rooting his story in the 'real' contemporary world, he preferred to create – or "subcreate", as he labelled the creative process of any artist (Tolkien 1997:132) – a fantastic world in which he would be able to express his ideas.[2] I consider that this 'decision' (I put this between inverted commas because, in the case of Tolkien, it would seem an inevitability, given his learning and interests) is fundamental to our understanding of the particular way in which *The Lord of the Rings* reflects certain characteristics of ironic myth, especially since it gave rise to the creation of a previously unknown literary chronotope, capable of hosting a very smooth, suggestive and, to some extent, even 'realistic' intertraditional dialogue.

Bakhtin's theories of the chronotope and the narrative dynamics of the novel give consistency to this idea insofar as Tolkien's work illustrates how the novel is able to liberate the genres of the past as it exercises its influence over them (Bakhtin 1989:483-484). However, the combination of the formal structure of the novel, the inclination towards literary encyclopaedia of the ironic myth and the creation of the Secondary World gave rise to such an insistent intertraditional dialogue that it seems impossible to define *The Lord of the Rings* as a novel only, given that the work is at the same time heavily indebted to the traditions of epic, romance and myth, in their varied expressions.

One of the most important differences between *The Lord of the Rings* and modernist novels written in the mode of ironic myth is that

---

[2] This reflects Tolkien's attitude towards what he perceived as absurd experiments, as expressed in his essay 'On Fairy-Stories': in order to renew our vision of the world we have to displace our modern perception of everyday reality, which is what fairy-stories achieve. See Tolkien (1997:146-147).

Tolkien does not resort to irony or parody, two literary devices that Bakhtin (1989:451) considers fundamental in order to liberate the 'dead' genres of the past. The rhetorics of irony and parody would, on the other hand, appear to be necessary for that purpose in a modern historical setting, as Joyce and other modernists discovered. Let us take a look at one example of how Joyce's novel *Ulysses* incorporates the medieval romance tradition, as the narrator portrays Leopold Bloom's visit to a hospital in Dublin:

> And whiles they spake the door of the castle was opened and there nighed them a mickle noise as of many that sat there at meat. And there came against the place as they stood a young learning knight yclept Dixon. And the traveller Leopold was couth to him sitten it had happened that they had ado each with the other in the house of misericord where this learning knight by cause the traveller Leopold came there to be healed for he was sore wounded in his breast by a spear wherewith a horrible and dreadful dragon was smitten him for which he did do make a salve of volatile salt and chrism as much as he might suffice. And he said now that he should go into that castle for to make merry with them that were there. (Joyce 1998:369)

Tolkien proposed a different method of incorporating the literary traditions of the past into the present, without relying on an ironic treatment.[3] In order to do so, he was faced with the difficult task of eluding

---

[3] The ironic treatment often yields abrupt contrasts, as in the example quoted above, so that the traditions do not merge efficiently but are rather separated even further. Rosebury (2003:154-155) argues that the absence of irony about value and about the literary work itself is what makes Tolkien's work fundamentally different from modernist works: "transparency, not ironic self-reference, is essential to *The Lord of the Rings*."

an *internal* dialogue with his own time, while at the same time making the work relevant for the contemporary reader. The invention of the Secondary World offered him possibilities that were unimaginable in the context of modernist strategies, and the result is a different treatment of the dialogue between past and present traditions that involves a constant exploration of its own constraints.

ARAGORN AND THE INTERTRADITIONAL DIALOGUE

One of the many striking features of *The Lord of the Rings* is the flexibility with which the main characters move between different narrative traditions. A particularly interesting case is Aragorn, who, depending on the interpretations we choose to make, can be regarded as a character from the traditions of the novel, the romance or the epic.[4] Connie Veugen's (2005:181-182) attempt at summarising Aragorn's heroic evolution from a hero of the high mimetic mode to a hero of romance is interesting, but at the same time grossly simplifying, as Veugen (2005:182) herself admits: "this transition is not as gradual or lineal as presented here. It is closely tied in with the overall story."

The transition *is* tied in with the overall story, but much more closely than Veugen seems ready to admit. I believe that the simplification referred to above is a direct result of strictly applying Frye's theory of modes to the analysis of *The Lord of the Rings*. This is the reason why I have chosen to carry out the analysis of Aragorn's heroic evolution with reference to the basic narrative paradigms outlined above, instead of a strict application of the hero's different degrees of power over his environment, which would follow Frye's categorisation into myth, romance, high mimetic, low mimetic and the ironic mode.

---

[4] See, for example, Flieger (1981), who sees him as a figure from romance, while Kocher's (1974) analysis often shows him as a novelistic character of flesh and blood. Shippey (2003) and Veugen (2005) tend to emphasize his romance and epic sides.

As the story unfolds, we perceive that Aragorn is much more than just a character moving from the high mimetic mode towards the mode of romance. He is continually informed by the novel, romance and epic traditions. What is more, this profound *mélange* yields a number of situations that outline the limits of the different traditions in dialogue, as we shall see.

The following analysis is an attempt to disclose the different stages in the heroic evolution of Aragorn from the point of view of the intertraditional dialogue, and at the same time to provide a glimpse of how the limits of this dialogue condition the narrative universe, the chronotope of Middle-earth, as it is presented in *The Lord of the Rings*.

In order to carry out the analysis as such, I will take into account two different narrative levels. The first one is the *generic level*, which is composed of what I perceive as the three fundamental Western narrative traditions – epic, romance, and novel. Within each of these traditions there are a number of sub-genres and possible combinations, such as the *chanson de geste*, the medieval romance, the adventure novel, etc., which will be considered as parts of the basic paradigms mentioned above.

The second narrative level is the *situational* one. This level is made up of four main influences that, depending on the circumstances, *may be* capable of altering the general direction of the intertraditional dialogue: the physical space, the characters, the theme, and the action. I will call any particular combination of these four influences a 'narrative zone'.

The analysis will follow the story line as it is developed in *The Lord of the Rings*, concentrating on the principal narrative zones that Aragorn crosses as the story unfolds.

ARAGORN IN BREE: EPIC AND ADVENTURE NOVEL

At the *Prancing Pony* in Bree, when Frodo lands after his clumsy manoeuvre while singing, the Ring has slipped on his finger and he disappears. This event gives rise to a change of tone in the narrative, marked by the explicit inclusion of elements that the hobbits perceive as decidedly foreign. The most prominent of these is Strider, who enters the scene to tell Frodo that he knows more about the Ring than the hobbits may think.

The figure of Strider reinforces the mysterious and threatening atmosphere that surrounds Bree and the inn. He has still not turned into the romance and epic hero that he will become later, but offers all the ambiguity of a novelistic character. This may have been initially a consequence of Tolkien's lack of knowledge about Aragorn when he first wrote the episode[5] – the study of the evolution of this narrative, *The Return of the Shadow*, makes it clear to us that Tolkien's original idea was that the hobbits should meet a kind of adventurer-hobbit in Bree, called "Trotter", who would later guide them through the Outside World. However, the character of Aragorn became more dominant and Tolkien changed the name to Strider, given that the distance between a hobbit adventurer called Trotter and the later, epic/romance hero Aragorn was too great.[6]

The name Trotter is also interesting from another point of view. The same name, attached to a character related to a somewhat similar episode, also appears in Dickens's *The Pickwick Papers*. In that episode, Pickwick and his servant Sam Weller arrive at a rural inn late at night, after a long journey. They travel incognito, and Sam, calling himself Walker, strikes up a conversation with the servant of another gentle-

---

[5] Regarding his first inclusion of this character in the story, Tolkien wrote: "Strider sitting in the corner at the inn was a shock, and I had no more idea who he was than had Frodo." (Tolkien 2000:254)

[6] Tolkien (1988).

man, with the aim of extracting information, which may be helpful to Pickwick. The other servant introduces himself as Trotter and tricks him with his apparently innocent attitude.[7]

The common features of the two episodes – the late arrival at a rural inn, the invented names, the similarity between characters, the search for information, and the ambiguous character of Trotter/Strider – may imply that Tolkien was looking for a model in sources close to the world of the Shire, a narrative zone to which he may have thought that his characters had returned.[8] However, he had to modify the narrative substantially when he discovered the potential of Aragorn. The result of the modifications is that Aragorn in Bree represents a *novelistic anticipation* of the great epic world which is waiting for the hobbits further on in the narrative. Tolkien was surely aware that it would have been absurd to introduce Aragorn as a genuinely epic hero in the almost burlesque environment of *The Prancing Pony*, and that the evolution towards epic characteristics should be gradual and carefully elaborated.[9]

The first step is the change of name, from Trotter to Strider, but there is plenty more evidence of Strider's potential as a character who transcends the limits of the novel. It is of course true that Strider is still very far from the epic hero he will later become,[10] but in the narrator's

---

[7] See chapter 16 in Dickens (2003:211-228).

[8] This is not the place to discuss it, but the Shire may be considered a narrative zone heavily informed by a combination of nineteenth-century rural, humoristic and adventure novels, such as those of Dickens, Jerome, Hardy on the one hand, and original fairy tales (Thackeray, Wilde, Lang, etc.) on the other. See Simonson (2006).

[9] Segura (2004:130) also comments on the change of tone in the narrative from the moment Aragorn enters the scene, which is when it becomes more similar to the heroic tone of the epic.

[10] Miller (2000:8, 198, 230), when discussing the epic hero's personality, claims that he should never try to hide his true identity; that he will be recognised as the hero he is due to his heroic presence, even if nobody knows who he is; and that his utterances are not primarily manifestations of intelligence, subtlety or sophistication, but rather used as an extension and/or anticipation of his physical strength.

first descriptions of him, we may find hints of several epic features. Miller (2000:135) claims that the epic hero feels comfortable in the wilderness, which is definitely the case with Strider: the first descriptions reveal that he is "weather-beaten", that his boots are worn and covered with mud, and that he wears "a travel-stained cloak of heavy dark-green cloth" (Tolkien 1992:172). Apart from this, Strider has dark hair with flecks of grey, something which Miller identifies as a sign of threat and a connection with the supernatural.[11]

This description emphasizes Strider's ambiguity and narrative potential, without exceeding the limits of what is permissible in the narrative zone of Bree, a border town in all senses, where the strangeness of the Outside World should be adequately blended with the more familiar Shire-related affairs.

In the chapter 'Strider', the hobbits have the opportunity of chatting privately with him, and it is here that the text shows a more exhaustive exploration of the limits of this character in the narrative zone of Bree.

Strider begins in novelistic terms, providing the hobbits with a plausible explanation for his presence in Bree, marked by a colloquial tone, and revealing that he is very much conscious of the lack of heroic standards in his physical appearance:

> '[...] Well, I have a rather rascally look, have I not?' said Strider with a curl of his lips and a queer gleam in his eye. 'But I hope we shall get to know each other

---

[11] Miller (2000:295) says that the ambiguity of Hagen of Tronegge, from the *Nibelungenlied*, is closely related to the colour of his hair. In Miller's view, Hagen's strange and contradictory connotations are considerably reinforced by the grey flecks in his hair: "[...] a man's hair, when it is not naturally but prematurely gray [implies] a character not quite wholly human, and perhaps inflated with strange instinct or uncanny power [...] The color/noncolor appears to threaten, by obscuring, the bright effulgence of the hero, and in the best interpretation will display, at least in the north, an otherworldy and inhuman connection."

> better. When we do, I hope you will explain what happened at the end of your song. For that little prank–' (Tolkien 1992:180)

Shortly after this, when Strider talks about the Black Riders, his diction becomes 'tainted' with a much more formal and serious tone, though it still retains certain colloquial features. The theme as such makes the narrator manipulate the light, which fades until an 'apparent' darkness dominates the room. In this romance-imbued atmosphere, Strider offers them his aid, something which Sam refuses violently, while the perspicacious Frodo notices the change of tone in his discourse: "'[...] I think you are not really as you choose to look. You began to talk to me like the Bree-folk, but your voice has changed.'" (Tolkien 1992:182)

Frodo, when explicitly mentioning this fact, is implicitly acknowledging both Strider's heroic potential and his inter-traditional flexibility. His observation gives the narrator license to continue elevating Strider's tone and heroic stature, but instead, he chooses to return to the path of the novel, having the comical and slightly ridiculous inn-keeper Barliman Butterbur reappear with a letter from Gandalf that he has just remembered. The letter corroborates Strider's status as friend, but Sam is still not convinced:

> 'You might be a play-acting spy, for all I can see, trying to get us to go with you. You might have done in the real Strider and took his clothes. What have you to say to that?' (Tolkien 1992:187)

Aragorn replies by arguing that if stealing the Ring had been his aim, he would have taken it already, and after speaking, he accompanies his discourse with a momentary manifestation of his epic potential:

> He stood up, and *seemed suddenly to grow taller. In his eyes gleamed a light, keen and commanding.* Throwing back his cloak, he laid his hand

> on the hilt of a sword that had hung concealed by his side. They did not dare to move. *Sam sat wide-mouthed staring at him dumbly.*
>
> 'But I am the real Strider, fortunately,' he said, looking down at them with his face softened by a sudden smile. 'I am Aragorn son of Arathorn; and if by life or death I can save you, I will.'
> (Tolkien 1992:187)[12]

With such a reply, Aragorn is appealing both to a novelistic reasoning based on logic – which Sam is asking for – and to the powerful arguments of the epic hero, whose physical appearance and arrogant, violent attitude inspires a natural respect: his body seems to grow taller and his eyes shine with undisputable authority. The combination of these two attitudes – one appealing to reason and the other based on Aragorn's awe-inspiring presence – convinces the hobbits, though it is Strider himself who concludes that he will be their guide. He keeps up this double attitude for some time, talking about his broken sword, the dangers they will have to face on the road, and Gandalf's mysterious disappearance, in formal and solemn terms that well fit the graveness of the situation, but mixed with exact data regarding time and place, which is mostly due to a novelistic impulse of rendering verisimilitude to the spatial-temporal relationships. However, little by little, the narrative equilibrium begins to lean dangerously towards the epic, and since this is not admissible in Bree, the narrative needs to introduce a novelistic counterbalance. Pippin's prosaic comment is more than efficient for that purpose:

> Pippin yawned. 'I am sorry,' he said, 'but I am dead tired. In spite of all the danger and worry I must go to bed, or sleep where I sit. Where is that silly fellow,

---

[12] Emphasis added.

> Merry? It would be the last straw, if we had to go out
> in the dark to look for him.' (Tolkien 1992:189)[13]

The problem is that such a statement turns the narrative dialogue upside-down, instead of just altering its course towards a more balanced dialogue between the novel and the epic. Pippin trivialises the situation to such an extent that Aragorn's reaction must necessarily be the same as that of Sam a moment before – wide-mouthed bafflement – and the narrative effect would be exclusively comic. Tolkien achieves the appropriate balance and rescues the dialogue by having Merry (the most intertraditionally flexible of the hobbits, after Frodo) reappear at the inn with news about the Black Riders. From this moment and on, a more natural and less tense interaction between the hobbits and Aragorn is established: the hobbits keep their novelistic and colloquial discourse, but without ridiculing the situation's epic gravity, while Aragorn adapts his solemn speech somewhat to the level of the hobbits.

> Strider looked at Merry with wonder. 'You have
> a stout heart,' he said; 'but it was foolish.'
> 'I don't know,' said Merry. 'Neither brave nor
> silly, I think [...]' (Tolkien 1992:189)

Through this dialogue between the epic and the novel, which is a fundamental feature of the chapter 'Strider', the two traditions end up in a kind of narrative compromise. However, the characteristics of the narrative zone of Bree – a border region with more elements of the novel than of the epic – make the dialogue lean more towards the novel. This is particularly clear in the figure of Aragorn, whose epic dimension is

---

[13] Shippey (2003:212), when discussing hobbit jokes, considers that they "reflect and by intention deflect the modern inhibition over high styles which we and they share." The statement also describes the effects of the hobbits' prosaic (novelistic) replies in the face of the more ceremonious and solemn discourse of other traditions.

considerably reduced. Far from being granted the overwhelming status of the epic hero that he will later enjoy, in Bree Aragorn is portrayed as a character with certain affinities to the role of the intimidating helper-friend from the tradition of the 19th-century British adventure novel.[14]

When discussing this type of character, Toda Iglesia (2002:108) underscores two basic features: his intimate association with amulets and magic artefacts, and his physical ugliness. Tolkien may or may not have been aware of these conventions, but it is interesting to notice that Aragorn will later exhibit certain traits which will take him far beyond the limitations of the role of the 'intimidating friend' of the adventure novel, and that the analogues with the magic artefact are reduced to a broken sword, shrouded in mystery and still not explicitly recognised as 'magical', while the ugliness becomes a somewhat shabby, though noble, physical appearance.

In Toda Iglesia's view, in terms of genre, the British 19th-century adventure novel is an attempt to mediate between the narrative traditions of the epic, the romance, and the novel, but it is also an expression of the Victorian era with its particular rites of passage undergone by young British men in remote areas of the empire.[15] This *mélange* should make it a perfect model for the narrative zone of Bree, a border region mixing the Shire and the Outside World, with certain Victorian connotations.[16] At the same time, it becomes a highly efficient narrative vehicle

---

[14] According to Toda Iglesia (2002:129), this type of friend usually enters the action as a spy or guide, using his extensive knowledge of the resources and dangers of the foreign terrain through which the hero travels, to facilitate the progress.

[15] Toda Iglesia (2002:23-33) highlights the combination of these traditions as one of the prime trademarks of the adventure novel, while arguing that the didacticism would be intimately associated with the imperialist ideology of the Victorian era.

[16] Bree, because of its historical relationship and geographical proximity to the Shire, retains at least some characteristics of the latter. The construction of the Shire as a narrative zone is deeply indebted to literary expressions of the Victorian and Edwardian eras, such as Dickens, Hardy, Jerome K. Jerome, etc. (see Simonson 2006). For an outline of the influence of the Edwardian adventure novel on *The Lord of the Rings*, see Lobdell (2004:1-24).

for the first stages of the journey during which the hobbits are initiated into the customs and the characteristics of the strange and dangerous Outside World.

Strider's way of talking and acting the day after the events at the inn reflects the conclusion that Tolkien may have reached with regards to the narrative treatment of this character: Aragorn, for the time being, has to renounce his fully epic traits and remain in the realm of the novel. Upon leaving Bree, Strider says: "I am afraid we shall have to try to get one pony at least. But so ends all hope of starting early, and slipping away quietly! We might as well have blown a horn to announce our departure." (Tolkien 1992:194)

A purely epic hero would not have expressed himself with the extreme indetermination of the first sentence – rather: "Bring a steed to me, Aragorn, son of Arathorn, heir of Gondor, or my wrath shall fall upon this village", or something of the kind – and he would definitely not have tried to hide or escape from his enemies. The main point of an epic hero's existence is to invest his name with glory, so one of his absolute priorities should rather be to announce to everybody that he sets out to carry out great and impressive deeds.[17] As Strider seems to indicate in the quotation above, the way in which they have to leave is neither purely epic nor successful from the point of view of the more pragmatic novel-hero, and this seems to him deeply unsatisfying. While they do attract the attention of the villagers, it is not because they want to, but because prosaic circumstances (the loss of the ponies) *make* their

---

[17] Normally, the epic hero of the pre-Christian era considers the matter of making his name known to the world through great deeds of prime importance, since it is his only way of being included in the songs of the poets and thus to become 'immortal'. The idea that this should be the main objective of all heroes is taken for granted, and so the protagonists will always know what their duty is. The notion of fighting is intimately related to the ambition of overcoming his mortality, the great enemy of all. The reference to the horn is also associated with the hero of the epic and *chanson the geste* traditions, which will be discussed when analysing the character of Boromir.

departure so conspicuous. Aragorn is not comfortable in this role, and his complaint is marked by the frustration of a hero with epic aspirations who is obliged by the limits imposed by the narrative dialogue to assume a role with considerably less power over his environment, and who finds that he is unsuccessful even in the comparatively easy and trivial novelistic task[18] of "slipping away quietly" from a sleepy town.

RIVENDELL: ROMANCE AND EPIC

In the chapter 'The Council of Elrond', Strider's importance in the narrative is steadily increased, until his role as one of the main protagonists of the story is firmly established. He finally emerges as Aragorn, a character with deep roots in the novel, romance, and epic traditions.[19] This, however, is achieved only after a long negotiation of the limits of the intervening narrative traditions.

From the point of view of the intertraditional dialogue, it is interesting to notice Aragorn's persistent difficulties to take on the epic hero's stance, even when he seems to assume several of the corresponding features. This can be clearly seen in his dialogue with Boromir, in which he is ostensibly invited to become more 'epic' in his manners, as we shall see.

Flieger (1981:48) claims that when Aragorn shows his sword, he "publicly puts off the Strider-figure, assuming his rightful identity and all

---

[18] Compared with the epic hero, the 'intimidating friend' of the tradition of the British 19th-century adventure novel is faced with different predicaments and can thus allow himself to be pragmatic about the relationship between honour and success, in this case avoiding an open confrontation with the enemy in order to escape unseen.

[19] Flieger's brilliant essay 'Frodo and Aragorn: The Concept of the Hero' (Flieger 1981) was, together with Shippey's (2003) perspicacious observations in the section titled 'The Council of Elrond', one of the first serious reflections on the negotiation of narrative traditions in the character of Aragorn in this episode. Both interpretations remain not only valid, but they are, to date, still the best studies of the traditions at work in the characterisation of Aragorn at Rivendell.

it implies." In my opinion, the statement is only true if we interpret Aragorn's "rightful identity" as a profound *mélange* of the novel, romance *and* epic traditions. In fact, the scene underscores just how difficult it is for him to shoulder the epic personality that the situation seems to require: facts are that he refrains from announcing himself as the true king (and much less from doing so *triumphantly*, as an epic hero would), and this very 'un-epic' hesitation makes it necessary for Elrond to reveal his identity.

This revelation implies a direct threat for Boromir, since Aragorn's kinship with Isildur would give him the right to claim the throne of Gondor, governed by Denethor, Boromir's father. He is not convinced by Aragorn's subsequent words about the sword and challenges him with his reply: "[...] the sword of Elendil would be a help beyond our hope – if such a thing could indeed return out of the shadows of the past." (Tolkien 1992:264)[20]

However, Aragorn is still surprisingly reluctant to give in to this invitation to heroic (epic) standards. When Boromir challenges him, Bilbo of all persons cuts in to recite an allegorical poem about Aragorn's birthrights. Only when his heroic stature has been certified by two different sources does Aragorn begin to answer Boromir in a more epically adequate manner, returning both the challenge and the boasting.

This reluctance is not so much due to limitations of the narrative zone of Rivendell, in which an epic or a *chanson de geste* hero may be fully projected (as Boromir's example has shown us), but it is rather a consequence of characterisation. Tolkien establishes a fundamental difference between the two rivals: Boromir's pride is matched against

---

[20] Regarding the boasting and the challenging, Miller (2000:234-237) observes that "two warriors implicitly recognize each other as men of a similar terrible kind through boasts."

Aragorn's humility.[21] This dichotomy seems to arise as a consequence of Tolkien's wish to make a different kind of hero out of the raw material that Strider has given him; a hero who is not fully epic, but who combines certain aspects of pagan courage – which Tolkien admired in the pre-Christian Scandinavian and Germanic cultures[22] – with characteristics of the Christian hero, such as patience, humility, and unyielding faith.[23]

Tolkien is thus interested in establishing a contrast between Aragorn and Boromir that underscores the spiritual integrity of the former and the moral fragility of the latter. In this process, the behaviour of Boromir helps defining the particular heroic features of Aragorn, and this is something that the narrator will exploit all through the journey from Rivendell to Amon Hen, as we shall see.

Aragorn receives the sword that belongs to him by birthright. From this moment onwards, Aragorn's identity will be intimately connected to his sword, and this will consolidate our new conception of him as an epic and romance hero *in spe*, partly because his mission is to recover his kingdom,[24] partly because the sword contributes to a concep-

---

[21] Shippey (2003:121), when discussing the difference in linguistic flexibility between Aragorn and Boromir, emphasizes the former's capacity of using colloquial speech, and "Boromir's slightly wooden magniloquence". This difference in diction is also indicative of Aragorn's humility as opposed to Boromir's pride.

[22] See Tolkien (1997a).

[23] Milton is a forerunner to Tolkien here, since one of his strategies for character-drawing in *Paradise Lost* was to emphasize the contrast between authenticity and truthfulness of the Christian hero and the falsehood of the secular epic hero. See Steadman (1969:15-16): "Milton juxtaposed Christian and secular ideals of heroic virtue within the same narrative framework and thus brought out the distinctive qualities of both. [...] The new [Christian heroic patterns] serve as a yardstick to measure – and castigate the old." This is particularly clear in the treatment of Adam and Satan.

[24] According to Miller (2000:134), the normal structure of the epic hero's adventures is the following: "hero is exiled, comes back to the center that sent him away, or to other centres of enclosed, rigid, restricting, old, and impacted power [...] he reacquaints the settled people with his name, or with a name". The same structure dominates the myth central to Arthurian romance: the fertilisation of the Waste Land and the mythic paradigm governing Aragorn's action, that Veugen (2005:180-181) calls the "hero-king myth".

tion of Aragorn as an epic hero with a basically Christian (romance) ethos. As symbols, the hilt of the sword represents the material world, while the blade symbolizes the materialisation of the spiritual dimension; and in the Christian tradition, swords are related to the spirit and word of God, with a will of their own. According to de Paco (2003:252), the habit of giving them names is a result of this.[25]

The *mélange* between the epic mission and the Christian ethos found in the figure of Aragorn is also implied by the contrast with Boromir in the scene where the Fellowship departs from Rivendell:

> Aragorn had Andúril but no other weapon, and he went forth clad only in rusty green and brown, as a Ranger of the Wilderness. Boromir had a long sword, in fashion like Andúril but of less lineage, and he bore also a shield and his war-horn.
> 'Loud and clear it sounds in the valleys of the hills,' he said, 'and then let all the foes of Gondor flee!' Putting it to his lips he blew a blast, and the echoes leapt from rock to rock, and all that heard that voice in Rivendell sprang to their feet.
> (Tolkien 1992:296)

While Aragorn's mission thus is typical of both the romance and the epic traditions,[26] it is interesting to see that the sword – the word and spirit of God in the Christian iconography – is the only weapon he needs. His simple clothing also indicates his humble stance compared to the more extravagantly dressed Boromir, who also carries a shield to

---

[25] Aragorn calls his sword Andúril, which means "the flame of the West".
[26] Kocher (1974:128) claims that the starting point for Aragorn's most difficult trials is marked by his departure from Rivendell. Indeed, after leaving Rivendell, Aragorn will be subjected to increasingly difficult tests that will eventually determine the destiny of the whole world. That issues of supreme – even universal – importance for large communities should be at stake is typical of epic narratives, such as *The Iliad*, *The Aneid*, or *Paradise Lost*.

protect himself – a detail hinting at his lack of faith – and a war-horn to announce his departure and acquaint the world with his name and deeds.

All through the journey towards Lórien and Amon Hen, the narrator continues defining Aragorn's heroic role by comparing him with Boromir, whose lack of self-control, patience and faith[27] stands out unfavourably against the calm backdrop of Aragorn's (and Gandalf's) Christian virtues. At the same time, Aragorn repeatedly shows that he is just as strong, skilful and courageous in battle as the Gondorian.[28] In this way, he is consolidated as the most complete hero of the two.

LÓRIEN: ROMANCE

Lórien is a narrative zone which, due to its close connection to romance paradigms, is particularly ill suited for a further exploitation of the epic potential of Aragorn and Boromir, who will both lose 'protagonism' in favour of Frodo and Sam. At Cerin Amroth, Aragorn exhibits an assimilation of the romance tradition in the scene where he recalls his first

---

[27] Boromir continually shows his lack of faith in Gandalf's suggestions: "All choices seem ill, and to be caught between wolves and the wall the likeliest chance. Lead on!" and "thither we are going against my wish. Who will lead us now in this deadly dark?" (Tolkien 1992:317 and 323, respectively) However, the scene that best shows his lack of faith, patience, self-control, and prudence is when he becomes tired of waiting for Gandalf to find the magic word at the Gates of Moria and throws a stone in the lake. This imprudence wakes up the *kraken*, a monster that threatens to kill the whole Fellowship, and may well be interpreted as a punishment of Boromir's moral weakness.

[28] At Caradhras, when Boromir volunteers to open up a path through the snow, Aragorn joins him. (It is significant that it is Boromir who later boasts of the feat: "'But happily your Caradhras has forgotten that you have Men with you,' said Boromir [...] 'And doughty Men too, if I may say it [...].'"(Tolkien 1992:309). Later on, when fighting the wolves, Aragorn and Boromir are shown as equally brave and strong; during the first battle with the orcs, the narrator says that "Boromir and Aragorn slew many" (Tolkien 1992:343), and in the decisive moment at the bridge of Khazad-dûm, both heroes try to help Gandalf while the rest are paralysed by fear: "'He cannot stand alone!' cried Aragorn suddenly and ran back along the bridge. 'Elendil!' he shouted. 'I am with you, Gandalf!' 'Gondor!' cried Boromir and leaped after him." (Tolkien 1992:349)

meeting with Arwen. The blood-stained epic hero we have seen a few pages before has now become a love-sick romantic who, contemplating a flower with a dreamy look in his eyes, pronounces a few sentimental words and takes Frodo's hand as they leave.

In this scene, Aragorn's epic potential is almost annihilated. His previous refusal, at Rivendell, to yield completely to the epic paradigms of characterisation; his Christian/romance traits (with love at the centre), and the invitation by the physical space, particularly adequate for the inclusion of romance elements,[29] make his romance conversion so credible that the reader even begins to suspect that he will leave his epic pretensions and turn into a solid romance knight. The scene anticipates his future flirts with this tradition – which will eventually lead to a complete transformation into the romance king once the war is won – but as he 'sobers up' after this interlude, his epic potential is not completely lost in the process.

FROM AMON HEN TO FANGORN: NOVEL, EPIC, AND ROMANCE

In the scene describing the death of Boromir at Amon Hen, apart from the evident analogy with *Le Chanson de Roland*,[30] we can also see a

---

[29] Regarding the connection between Lórien and elves and the tradition of medieval romance, Shippey (2003:55-65) considers the medieval poem *Sir Orfeo* to be the text that inspired Tolkien most when creating his elves. Lórien also has a clear connection to the Middle-English poem *Pearl*, in which the poet sees his dead daughter in a paradisiacal land across a river he cannot cross. The members of the Fellowship, by contrast, are able to cross the river (Silverlode) that separates them from Lórien and thus enter an immaculate and paradisiacal realm. See Shippey (2003:218) and Kaufmann (1975).

[30] The analogy with the protagonist of *Le Chanson de Roland* is clear: like Roland, Boromir blows the horn in order to make his allies aware of the attack, but it is too late; he, too, dies with many wounds after killing a large number of enemies that are compared to insects. Miller (2000:323) describes the death of Roland in the following way: "[Roland] has not one 'knee-loosing' mortal wound [...] but a great many. [...] It is as if he had been slowly bitten to death by a swarm of enemies figured as animals or even insects." Even the friends of both are similar: Olivier is marked by

parallel between the heroic couples Aragorn/Boromir, on the one hand, and Hector/Achilles on the other. While Hector as a character is marked by both his sense of responsibility and his battle courage, Achilles is intimately connected with uncontrolled and destructive wrath. From my point of view, it is not the Homeric version of these heroes that comes closest to the treatment of the heroic couple Aragorn/Boromir, but rather Benoit de St. Maure's *Le Roman de Troie*, which, according to King (1987:231), is also the first version that emphasizes the difference between the villain and the courtly knight in the characters of Achilles and Hector:

> Benoit's Achilles can't play the courtly game well because he is the plaything of his own twin sexual and aggressive passions [...] Hektor channels his energies in a more productive way: he has achieved wisdom and the courtliness that goes with it.

The parallels to the scene of Boromir's death is significant, because Tolkien's treatment also reminds us of Aragorn's romance (and Christian) potential, even in the moments most heavily informed by epic or *chanson de geste* standards, such as Boromir's heroic feats waging battle against the orcs and his subsequent (and, of course, highly appropriate) death. The scene shows Aragorn's double affinities as he forgives Boromir both due to his traditionally heroic death and to his repentance:[31] his reaction is motivated by pity and forgiveness – Christian virtues – on the one hand, and by the epic hero's ethos, centred on the

---

his wisdom, as is Aragorn, while Roland is characterized by his impetuosity, courage, strength and fury in battle. See Day (2003:173).

[31] See Kocher (1974:132): "Aragorn shifts none of the blame to Boromir, whose sincere repentance and heroic death in battle [...] completely redeem him in Aragorn's eyes."

virtue of a death on the battlefield, being the epic hero's most efficient method of investing his name with lasting glory,[32] on the other.

The chapter 'The Departure of Boromir' shows, among other things, the persistent limitations of Aragorn as a traditional epic hero. From the moment we first met him, in Bree, we have perceived his inherent epic potential, which to a great extent has been held in check by the other members of the Fellowhip: the hobbits, who have brought him into dialogue with the novel; Gandalf, who has eclipsed him as a leader; and Boromir, whose egotism and lack of moral strength Aragorn has been made to counterbalance with a constant exhibition of his mixture of epic and romance/Christian virtues, and whose presence and remarks have questioned his 'protagonism'.

At this stage of the narrative, all these characters have conveniently disappeared, and Aragorn is presented with an opportunity to put his full epic potential on display: the most recent action has been marked by *chanson de geste* standards; and the comrades that remain – Gimli and Legolas – do not pose an obstacle for his epic fulfilment because of their narrative neutrality.

In short, everything seems to indicate that Aragorn will finally turn into a pure epic hero, and when he makes the decision to follow the orcs, the narrator elevates the tone to the high diction of the epic:

> '[...] With hope or without hope we will follow the trail of our enemies: and woe to them, if we prove the swifter! We will make such a chase as shall be accounted a marvel among the Three Kindreds: Elves,

---

[32] The Scandinavian saga tradition, which may be seen as a 'lighter' and more prosaic and domestic version of the older epics and the medieval *chansons de geste*, also shows this *ethos*. This is due mainly to its strong connections to Nordic mythology and its emphasis on earthly fulfilment by heroic deeds – an attitude that would persist even after the Scandinavian countries were officially converted. Tolkien found the combination of pagan courage and the Christian *ethos* as encountered in *Beowulf* particularly attractive (see Tolkien 1997a).

Dwarves, and men. Forth the Three Hunters!'
Like a deer he sprang away. Through the trees he sped. On and on he led them, tireless and swift, now that his mind was at last made up [...].
(Tolkien 1992:440)

Aragorn's tone and boastful attitude, together with the wish that the heroic feats be turned into a matter of legend and the physical strength conferred by his new-found determination, all help setting the scene for a further exploitation of his epic side. It remains to be seen, however, whether the nature of the mission corresponds to the demands of the epic.

During the first part of the hunt for the hobbits, Aragorn, Gimli and Legolas cover a distance of forty-four leagues (around two hundred kilometres) on foot in only four days, crossing the great plains of Rohan. In spite of this impressive feat, they do not manage to hunt down the orcs. Aragorn and Gimli believe that their failure is due to Saruman's influence (Tolkien 1992:448), but there may be other reasons involved: the rescue of Merry and Pippin is not an epic mission. Aragorn, the king in exile, is getting farther and farther away from Minas Tirith, where he should be going to fight the Enemy and claim kingship. And for what reason? To save two hobbits, who at this moment seem totally insignificant for the outcome of the conflict between Sauron's forces and those of the Free Peoples. Such a mission is bound to fail from the point of view of a purely epic narrative tradition.[33] Aragorn himself seems to acknowledge this constraint when they temporarily interrupt the pursuit for lack of light, but even so, he wants to go on:

---

[33] The epic greatness of the hunt is related to the physical feats of strength and endurance, not its objective. Because of this, the mission fails from a result-oriented epic standpoint, while it is a success from the point of view of the romance, which emphasizes the knight's spiritual education.

> [...] Gimli murmured [...]: 'Would that the Lady had given us a light, such a gift as she gave to Frodo.'
> 'It will be more needed where it is bestowed,' said Aragorn. 'With him lies the true Quest. Ours is but a small matter in the great deeds of this time. A vain pursuit from its beginning, maybe, which no choice of mine can mar or mend. Well, I have chosen. So let us use the time as best we may!'
> (Tolkien 1992:446)

Éomer and the Riders of Rohan attempt to put Aragorn back on the epic track, killing off the orcs and offering him horses in exchange for a promise to go straight to Edoras as soon as he has confirmed the absence of hobbits among the dead orcs. Éomer, during their meeting, inspires Aragorn to speak and behave like an epic hero,[34] proudly affirming his rank in almost boastful words, but instead of joining the *Rohirrim* in the war against Saruman he stubbornly rejects the offer and decides to continue the search for the hobbits.

After finding the funeral pyre for the orcs containing no hobbit-remains, Aragorn, Gimli and Legolas camp below a tree at some distance from the forest of Fangorn. Both the nightfall, which, due to the lack of sufficient light, hinders normal perception of reality, and the proximity of the legendary Fangorn Forest invite the romance tradition to take part in the dialogue and make the strange behaviour of the sheltering tree coherent and even feasible:

> It may have been that the dancing shadows tricked their eyes, but certainly to each of the companions the boughs appeared to be bending this way and that so as to come above the flames, while the upper branches were stooping down; the brown leaves now stood out stiff, and rubbed together like many cold

---

[34] See Kocher (1974:133).

> cracked hands taking comfort in the warmth.
> (Tolkien 1992:462)

Shortly after this, a silent old man appears, only to vanish instantly again, without leaving any trace.

The world has become mysterious with the nightfall, and the strange events reinforce the presence of romance paradigms in the narrative dialogue, which will incline the balance towards this tradition on the following day, as the adventurers enter the Forest of Fangorn to look for the hobbits.

As they lose the horses and leave the realm of Rohan behind, Aragorn also loses his epic bearings, delving into a romance territory that leads him further away from his 'true' quest[35]. The atmosphere in the forest is oppressive and the orientation becomes increasingly difficult. Gimli is the first to acknowledge the slight chances of success of their enterprise and tries to convince Aragorn to change his mind:

> 'If we do not find them soon, we shall be of no use to them, except to sit down beside them and show our friendship by starving together.'
> 'If that is indeed all we can do, then we must do that,' said Aragorn. 'Let us go on.'
> (Tolkien 1992:512)

There is a significant difference between the attitude of Aragorn, who feels that it is his duty not to lose faith, and that of Gimli, which is more pragmatic and realistic. Aragorn's obstinate stance will be rewarded by

---

[35] Quint (1985) argues that the narrative movement towards romance standards in an epic narrative is often marked by a digression that breaks the structure of the central action. As an example, he discusses an episode from *Gerusalemme Liberata*, in which Reinaldo, the protagonist, allows himself to be led astray from his historical (epic) mission and experience a romance adventure in which the events suddenly become disconnected from each other and from the overall plot. When Reinaldo sobers up and rejoins the main action, the epic presents him with a clear objective and organises the events in a coherent narrative.

the reappearance of Gandalf (which is portrayed much as a haphazard encounter with a romance wizard), but – and this is important – only after he has shown an unshakeable faith in the success of his chosen mission, which had been little less than impossible to begin with.[36]

The assertion, on behalf of a spiritual authority such as Gandalf, that he has successfully passed a moral test, gives Aragorn the final license to abandon the hunt for the hobbits and to embark on epic ventures:

> [...] 'Come, Aragorn son of Arathorn!' he said. 'Do not regret your choice in the valley of the Emyn Muil, nor call it a vain pursuit. You chose amid doubts the path that seemed right: the choice was just, and it has been rewarded. For so we have met in time, who otherwise might have met too late. But the quest of your companions is over. Your next journey is marked by your given word. You must go to Edoras and seek out Théoden in his hall. For you are needed. The light of Andúril must now be uncovered in the battle for which it has so long waited. [...]'
> (Tolkien 1992:522)

In this way, everything is finally set for a full exploitation of Aragorn's epic potential: his romance/Christian virtues have been tested and confirmed, whereby he has obtained permission to carry out epic deeds.

---

[36] Hope is one of the main virtues in Tolkien's moral universe. As we have seen, the way Tolkien merges different traditions clears the way for its applicability to modern times and expresses an attitude that we might call an 'intertraditional literary myth of hope'. As Aragorn is one of the most important representatives of this myth, it is important that he should not lose faith in the mission and yield to the less spiritually informed ambitions of the purely epic hero.

MEDUSELD AND HELM'S DEEP: EPIC

It has been a commonplace in Tolkien criticism to compare the arrival at Meduseld, Théoden's *burh*, with the parallel episode in the Old English epic *Beowulf*, in which the eponymous hero enters Heoroth, the home of the Danish king Hrothgar, to help him fight the monster Grendel.[37]

We have now entered a territory close to Northern Europe during the early Middle Ages, of whose narrative traditions *Beowulf* is the most notable representative, and this is reflected in Aragorn's behaviour as they approach Meduseld. At the gates, he engages in a violent argument with the doorward, showing us a side of his personality far removed from the long-suffering romance knight, ready to face the risk of failure and humiliation for the sake of spiritual growth: now, he refuses to leave his sword outside the Hall and defies both the doorward and the king by proudly affirming his identity, up to a point where armed combat seems inevitable:

> 'It is not clear to me that the will of Théoden son of Thengel, even though he be lord of the mark, should prevail over the will of Aragorn son of Arathorn, Elendil's heir of Gondor.' (Tolkien 1992:533)

---

[37] For example, St. Clair (1996:64); Tolley (1993:155-156), and Shippey (2003:124). The verses sung by Aragorn as they pass the grave mounds of the dead kings of Rohan also help setting the scene, because of their similarity with the elegiac Old English poem *The Wanderer*. Kelly (1968:170-200) concludes that the poetry of Rohan and of the Anglo-Saxons show similarities in intonation, alliteration, repetition, and word order. The song that Aragorn sings is could be seen as a paraphrase of the Old English poem *The Wanderer*. Aragorn's version reads like this: "Where now the horse and the rider? Where is the horn that was blowing? / Where is the helm and the hauberk, and the bright hair flowing?" The similarity with 'The Wanderer' is undeniable: "Where is the horse now, where the hero gone? / Where is the bounteous lord, and where the benches / For feasting? Where are the joys of the hall?" See Hamer (1970:181).

Aragorn's formerly humble attitude has been replaced by the arrogant and challenging stance of the epic hero,[38] triggered by the physical space, the action, and the characters. It is only after Gandalf's persistent mediation that Aragorn finally accepts the doorward's conditions.

The scene that shows Théoden's recovery and Gríma's subsequent downfall is marked by a strong emphasis on Christian virtues, such as hope, mercy, forgiveness and generosity,[39] all of which are diametrically opposed to the warrior ethics of the pre-Christian epic hero. Perhaps as a consequence of this, Aragorn hardly intervenes in the dialogue; he cannot mar his new and fully-grown epic identity by falling into the 'pit' of mercy.

However, Tolkien has not finished torturing the recently converted epic hero with foreign influences. Éowyn, the king's niece, enters the scene, hopelessly falling in love with Aragorn. The episode is not more than a brief interlude, but it is enough to remind us of Aragorn's courtly – romance – side, given that he acts with her as a typical knight of medieval romance would; courtly and kindly but always true to his lady.[40] At the same time it is significant that Éowyn should be a basically epic heroine,[41] which reduces the parallelism to the courtly love scenes

---

[38] See Miller (2000:234).

[39] Théoden is convinced by Gandalf's message of hope, while Gríma is forgiven and offered a place in the cavalry at the king's side. He rejects the offer with disdain but is nonetheless given a horse and permission to leave.

[40] Courtly love and its consequences – in this case, the constant testing of Aragorn's fidelity towards Éowyn – is one of the most prominent themes in medieval romance. The best known example is, perhaps, *Sir Gawain and the Green Knight*, in which the protagonist is afflicted by his hostess' constant invitations to adulterous love that he must resist. On the influence of this work on *The Lord of the Rings*, see Miller (1991) and Chance (1986).

[41] As a character, Éowyn shares many features with the amazons, the female warriors of *The Iliad* and *The Aneid*, and with Brynhild of the *Völsungasagan* / Brunhilda of the *Nibelungenlied*. For a more exhaustive exploration of these analogues, see Day (2003:157) and Fenwick (1996).

from the medieval romance tradition to a minimum, albeit it does not suppress it entirely.[42]

In the following chapter, 'Helm's Deep', the dialogue between romance and epic is particularly evident in the different attitudes towards war, as shown by Gimli and Legolas, on the one hand, and Aragorn, Éomer and Théoden, on the other. For the former, the battle is an entertainment, good sport that inspires competitiveness:

> 'Twenty-one!' cried Gimli. He hewed a two-handed stroke and laid the last Orc before his feet. 'Now my count passes Master Legolas again!'
> [...] 'Good!' said Legolas. 'But my count is now two dozen. It has been knife-work up here.'
> (Tolkien 1992:559)[43]

As opposed to this romance attitude, Aragorn and Théoden exhibit an epic attitude towards battle. For them, war is a serious matter and despair is only grimly held in check by the desire to gain immortality through heroic deeds that are to be praised in song by poets:

> 'The end will not be long,' said the king. '[...] When dawn comes, I will bid men sound Helm's horn, and I will ride forth. Will you ride with me then, son of Arathorn? Maybe we shall cleave a road, or make an end as will be worth a song – if any be left to sing of us hereafter.'

---

[42] Miller (2000:46-47) argues that "the feminine element in romance epics breaks and reforms the narrative frame." This is an effect that will be more clearly appreciated in the next meeting between Aragorn and Éowyn.

[43] Compared to the austere epic hero, the romance knight shows a far more leisurely attitude towards battle, marked by what we might call an enthusiastic desire for competition and good sport.

> 'I will ride with you,' said Aragorn.
> (Tolkien 1992:562-563)[44]

ISENGARD: NOVEL

The ease with which Aragorn shifts to the novel tradition during the sojourn at Isengard is also worth a comment. In this episode, Merry and Pippin take on the role of masters of ceremony: they bring food and pipe-weed to the weary travellers and organise a kind of novelistic picnic at the gates of Orthanc – much like a group of tourists would at the gates of some medieval castle – in the jocose and carefree tradition of Jerome's humoristic holiday novels,[45] before filling in the informative gaps for their friends and for the reader.

Gimli's interventions reinforce the presence of the novel tradition, as he asks, in a similarly humoristic tone, for food and a comfortable place to eat, a story well told,[46] and pipe-weed to enhance the pleasure of listening to the hobbits' tale. Aragorn remains rather austere

---

[44] In Miller's (2000:220) view, "[the epic hero is] playing out a suicidal scenario [accepting] a confrontation from which he cannot possibly escape alive. [...] he presents himself as victim, but he will not go quietly, and most often he will not go alone. [...] [He] dooms himself and his men." Aragorn shows indulgence and even sympathy for Legolas and Gimli's competition (Tolkien 1992:561), but he does not take part in it. Dickerson (2003:42) claims that the competition between the elf and the dwarf is not the central event in the treatment of this episode, given the comparatively limited space it is allotted by the narrator, while Chance (2004:221) underscores the analogues between the descriptions of the battle and descriptions found in Old English heroic poetry, such as *The Battle of Maldon* or *Brunanburh*, that share many features with the Northern current of epic poetry represented by *Beowulf*. Segura (2004:188) observes that the treatment of time during the battle at Helm's Deep transmits a sense of despair, something which reinforces the epic elements in this episode.

[45] *Three Men in a Boat* comes to mind. There are many similarities between the interaction of the characters in this novel, on the one hand, and that of the hobbits, on the other (especially during the first part of the journey through the Shire).

[46] With a story well told, Gimli refers to novelistic standards of 'truth' – a chronologically and geographically coherent and full picture – as his subsequent questions show.

at first, but as he sits down to enjoy the lunch he shows a clear tendency to slacken the rigidly epic traits that have dominated his personality during the last chapters:

> 'Now let us take our ease here for a little!' said Aragorn. 'We will sit on the edge of ruin and talk, as Gandalf says, while he is busy elsewhere. I feel a weariness such as I have seldom felt before.' He wrapped his grey cloak about him, hiding his mail-shirt, and stretched out his long legs. Then he lay back and sent from his lips a thin stream of smoke.
> (Tolkien 1992:586)

Now, invited to take part in a novelistic discourse by the hobbits, the action (picnicking) and the type of conversation (prosaic and colloquial, basically aimed at filling in the missing gaps of the plot), the 'Beowulfian' hero leaves the epic issues to Gandalf and Théoden, covering his shining armour with the travel-stained coat and making himself comfortable on the ground to smoke and chat. He admits his double personality with a natural ease, assuming once more the stance of a character from the adventure-novel.

MINAS TIRITH: EPIC AND ROMANCE

When Aragorn arrives at the fields of Pelennor, commanding a fleet of ships with black sails,[47] it is in the midst of general despair. His bearing as

---

[47] Day (2003:161-162) argues that the main connection between Aragorn's return and Theseus' homecoming after his adventure in Crete is the despair that strikes the inhabitants of the city when seeing the black sails. This and other analogues enhance the connections between Minas Tirith, on the one hand, and the classical cities of Athens and Troy on the other, reinforcing Aragorn's own relationship to the main narrative traditions associated to that epoch: epic and heroic poetry, and myth. See Greenman (1992).

he shows his true identity, unfolding the standard[48] and accomplishing prodigious feats of arms, is decidedly epic, but as he prepares to enter the city, his attitude changes radically: he is suddenly reluctant to enter the city in triumph and hides his banner, removes the star from his brow and covers his coat of mail with his elvish cloak. His official reason for doing so – to avoid trouble with the people of the city – is of a certain relevance as it shows his romance/Christian prudence, but there may be other motivations involved, related to the limits imposed by the inter-traditional dialogue.

Miller (2000:119-120) argues that the city is easily turned into a serious threat for a battle-waging epic hero: on the one hand, it puts constraints[49] on his previously unlimited range of action, and, on the other – which is most important – it limits his normal 'epic' behaviour, which is necessarily violent and aggressive:

> In the heroic tradition [...] the city is a trap for heroism. So is marriage, which usually means submission to the ideal systems of contractual kingship, continuation, and social rules [...] In the usual epic scenario, the hero is prepared to go to any lengths to avoid the fate of Héktor – not death, but death on the defensive, trapped in the constricting bonds and artefacts

---

[48] The unfolding of standards and banners symbolizes, according to de Paco (2003:181), the exaltation of the bearer's identity, but also the victory of Christ after his glorious resurrection. Tolkien has once more succeeded in finding a symbol closely related to Aragorn that is capable of integrating both epic (pagan) and Christian aspects, at least if we interpret Aragorn's trip through the Underworld of the Paths of the Dead as a kind of death and resurrection that culminates in a glorious return. The connection between Aragorn and Christ will be reinforced as he enters Minas Tirith, as we shall see.

[49] As opposed to modern cities, the cities of early Mediterranean civilisations (for example, Troy), were normally protected by walls that surrounded the whole urban area. Minas Tirith has a similar structure, but with seven walls instead of only one, which means that the further towards the centre (where we find the Citadel and the tower of Ecthelion, the steward's residence that the new king must take back) Aragorn proceeds, the more constricted he will become.

of culture, rather than death on the offensive, assaulting that culture.

It is evident that Aragorn's aim is to take command of the city, marry Arwen, and become king of Gondor and of all the Free Peoples. However, he still has to command his troops in the final battle against Sauron, and to enter the city in triumph would diminish his violent potential as an epic hero. In the end he prefers to enter the city incognito, with the exterior signs of his epic identity hidden and his armour covered.

There may be further reasons for his prudence. By hiding the epic side of his identity, he also paves the way for the future events, in which he acts as the healer and renewer of the kingdom.[50] As before when rejecting Éowyn's offer of love in Édoras and at Dunharrow, and when unfolding the banner to reveal his identity to the armies on the Pelennor, Aragorn's entrance into Minas Tirith to heal the wounded and ill does not imply a complete rejection of one narrative tradition in favour of another,[51] but rather a *significant* narrative shift towards the tradition of romance that at the same time retains its connections with the epic.

---

[50] See Kocher (1974:140): "On the plains of Pelennor, [Aragorn] overcomes the enemies of Gondor by arms. But Gondor itself he overcomes by love." Flieger (1981:49-50) links Aragorn's double role of healer and renewer to the romance tradition. This is particularly evident in the scene in which Aragorn heals Faramir and Éowyn. Here, the theme of the new king who arrives to heal the kingdom – his name Envinyatar means 'the Renewer', as Aragorn himself points out (Tolkien 1992:897) – and that of Éowyn's unrequited love, reinforce the presence of the romance tradition. This can be seen in the descriptions of the effects of *athelas*, which brings a virginal air to the room, "as if it had not before been breathed by any living thing and came new-made from snowy mountains high beneath a dome of stars." (Tolkien 1992:902)

[51] With regard to the theme of healing in the epic tradition, Miller (2000: 325-326) observes that Achilles possesses the ability to heal, but he does not use it because "the [epic] hero's business is always to deal out death." The point is that even if healing is not a priority for an epic hero, it is not totally foreign to him.

VICTORY: ROMANCE

From the episode of the Fields of Cormallen and on, Aragorn's intertraditional flexibility is almost completely reduced to his romance side. The scene showing him seated on a throne in the clearing of the forest of Ithilien with the sword on his knees, acting like a benevolent and wise king, is a proper introduction for what is to come.

The romance tradition continues to dominate the narrative when the heroes return to Minas Tirith. At this stage, Aragorn appears as the renewer king of medieval romance: wise, strong, in the prime of life, and with healing powers: "ancient of days he seemed and yet in the flower of manhood; and wisdom sat upon his brow, and strength and healing were in his hands, and a light was about him." (Tolkien 1992:1004) This time he enters the city in triumph, and the narrator emphasizes the renewed splendour of the streets. However, Aragorn the romance king lacks a queen to become complete and to fulfil the mythical pattern. The problem is that the White Tree of Gondor is dead, and Aragorn cannot get married until it flowers again.

Gandalf enters the scene once more, and acting as a divine messenger, he takes Aragorn to Mount Mindolluin, where he explains to him what should be done, showing him a sapling that, against all odds, has sprouted from the rocky ground. Aragorn plants the sapling where the old tree used to stand and marries Arwen on the day of the summer solstice. Both things are intimately connected to the medieval and Renaissance world-view, where the king and queen are at the centre, and in direct connection with God.[52] As we have seen, virtually everything in this episode is related to the concepts of fertility and renewal (the marriage, the flowering tree and a general renaissance of the arts and culture

---

[52] In the Christian (and hence, romance) iconography, the tree symbolizes a bridge between heaven and earth, as does the union between the king and queen (see de Paco 2003:145, 347).

in the city)⁵³ which by analogue with the central myth in Arthurian romance – we may well call it the fertilisation of the Waste Land – puts the narrative in close contact with medieval romance.

One of the reasons for this may be that Aragorn, after the triumph at the Black Gate, takes on the role of king, whereby he loses his epic traits. This is largely due to the fact that the figure of the king, and all it implies in terms of responsibility and stability, is opposed to the attitude and fundamental ambitions required of the epic hero (Miller 2000:140-141). In this way, Aragorn's 'rebirth' marks the beginning of the Fourth Age, but at the same time he is reduced to the stereotype of the renewer king and becomes so inflexible that he is no longer able to take part in the intertraditional dialogue.⁵⁴

CONCLUSIONS

The character of Aragorn is a clear example of how the limits imposed by the narrative zones that, in turn, are informed by different narrative traditions in dialogue, play a crucial role in the character-drawing in *The Lord of the Rings*. In the case of Aragorn, the dialogue between different traditions is primarily exploited in order to create a character that shares affinities both with pagan and Christian paradigms, and his heroic evolution shows much of this internal struggle until he finally settles in the role of the benevolent romance king.

The novelistic environment of Bree – characters, action, and physical space – and the scenes in which the hobbits dominate the narra-

---

[53] See Day's (2003:172-174) comparison between Aragorn and Charlemagne. Moorman (1968:203) argues that the central myth of *The Lord of the Rings* should be the founding of the city. This reduces the scope of applicability too drastically, but it makes sense if we expand the implications of that enterprise to the bringing of hope to a spiritually wounded culture by the use of intertraditional elements; the myth would then be related to something like an integration of Western narrative and cultural traditions into one great code of wide applicability.

[54] See Kocher (1974:142): "Aragorn the man recedes to Aragorn the King."

tive, such as the 'picnic' at Orthanc, considerably tone down his epic side, while Aragorn's romance side is brought out when the narrative zone is significantly influenced by the themes of courtly love (as in his interaction with Arwen and Éowyn) and moral tests (the hobbit hunt, Éowyn); the physical space of forests (Lórien, Fangorn and Ithilien); and his success in bringing back growth and fertility to the kingdom (Ithilien and, once the War of the Ring is over, Minas Tirith).

Aragorn's epic dimension is most fully exploited in his dealings with purely epic characters, such as Théoden or Éomer; in the physical space dominated by warrior cultures (Meduseld); actions related to war, warrior ethics and heroic feats (the physical prowess involved in the hunt for the hobbits, the argument in front of Théoden's hall; the battles of Helm's Deep and Pelennor).

The consciousness of the narrative dynamics that govern this particular kind of intertraditional dialogue, where the traditions shape the narrative as they bleed into each other in the different narrative zones that make up the global chronotope of Middle-earth, will hopefully clear the way for what I perceive as four possible advances in Tolkien studies: to produce relevant criticism concerning genre in *The Lord of the Rings*; to provide new clues for an understanding of many of its apparent contradictions; to bridge the gap between the two main traditional fields of Tolkien criticism (source-hunting, on the one hand, and the disclosure of its contemporaneous character, on the other); and to put this work in a *meaningful* relationship with modernism by showing both similarities and differences, with reference to the concepts of ironic myth and the intertraditional dialogue.

MARTIN SIMONSON took his degree in English Philology at the University of the Basque Country in Vitoria, Spain, and holds a Ph.D. in English Literature from the same university. His doctoral thesis focused on the narrative dynamics of *The Lord of the Rings*. He has contributed with essays on Tolkien in *Reconsidering Tolkien* (2005), and in *Tolkien Studies* 3 (2006). He is currently head of the English department at Colegio San Viator in Vitoria.

References

Bakhtin, Mikhail, 1989, 'Las Formas del Tiempo y del Cronotopo en la Novela: Ensayos de Poética Histórica', in Mikhail Bakhtin, 1989, *Teoría y Estética de la Novela* (first published 1975; translated from Russian by H. Kriúkova and V. Cazcarra), Madrid: Taurus, pp. 237-409.

Battarbee, Keith J. (ed.), 1993, *Scholarship & Fantasy: Proceedings of The Tolkien Phenomenon, May 1992, University of Turku, Finland*, (Anglica Turkuensia 12), Turku: University of Turku.

Chance, Jane, 1986, 'Tolkien and his Sources', in Miriam Youngerman Miller and Jane Chance (eds.), 1986, *Approaches to Teaching Sir Gawain and the Green Knight*, New York: MLA, pp. 151-155.

---, 2004, '*The Lord of the Rings*: Tolkien's Epic', in Rose A. Zimbardo and Neil D. Isaacs (eds.), 2004, *Understanding The Lord of the Rings. The Best of Tolkien Criticism*, Boston and New York: Houghton Mifflin, pp. 195-232.

Day, David, 2003, *The World of Tolkien: Mythological Sources of The Lord of the Rings*, London: Mitchell Beazley, Octopus Publishing Group.

De Paco, Albert, 2003, *Diccionario de Símbolos*, Barcelona: Editorial Optima.

Dickens, Charles, 2003, *The Posthumous Papers of the Pickwick Club*, (first published 1836-1837), London: Penguin Books.

Dickerson, Matthew, 2003, *Following Gandalf. Epic Battles and Moral Victory in The Lord of the Rings*, Grand Rapids, MI: Brazos Press.

Fenwick, Mac, 1996, 'Breastplates of Silk: Homeric Women in *The Lord of the Rings*', in *Mythlore* 21, 1996, pp. 17-23.

Flieger, Verlyn, 1981, 'Frodo and Aragorn: The Concept of the Hero', in Neil D. Isaacs and Rose A. Zimbardo (eds.), 1981. *Tolkien: New Critical Perspectives*, Lexington, Kentucky: The University Press of Kentucky, pp. 40-62.

Frye, Northrop, 1971, *Anatomy of Criticism*, (first edition 1957), Princeton: Princeton University Press.

Greenman, David, 1992, 'Aeneidic and Odyssean Patterns of Escape and Return in Tolkien's 'The Fall of Gondolin' and *The Return of the King*', in *Mythlore* 18, 1992, pp. 4-9.

Hamer, Richard (ed. and trans.), 1970, *A Choice of Old English Poetry*, London: Faber and Faber.

Joyce, James, 1998, *Ulysses*, (first edition 1922), Oxford: Oxford University Press.

Kaufmann, U. Milo, 1975, 'Aspects of the Paradisiacal in Tolkien's Work', in Jared Lobdell (ed.), 1975, *A Tolkien Compass*, La Salle, Illinois: Open Court, pp. 143-152.

Kelly, Mary Quella, 1968, 'The Poetry of Fantasy: Verse in *The Lord of the Rings*', in Neil D. Isaacs and Rose A. Zimbardo (eds.), 1968, *Tolkien and the Critics. Essays on J.R.R. Tolkien's The Lord of the Rings*, Notre Dame and London: University of Notre Dame Press, pp. 170-200.

King, Katherine C., 1987, *Achilles: Paradigms of the War Hero From Homer to the Middle Ages*, Berkeley: University of California Press.

Kocher, Paul, 1974, *Master of Middle Earth: the Achievement of J.R.R. Tolkien*, (first edition 1973), Harmondsworth: Penguin.

Lobdell, Jared, 2004, *The World of the Rings: Language, Religion, and Adventure in Tolkien*, (revised edition, first edition 1981: *England and Always: Tolkien's World of the Rings*), Chicago & LaSalle, Illinois, Open Court.

Miller, Dean A., 2000, *The Epic Hero*, Baltimore, Maryland: The John Hopkins University Press.

Miller, Miriam Youngerman, 1991, '"Of sum mayn meruayle, that he myht trawe": *The Lord of the Rings* and *Sir Gawain and the Green Knight*', in *Studies in Medievalism*, 1991, 3.3, pp. 345-365.

Moorman, Charles, 1968. 'The Shire, Mordor, and Minas Tirith', in Neil D. Isaacs and Rose A. Zimbardo (eds.), 1968, *Tolkien and the Critics. Essays on J.R.R. Tolkien's The Lord of the Rings*, Notre Dame and London: University of Notre Dame Press, pp. 201-217.

Quint, David, 1985, 'The Boat of Romance and Renaissance Epic', in Kevin Brownlee and Marina Scordilis Brownlee (eds.), 1985, *Romance: Generic Transformation from Chrétien de Troyes to Cervantes*, Hanover: University Press of New England, pp. 179-182.

Rosebury, Brian, 2003, *Tolkien: A Cultural Phenomenon*, (revised and enlarged edition; first published 1992), Houndmills: Palgrave Macmillan.

Segura, Eduardo, 2004, *El Viaje del Anillo*, Barcelona: Minotauro.

Shippey, Tom A., 2003, *The Road to Middle-earth*, (third edition, first edition 1982), Boston: Houghton Mifflin.

Simonson, Martin, 2005, '*The Lord of the Rings* in the Wake of the Great War: War Poetry, Modernism, and Ironic Myth', in Thomas Honegger (ed.), 2005, *Reconsidering Tolkien*, (Cormarë Series 8), Zurich and Berne: Walking Tree Publishers, pp. 153-170.

---, 2006, 'Three is Company: Novel, Fairy Tale, and Romance on the Journey Through the Shire', in *Tolkien Studies* 3, 2006, pp. 81-100.

St. Clair, Gloriana, 1996, 'An Overview of the Northern Influences on Tolkien's Works', in Patricia Reynolds and Glen H. GoodKnight (eds.). 1996, *Proceedings of the J.R.R. Centenary Conference. Keble College, Oxford, 1992*, (*Mythlore* 80/*Mallorn* 30), Milton Keynes and Altadena: The Tolkien Society and The Mythopoetic Press, pp. 63-67.

Steadman, John M., 1969, *Milton and the Renaissance Hero*, London: Oxford University Press.

Stevens, John, 1973, *Medieval Romance: Themes and Approaches*, London: Hutchinson University Library.

Toda Iglesia, Maria A., 2002, *Héroes y Amigos: Masculinidad, Imperialismo y Didacticismo en la Novela de Aventuras Británica, 1880-1914*, Salamanca: Ediciones Universidad de Salamanca.

Tolkien, John Ronald Reuel, 1988, *The Return of the Shadow*, (edited by Christopher Tolkien; *History of Middle-earth* volume 6), London: Unwin Hyman.

---, 1992, *The Lord of the Rings*, (one volume edition with the text of the second edition; first edition 1954-55; second edition 1966), London: HarperCollins.

---, 1997a, 'Beowulf: The Monsters and the Critics', in J.R.R. Tolkien, 1997, *The Monsters and the Critics and Other Essays* (edited by Christopher Tolkien; first edition 1983; originally Sir Israel Gollancz Memorial Lecture, read 25 November 1936; first published in 1937), London: HarperCollins, pp. 5-48.

---, 1997b, 'On Fairy-Stories', in J.R.R. Tolkien, 1997, *The Monsters and the Critics and Other Essays* (edited by Christopher Tolkien; first edition 1983; originally Andrew Lang Lecture given on 8 March 1939, first published in 1947), London: HarperCollins, pp. 109-161.

---, 2000, *The Letters of J.R.R. Tolkien*, (edited by Humphrey Carpenter, with the assistance of Christopher Tolkien; first edition 1981), Boston and New York: Houghton Mifflin.

Tolley, Clive, 1993, 'Tolkien and the Unfinished', in Keith J. Battarbee (ed.), 1993, *Scholarship & Fantasy: Proceedings of The Tolkien Phenomenon, May 1992, University of Turku, Finland*, (Anglica Turkuensia 12), Turku: University of Turku, pp. 151-164.

Veugen, Connie, 2005, '"A Man, Lean, Dark, Tall": Aragon Seen Through Different Media', in Thomas Honegger (ed.), 2005, *Reconsidering Tolkien*, (Cormarë Series 8), Zurich and Berne: Walking Tree Publishers, pp. 171-209.

Zimbardo, Rose A. and Neil D. Isaacs (eds.), 2004, *Understanding The Lord of the Rings. The Best of Tolkien Criticism*, Boston and New York: Houghton Mifflin.

Slow-Kindled Courage. A Study of Heroes in the Works of J.R.R. Tolkien

ANNA SLACK

Abstract

It is posited that in the dislocation between literature's example and reality's experience, the Great War created a backlash against the linguistic and ideological form of heroic literature, eliciting a sense of 'disenchantment' for concurrent poets and writers. Heroes in Tolkien's fictions are examined as an attempt to reinstate these older frameworks of heroism, especially at levels of sophrosynic achievement or Christian mimesis. Discussion covers the historical context of the Great War, models of heroism upon which Tolkien drew, Tolkien's own theory regarding the links between the primary world of history/reality and the secondary world of literature, and the crossing of these issues to elicit the heroes of his fiction. Exploration of Tolkien's heroes illustrates the way in which Tolkien attempts to escape the prevailing disenchantment of his age, but concludes that his heroes are ultimately symptomatic of the time in which he wrote.

> *We all have a problem with heroes. We want them*
> *so badly that we keep inventing new ones.*
> Burrow (2004:14)

If literature is a mimetic art, then heroes in literature both reflect and answer the need for heroes in the real world. *The Iliad*, *The Aeneid*, the Bible, *Beowulf,* historiographic works such as those of Wace or Layamon: all exemplify the curious overlap between the secondary world of literature and the primary world of history. This dialogue between reality and fiction is a complex system of encouragement and self-perpetuation for writers and readers alike.

In this article, Tolkien's heroes are examined in terms of their antecedents, the heroic spaces created for them, and the ways in which they enter into the aforementioned dialogue with history via the historical moment of their creation.

'FAIRIES AND FUSILIERS'

In Tolkien's time history and literature were closely intertwined in creating a model of heroism. Partially due to the amount of literature preserved, the Great War is one of the most-documented conflicts in western history. Generally speaking, the prevailing initial literary voice of the trenches came from officers and soldiers who were themselves educated on epics: *The Iliad*, *The Aeneid*, *Paradise Lost*. These possess a high-linguistic register that praises courage, honour and glorious death in battle, *Paradise Lost* doing so in its Homeric depiction of Satan. The trench-writers applied this style of thought and linguistic expression to a new conflict; for example, Rupert Brook's *Peace* captures a sense of language that originates ideologically in Homer:

> Now God be thanked Who has matched us with His hour
> And Caught our youth, and wakened us from sleeping
> [...]
> Glad from a world grown old and cold and weary,
> Leave the sick hearts that honour could not move,
> And half-men, and their dirty songs and dreary,
> And all the little emptiness of love!
> (Stallworthy 1984:162)

This elucidation of honour and shame shows war as the ideal occupation of youth. Married to the Homeric framing ("hearts that honour could not move") is a redemptive bellicosity influenced by Christianity: "[...] we have found release there, / Where there's no ill, no grief [...]"

But this glorious view was disturbed by the sheer scale of the war; linguistic traits characteristic of the Classics and the Christian faith, used previously to aggrandise battle, were employed to sing a different song:

> What passing bells for these who die as cattle?
> Only the monstrous anger of the guns.
> Only the stuttering rifles' rapid rattle
> Can patter out their hasty orisons.
> No mockeries for them from prayers or bells,
> Nor any voice of mourning save the choirs, –
> The shrill, demented choirs of wailing shells;
> And bugles calling for them from sad shires.
> (Owen 1933:80)

In merging heroic/Christian language, Owen challenges views that automatically confer heroism on war. He does the same in *Strange Meeting*, where the poem's dream-like frame is reminiscent of Odysseus' and Ajax's meeting in *Odyssey* XI; the title of 'Arms and the Boy' plainly references *The Aeneid*'s opening line, "Arma uirumque cano" ('I sing of arms and of the man'), emphasising soldiers' youth. An archaic linguistic register associated with the values of war is consistently employed to undermine them, for Owen's subject was "the pity of war", not its heroism.

Siegfried Sassoon wrote likewise. Keenly aware of "one [...] who reads / Of dying heroes and their deathless deeds" (*Remorse*, Sassoon 1961:86), his concern was to highlight the bitter difference between perception and reality. *The Hero*, for example, depicts the "gallant lies" told to keep up heroism's façade for an Every-Woman whose son has been killed. Sassoon was also aware of the point where history, literature and war interlocked. In *Songbooks of the War* he writes:

> In fifty years, when peace outshines
> Remembrance of the battle lines,
> Adventurous lads will sigh and cast
> Proud looks upon the plundered past
> [...]

> And dream of lads who fought in France
> And lived in time to share the fun.
> (Sassoon 1961:86-87)

These poets sought to reflect the conflict of their time. Given the accepted canon of war poetry, prominently showcasing Owen and Sassoon, it can be said that the anti archaic-language backlash succeeded. That those dying were so young seems however to have turned the tide against more than the classics; this disenchantment of war also lashed out against fairy story:

> The child alone a poet is:
> Spring and fairyland are his
> [...]
> Wisdom made him old and wary
> Banishing the Lords of Fairy.
> Wisdom made a breach and battered
> Babylon to bits: she scattered
> To the hedges and the ditches
> All our nursery gnomes and witches
> [...]
> None of all the magic hosts,
> None remain but a few ghosts
> Of timorous heart, to linger on
> Weeping for lost Babylon.
> (*Babylon*, Graves 1995:50)

Here the advent of wisdom is associated with war ('breach', 'battered', 'ditches'), and the death of faërie. John Garth (2003:292) writes: "Graves' image of the end of innocence – wisdom scattering the nursery fairies – indicates the literal meaning of disenchantment. The Great War had broken a kind of spell." The broken spell created a post-world-war anxiety about heroic nature, hitherto defined by Homer, Virgil and the fantastic. "The Western Front made the fairy aesthetic seem both desperately necessary and hopelessly anachronistic" (Diane Purkiss, cited in Garth [2003:303]).

Tolkien, himself a trench-soldier, countered this linguistic and ideological background, offering a divergent approach: his "[...] real taste for fairy stories was wakened by philology on the threshold of manhood, and quickened to full life by war" ('On Fairy-Stories', Tolkien 2001:42). Linguistically and ideologically, Tolkien's writing resounds with archaisms, and in this literary etymology he tries to resurrect the values dethroned by the writings of his contemporaries. In responding to the disregard of heroic language, Tolkien's writing challenges the economy of truth represented by the canon of 'disillusioned' writers like Owen and Sassoon. Tolkien's writing reflects his desire to rekindle a model of heroism despite the trend of history. A childhood friend had remarked to him that as writers they "had been granted some spark of fire [...] that was destined to kindle a new light, or, what is the same thing, rekindle an old light in the world" (Garth 2003:308). For Tolkien, this spark resided in the mythopoeic realm of faërie.

PRISONERS AND DESERTERS: TOLKIEN'S THEORY OF FAËRIE

The function and appeal of fairy tales and similarly fantastic stories has long been discussed. Relatively few detailed analyses have been completed, though notable among these are the Brothers Grimm, Propp, Jung, Campbell, C.S. Lewis, Tolkien himself and Bettelheim. All agree that these stories fulfil an important need, although explanations differ. Jung discusses the appeal and function of myth in terms of archetypes (such as the Shadow, the Animus/Anima, and the Syzygy). In *The Uses of Enchantment*, Bettelheim posits that fairy tales give symbolic form to trying situations for children: "The fairy tale simplifies all situations [...]. Its figures are clearly drawn [...]. All characters are typical rather than unique" (Bettelheim 1976:8). The formative system provided by stories and heroes for children is also examined by Margery Hourihan in

Deconstructing the Hero. In 'On Fairy-Stories', Tolkien states that these tales have a 'prophylactic' effect for adults, whose oversight in critical thought he laments. He describes the main veins of this effect as recovery, escape and consolation, which in turn resolve themselves at their highest point into what he termed 'eucatastrophe'. In his distinctions of these functions, Tolkien asserted that a reader sought stories to escape from the world and recover the means to view it clearly, thereby returning to it renewed. In this he has common ground with writers like Bettelheim, except Tolkien's theory is transgenerational. Aware that some critics were quick to call an adult taste for fairy stories escapism or "juvenile trash" (Wilson 1956:314), Tolkien used his three-part-theory to distinguish between the "escape of the prisoner and the flight of the deserter" ('On Fairy-Stories', Tolkien 2001:61). The crux of his position was in the fact that after reading, readers returned to the world rather than making a constant withdrawal from it (the act of deserting). That Tolkien uses terms like 'deserter' reflects the conflict of his time, linking war, faërie and theory together. With his theory in mind, it would be reasonable to expect Tolkien's heroes to bring a sense of recovery to his works.

MODELS OF HEROISM: *KLEOS* AND *SOPHROSYNE*

Hero-theory runs from ancient Greece to more modern writers like Thomas Carlyle and Lucy Hughes-Hallett. For the purposes of this article, literary heroism is broadly viewed as a bipolar delineation between *kleos* and *sophrosyne*.

Kleos is the Greek word for renown or glory; personal renown is paramount in this heroism. Hughes-Hallett (2004:1) suggests that these heroes are "superb spirit[s] [...] associated with courage and integrity and a disdain for the cramping compromises by means of which the unheroic majority live their lives – attributes that are widely considered noble." The distinction between unheroic majority and hero sets the latter 'higher' than others on the mortal scale; this is suggested by frequently antagonistic roles between heroes and other figures of authority such as kings. The primary example of this hero is Achilles: offered the choice between living a long and comfortable life but having no fame, and going to war, dying young and winning great glory, he chooses the latter.[1]

Not every hero seeking renown falls under Achilles' category. *Kleos* could be further defined as the constant quest for renown (Achilles), the quest for another object (Beowulf or Siegfried), and the romance quest on behalf of a lady (Yvain or Lancelot). Norse and Classical heroes would be concerned with their reputation or their quest, while romance heroes often possess spiritual undertones, especially in the ornate, religiously-inspired modes of address of *fin'amor*.

Opposed to *kleos* is *sophrosyne*, the virtue of heroic temperance. Considered a fatal flaw of excess in tragedy (where it constitutes vital inaction), and often associated with women or the young, it was Christianity during the Mediaeval and Renaissance periods which facilitated the shift towards *sophrosyne* as a heroic virtue. Examples of sophrosynic heroes would be mediaeval hagiographies, Guyon in *The Faërie Queene*, or Milton's Christ in *Paradise Regained*. *Sophrosyne* is "[...] very difficult to give to a literary hero, because inaction is a highly undramatic mode of behaviour" (Jordan 1989:4); it necessitates the substitution of psychological/spiritual action for physical heroics.

These templates highlight a fundamental divide in literature's heroic roles; a *kleos* hero, of noble birth, perhaps divinely-engendered, was predetermined for great things. He was to excel in matters of prowess for his own advancement and glory, or for the honour of his lady. A sophrosynic hero was to imitate a higher standard: Christ. A variation on being divine offspring, the hero was to seek God's glory and will over his own.

---

[1] See Homer, *The Iliad*, pages 34 and 339.

This Christian mimetic (heroes mirroring Christ) was certainly one that Tolkien strove to create; eucatastrophe is defined as:

> a piercing glimpse of joy [...] [that] rends indeed the very web of story. [...] [I]n the 'eucatastrophe' we see in a brief vision that the answer may be greater – it may be a far-off gleam or echo of *evangelium* in the real world. [...] [T]he Great Eucatastrophe, [t]he Christian joy is [...] high and joyous. Because this story is supreme; and it is true. Art has been verified. God is the Lord, of angels, and of men – and of elves. Legend and history have met and fused.
> ('On Fairy-Stories', Tolkien 2001:70-73)

Tolkien calls this the "true form of fairy tale [...] its highest function" ('On Fairy-Stories, Tolkien 2001:68). Thus we may assume that Tolkien's heroes should enter the heroic tradition at a level which corresponds to the Christian one. The modern hero is a fusing of *kleos* and *sophrosyne*; he must act morally and often exhibit physical prowess, but only when vital. Like the trench-soldiers, he is an unheroic figure in a heroic circumstance. That Tolkien chooses to write in the sophrosynic tradition opposes this view.

Tolkien's stance was not unique; 'On Fairy-Stories' and eucatastrophe were fermented in the creative arena of the Inklings, a group of Oxonians who met regularly to translate Norse sagas and read each others' work. Other Inklings included C.S. Lewis and Charles Williams: their works (e.g. *The Cosmic Trilogy, The Chronicles of Narnia, War In Heaven, The Greater Trumps*) all exhibit the same 'Christianised' theory of the relation of story/story-telling to the real world. In Williams' fictions, for example, characters come to learn that the super-spiritual bubbles away intensely within the bounds of the world in which they live. In the autobiographical *Surprised by Joy*, C.S. Lewis states that the joy he has been describing would be called 'eucatastrophe' by Tolkien. As in his youth, Tolkien was involved with a group of writers that sought to influence the world. By accenting the spiritual in their writings, these writers presented fictitious framings of Ephesians 6:12 (*King James Bible*): "[...] for we wrestle not against flesh and blood, but against principalities, against powers, against the rulers of darkness of this world, against spiritual wickedness in high places." Interestingly, this Pauline letter then applies the topoic motions of arming the epic hero to Christians:

> Stand, therefore, having your loins girt about with truth, and having on the breastplate of righteousness; and your feet shod with the preparation of the gospel of peace; Above all, taking the shield of faith, wherewith ye shall be able to quench all the fiery darts of the wicked. And take the helmet of salvation, and the sword of the Spirit, which is the word of God.
> (*King James Bible*, Ephesians 6:14-17)

This makes the Christian a hero with an epic level of prowess – but, as *sophrosyne* dictates, it is a spiritual prowess.

TOLKIEN'S HEROES

Tolkien's heroes draw on the traditions outlined above, his scheme of heroism modulating as his writing progresses and exhibits different heroic spaces. Considered here are Beren and Túrin in *The Silmarillion*; Bilbo in *The Hobbit*; Aragorn and Frodo in *The Lord of the Rings*. Tolkien was engaged in depicting heroism for a culture sunk increasingly in disillusion. If, as Aldous Huxley (cited in Sale 1973:1) observes, "civilisation has absolutely no need of nobility or heroism", the question is what Tolkien's heroes – written for the superficially anti-heroic modern reader of the post-war critical environment – reflect of his time.

BEREN AND TÚRIN: A BACKWARD GLANCE?

In *Modern Heroism*, Robert Sale suggests that for Tolkien, *The Silmarillion* is "a nostalgic glance [...] back to a world he would much rather have lived in" (Sale 1973:228). Sale asks how Tolkien can create heroes of an older tradition as a modern author, and hints at the Great War when he says: "If despair is created by the sense that History has overwhelmed the world, then the heroism will be created in defiance of that same history" (Sale 1973:11). Because Tolkien-as-author feels the pressure of history, Beren and Túrin feel it too. Despite his fictional setting, Tolkien's content points to his modern position.

A synopsis of Beren's heroism evokes a romance quest; he has to claim one of the Silmarils from the Iron Crown of Morgoth, deliver it to King Thingol, and thereafter claim the hand of Lúthien, whom he loves. But the story also operates on a darker level; the Silmarils carry a dreadful curse into which many have already been drawn; Beren is a stranger at court, dispossessed and the last of his people. Lúthien is an elf who must give up her immortality for Beren. Unusually active for a woman in a romance, she refuses to be left behind by Beren and the narrative follows her in as much detail as it does Beren.

Tolkien was obviously aware of this measure in heroics whose balancing unbalances the romance-quest. Lúthien belongs to a tradition of prominent women that goes back to Marie de France, Chrétien de Troyes and later Spenser. But unlike Spenser's handling of Una and Redcrosse, Tolkien cannot balance his narrative in a fashion appropriate to his genre. Attempting to re-confine his heroine, Tolkien gives Lúthien a hound as companion who defeats Sauron and battles with Morgoth's wolf at the tale's end. Nevertheless, Lúthien is made conspicuous by her heroism. She rescues Beren from Sauron, sings Morgoth to sleep (facilitating the seizure of the Silmarils), heals Beren more than once, and pleads for his life to be returned to him in the Halls of the Dead. But Lúthien is not of Britomart's class; her prowess is not in arms.

The story counterpoises Beren's doom and Lúthien's voice; Lúthien consistently tips the possession of heroic status towards herself. Beren is weighed down by the grief of his humanity, but Lúthien, in her constant active role, is an artist within the tale who directly affects its ending. In persuading the divine agents, the Valar, to grant Beren his life, she becomes what Tolkien would call a 'sub-creator'; a position conferred upon her by her voice, which originates in her elven descent and connection therein to faërie. Faërie is a world with which Beren, fashioned by 'doom', cannot compete.

This extra-literary weight on the text is created by the author's position in history; the narrative is skewed between the typical hero-of-the-sword, and the artistic heroism of language figured in Lúthien. For example, there is more awe in the text when Huan the hound speaks (linguistic heroism) than when he wrestles with Carcaroth (physical heroism). When Beren names Lúthien *Tinúviel*, he establishes the romance element of the narrative in foregrounding his love for her. But in the same breath he surrenders his position as hero to her by ceding to linguistic-heroism: "Then the spell of silence fell from Beren, and he called to her, crying *Tinúviel*; and the woods echoed her name" (*Silmarillion*, Tolkien 1999b:193). Beren's surrender of narrative and heroic primacy began when he entered the woods that were the realm of the Elves; here the woods themselves confirm that the silence of physical heroism is to be replaced by the voice.

The dominance of Lúthien's heroism is asserted at the tale's end when conclusion itself is tackled:

> The song of Lúthien before Mandos was the song most fair that ever in words was woven, and the song most sorrowful that ever the world shall hear [...] and Mandos was moved to pity, who never before was so moved, nor has been since.
> (*Silmarillion*, Tolkien 1999b:220)

The narrator also writes: "Thus [with Beren's death] ended the Quest of the Silmaril; but the Lay of Leithian, Release from Bondage, does not end" (*Silmarillion*, Tolkien 1999b:220). Tolkien acknowledges the dualism of the heroism in his story, a conflict that lies in inter-weaving several modes and heroes into one story. What reflections does a tale where the artist (Lúthien) is more overtly heroic cast upon the narrator? At its outset, the narrator tells us that what we are reading is "told in fewer words" than older versions and "without song" (*Silmarillion*, Tolkien 1999b:189), pointing to the fact that the story-teller has little grasp of the tale's principal heroic ethic, words. But is this to give more space to Lúthien? Does the narrator's alignment with linguistic heroism explain why Beren's physical heroism seems less important? Downplaying the narrator's own craft may reflect the fact that Lúthien, primary exponent of the faërie heroism of tongue, is "now lost" (*Silmarillion*, Tolkien 1999b:221). The dehabilitation of the narrator in the loss of faërie suggests the literary losses incurred in the disenchantment of Tolkien's contemporaries.

The power attributed to language in *The Silmarillion* reflects Tolkien's love of philology. Robert M. Adams (1981:169) observes: "Tolkien has a fascination with names [...] that will probably seem excessive to anyone whose favourite light reading is not the first book of Chronicles." For example, Túrin's story begins: "Rían, daughter of Belegund, was the wife of Huor, son of Galdor; and she was wedded to him two months before he went with Húrin his brother to the Nirnaeth Arnoediad" (*Silmarillion*, Tolkien 1999b:235). The Biblical comparison is further evidenced in Tolkien's love of family trees, shown in *The Silmarillion* and the Appendices to *The Lord of the Rings*. The tale of Túrin Turambar is filled with names and the act of naming. One may assert this to be an extension of faërie heroism: power in words equals power in names.

Throughout 'Beren and Lúthien', Beren is accorded names befitting his deeds e.g. Erchamion ('One Hand') or Camlost ('The Empty-Handed'). These create a progressive heroic identity; though not making Beren heroic, they reflect his achieved heroism. Compare this to Genesis 17 or 35, where Abram and Jacob both have their names changed *post factum* to reflect their new status: Abram ('Exalted Father') becomes Abraham ('Father of Many') when he commits himself to God, and Jacob (figuratively 'He deceives') becomes Israel ('He struggles with God').

Túrin names himself, and frequently the event eliciting this naming is one he has falsely interpreted, as when he names himself Neithan ('The Wronged') refusing the king's pardon "in the pride of his heart". The sheer volume of names (seven in all) attributed to Túrin in the narrative bear witness to his attempt to mould his own heroism. Túrin is overshadowed by Beren ("This man is not Beren – a dark doom lies on him!" *Silmarillion*, Tolkien 1999b:251), and in response he reaches for a way to turn himself into a hero.

Túrin's final name, Turambar ('Master of Doom') is a hubristic self-sentence. Empowered by the names he has given himself, Túrin tries to assert authority over the narrator of the text as well as the characters within it when he states that he has mastered his 'dark doom'. Unlike Beren, who accepts his doom, Túrin constantly pulls away from it in his act of naming, and in doing so only succeeds in becoming stuck fast. As a result, Túrin's story feels strongly governed by *wyrd*, the Norse fate. Ironically, Beren receives life for accepting his doom; Túrin receives death resisting it at every turn. Though Beren's strategy may be more 'Christian', it does not reward him with eternal life as a Biblical parallel might suggest; in this, Beren reflects the culture of disillusionment and foreshadows Frodo.

Both Beren and Túrin struggle in their heroic spaces because they are created 'backwards' as insertions into a tradition long passed. Beren and Túrin are forgeries, albeit intelligent ones. As a modern Christian,

Tolkien cannot help but create characters that cannot quite sup with Achilles or Beowulf. This is exemplified in Túrin's encounter with Glaurung the dragon: while Túrin's literary predecessor, Siegfried, slew the dragon and claimed his prize, Túrin falls prey to Glaurung's voice, and as a consequence loses everything. Glaurung acknowledges Túrin's *kleos*-naming when he goads him: "Then surely in scorn they will name thee, if thou spurnest this gift" (*Silmarillion*, Tolkien 1999b:256). It is Túrin's future reputation that Glaurung manipulates. In steering Túrin from the rescue of Finduilas (a romance quest), Glaurung denies Túrin the chance to become the hero of another genre. In this single moment, Túrin fails to belong either to the heroic genre (by discerning the dragon's guile as Siegfried with Fáfnir), or the romantic one. The result is a tragic matrix that ends with Túrin marrying his sister, and with both their deaths.

Beren and Túrin exemplify key aspects of Tolkien's heroic scheme; clearly language, name and deed all have a part to play in framing a hero. Epic, Norse and Mediaeval traditions were part of his thinking, and the Middle-earth of *The Silmarillion* provides a place where these heroes can exist. *The Silmarillion* explores heroic temperament, with his heroes' fate as the first residue of war's disenchantment, for the heroism of Middle-earth's heroes is never questioned. When Tolkien began to write *The Hobbit* in the 1930s, Middle-earth's heroic space changed to accommodate the new protagonists.

BILBO BAGGINS: A 'MODERN' HERO

"In a hole in the ground there lived a hobbit" (*Hobbit*, Tolkien 1999a:3); so begins Tolkien's first published fiction. Middle-earth has changed; *The Silmarillion*'s narrator would not write this way, nor would his heroes live in such a hole, even if it "mean[t] comfort" (*Hobbit*, Tolkien 1999a:3). But in essence the author's premise remains; emphasis in the opening words is not on defining what a hobbit is, but a detailed description of where one lives. Middle-earth is still an arena fashioned for its heroes, though the shift in tone and locale alerts us to the shift in hero. Hobbiton is not a heroic setting, and Bagginses "never [have] any adventures or [do] anything unexpected" (*Hobbit*, Tolkien 1999a:3). The narrator tells us that this story will be about one who breaks away from that mould: "He may have lost the neighbours' respect, but he gained – well, you will see whether he gained anything in the end" (*Hobbit*, Tolkien 1999a:4). This is an active invitation to consider the hero's achievements.

Bilbo is defined as stereotypical of the English upper-middle-class (with emphasis on decorum and social niceties); we are asked to weigh his 'fame' at home against the fame achieved in his quest. In this sense, Bilbo is anti-heroic. He is anti-heroic also in being neither wise nor strong, but hired as a burglar. Conducted by dwarves (who, with the almost concurrent appearance of Walt Disney's *Snow White*, may not have been viewed seriously), the quest would have no place in 'epic' literature. Although the dispossessed dwarves hold the quest highly ("a journey from which some of us, perhaps all of us, may never return", *Hobbit*, Tolkien 1999a:17), Bilbo does not appreciate its epic quality (at the thought of not returning, he faints), and the reader may therefore be less inclined to. A character like Bombur is clearly not designed for the epic tradition. Tolkien initially creates a miniature epic world, and carefully expands it until it becomes a full-blown mythological canvas seen through the eyes of an anti-mythic character.

This distinction is demonstrated in Bilbo's progression from bumbling protagonist to hero: in rescuing the dwarves from the spiders in Mirkwood or Thranduil's dungeons, the hobbit is drawn into heroic circumstances. The reader expects the conversation with Smaug to be the work's climax; it is certainly envisioned as such by the questing characters. That the story does not end with the slaying of the dragon indicates movement from fairy-tale to mythic canvas; but Bilbo retains a common sense that curtails him from either faërie or epic heroism. His unconsciousness at the Battle of the Five Armies reflects his dislocation in the narrative. Bilbo's heroism reaches its height when he relinquishes the Arkenstone to Bard;

> 'I hope you will find it useful.'
> The Elvenking looked at Bilbo with a new wonder. 'Bilbo Baggins!' he said. 'You are more worthy to wear the armour of elf-princes than many that have looked more comely in it.'
> (*Hobbit*, Tolkien 1999a:251)

Here Tolkien highlights and reconciles the incongruity he has cultivated throughout the work. Much of the tale's humour stems from Bilbo's anachronism, the unheroic character in a heroic world. In the above quotation, the two are conflated so that the reader sees that as Bilbo can be measured on the scale of Elven-princes he is not such a misfit hero after all. Tolkien does similarly with Thorin's final words:

> There is more in you of good than you know, child of the kindly West. Some courage and some wisdom, blended in measure. If more of us valued food and cheer and song above hoarded gold, it would be a merrier world.
> (*Hobbit*, Tolkien 1999a:266)

Here Bilbo is not so much affirmed into the heroic tradition as made equal to it in what he loves. However, upon his return to Hobbiton, he has "lost his reputation [...] he was no longer quite respectable" (*Hobbit*, Tolkien 1999a:278). Affirmation of heroic equity can pass from mythic to non-mythic, but not from the non-mythic to the mythic: Achilles may dub a trench-soldier heroic, but the trench-soldier cannot claim it for himself. Bilbo comes from the later arm of the sophrosynic tradition; he is a 'moral' hero, who acts when it is right to do so, rather than not acting at all. Nothing he does is for fame or reputation, although this is the way in which he is then measured. *The Hobbit* reflects the perception of reputation and heroism that had been shifted and confused by the Great War; within the frame of children's story Tolkien touches on the concerns of disenchantment and problems for a modern hero.

SPIRITUAL MIMESIS: *THE LORD OF THE RINGS*

Tolkien staunchly stated that *The Lord of the Rings* was not an allegory, and that he "much prefer[ed] history, true or feigned, with its varied applicability to the thought and experience of the reader" (*LotR*, Tolkien 1995:xvii) In this regard, *The Lord of the Rings* seems to present itself as historiography; this fused ground of history and myth allows Tolkien to attempt to mirror the spiritual realm in his literature. Tolkien's most prominent heroes, Frodo and Aragorn, are sophrosynic heroes reflecting two aspects of Christ; servant and king. Like Bilbo, they are anachronistic: although in narrative terms they prefigure Christ, in the author's terms they are His descendants. As mimetic heroes, they imitate Christ rather than seeking their own glory, though in this imitation, particularly Frodo's imitation, *The Lord of the Rings* also grapples more with eucatastrophe and disenchantment than Tolkien's earlier works.

Structurally, it is suggested that Frodo and Aragorn are flip sides of the same coin. C.S. Lewis (2004:12) observes: "All the time we know that the fate of the world depends far more upon the small movement than on the great." Tolkien's interweaving of plot in *The Two Towers* and *The Return of the King* is highly complex, and Lewis' comment highlights the way in which heroism is split between Frodo and Aragorn accordingly. As a returning king, Aragorn inherits the *kleos* tradition, succeeding Beren and Túrin. In his love for Arwen he explicitly replays Beren's story; like Beren and Túrin he has many names.

One may easily point to Aragorn and claim that Tolkien is reframing the Arthur myth: Aragorn has a magic sword, comparable in its Elven-craft to Calibeorn in Layamon's *Brut*. Caught in a love triangle (between Eówyn and Arwen), Aragorn is the true but unknown king of Gondor, who with a wizard's help regains his throne. At this level the resemblance is striking, but Aragorn is far more modern than Malory's or Tennyson's Arthur. As king he is the story's figurehead, though he bows under the role's weight. In history and legend, kings are expected to be steadfast and wise in their decisions. Literature excels at highlighting instances where they are not (Homer's Agammemnon, Shakespeare's Lear). Within the frame of *The Lord of the Rings* we are aware of kings who failed at crucial times (Isildur).

Both author and Aragorn are aware of this burden, and as a result Aragorn is defined by the crisis of choice: "I am not Gandalf, and though I have tried to bear his part, I do not know what design or hope he had for this hour, if indeed he had any […]" (*LotR*, Tolkien 1995:387); "All that I have done today has gone amiss […] What is to be done now? […] An evil choice is now before us" (*LotR*, Tolkien 1995:405). Unlike Túrin, Aragorn is concerned that he makes the right choice for the sake of his heart rather than his historical reputation ("my heart speaks clearly at last", *LotR*, Tolkien 1995:409). Aragorn's progressing desire to perform his role affects his names. He begins as Strider; in 'The Council of Elrond' he is announced by his proper name, Aragorn (*LotR*, Tolkien 1995:240); in 'Farewell to Lórien' Galadriel says "In this hour take the name that was foretold for you, Elessar, the Elfstone of the house of Elendil!" (*LotR*, Tolkien 1995:366). Aragorn receives names according to his destiny; only in accepting his right to choice does he announce himself by his own names:

> 'I am Aragorn, son of Arathorn, and am called Elessar, the Elfstone, Dunadan, the heir of Isildur Elendil's son of Gondor. Here is the Sword that was

> Broken and is forged again! Will you aid me or thwart me? Choose swiftly!'
> [Aragorn] seemed to have grown in stature while Éomer had shrunk; and in his living face they caught a brief vision of the power and majesty of the kings of stone. For a moment it seemed to the eyes of Legolas that a white flame flickered on the brows of Aragorn like a shining crown. (*LotR*, Tolkien 1995:423)

Aragorn's claim to his heroic space engenders a tier of three responses; first, growth in stature, both literally and metaphorically. Second, a "vision of power and majesty" that links him historically with previous kings. Only Legolas sees the "white flame […] like a shining crown". This may be a simple foreshadowing of the crown that Aragorn will wear. In Middle-earth, the Elves are continuously associated with the spiritual level, and Legolas alone sees a reflection of this realm. The flame is comparable to the prophetic fire encircling Iulus' head at the close of *Aeneid II*, or the gospels' account of the dove descending on Jesus at his baptism. Aragorn is spiritually empowered to fulfil his role.

Aragorn is also defined antithetically by Denethor. A steward, not a king, Denethor refuses to relinquish his power. Like Aragorn, he embodies the matrix formed by power and choice, but is associated with a 'fey' mood, and destructive linguistic visions surround him:

> We will burn like heathen kings before ever a ship sailed hither from the West. The West has failed.
> (*LotR*, Tolkien 1995:807)

In correspondence with a spiritual heroism modelled on Ephesians, where Aragorn represents the kingly side of Christ as a hero, that this is the only place in the text where 'heathen' appears is of note. In conjunction with the association of 'the West' with Christendom in literature, this suggests that Denethor represents those who will not imitate

Christ in dispensing their power. This is supported by the scriptural resonance of *The Return of the King*, title of the final book.

What distinguishes between Aragorn and Frodo? W.H. Auden wrote: "One type [of quest hero] resembles the hero of Epic; his superior *arete* is manifest to all. [...] The other type, so common in fairy tales, is the hero whose *arete* is concealed" (Auden 2004:37). While Aragorn claims his *arete* in the text, Frodo laments the right bestowed upon him ("I wish it had never, never, been found", *LotR*, Tolkien 1995:891). His heroism is in his acceptance of his role, even though he is not a king and no great glory will follow. Unlike Bilbo, Frodo is more than a moral hero; the text is riddled with suggestions that providence has chosen Frodo to destroy the Ring: "Behind that there was something else at work, beyond any design of the Ring-maker [...] you [...] were meant to have it" (*LotR*, Tolkien 1995:55). When Frodo takes the task we are told:

> At last with an effort he spoke, and wondered to hear his own words, as if some other will was using his small voice.
> 'I will take the Ring,' he said.
> (*LotR*, Tolkien 1995:263-264)

Frodo has constantly to choose to serve; he is empowered to do that in part by providence, in part by his own inclination towards courtesy. Both facets mesh when he spares Gollum, a deed performed out of pity. Frodo is defined like Aeneas in terms of his *pietas* (his right-choosing), and like Gawain in terms of his courtesy; he is frequently referred to as a 'courteous halfling', and even astounds Galadriel ("here she has met her match in courtesy", *LotR*, Tolkien 1995:356). It is in Frodo that imitative spiritual heroism is most clearly expressed in *The Lord of the Rings*. While Aragorn has the re-forged Andúril, Frodo's key possession is the phial of Galadriel, whose purpose accents the spiritual level of his quest: "May it be a light to you in dark places, when all other lights go out"

(*LotR*, Tolkien 1995:367). This echoes Psalm 27: "The Lord is my light and my salvation".

Like Aragorn, Frodo is seen at moments 'as though in a vision', again suggesting the spiritual ethic that permeates the fabric of the text. When Frodo spares Gollum, we read:

> For a moment it appeared to Sam that his master had grown and Gollum had shrunk: a tall stern shadow, a mighty lord who hid his brightness in grey cloud, and at his feet a little whining dog.
> (*LotR*, Tolkien 1995:604)

Again one character shrinks while the other seems taller; as with Aragorn, the comparison affirms Frodo's heroic status. Frodo is a truly sophrosynic hero; but as the Ring grows in power it stifles his ability to choose: "Lead me! As long as you've got any hope left. [...] I'll just plod along after you" (*LotR*, Tolkien 1995:907). The arena shifts from one visible to the reader to an all-encompassing spiritual one:

> No image of moon or star are left to me. I am naked in the dark, Sam, and there is no veil now between me and the wheel of fire. I begin to see it even with my waking eyes, and all else fades.
> (*LotR*, Tolkien 1995:916)

The spiritual is intensely physical for Frodo, but the reader sees only what Sam sees: "Anxiously Sam had noted how his master's left hand would often be raised as if to ward off a blow, or to screen his eyes from a dreadful Eye that sought to look in them" (*LotR*, Tolkien 1995:914). Tolkien both highlights and undercuts the unfolding heroism; he distances the reader by giving psychological action viewed second-hand, but closes the gap in giving Sam's vision of the spiritual realm. When Gollum and Frodo meet again after Shelob's lair, Sam's vision sets the scene for Mt Doom:

> Then suddenly [...] Sam saw these two rivals with other vision. A crouching shape, scarcely more than the shadow of a living thing, a creature now wholly ruined and defeated, yet filled with hideous lust and rage; and before it stood stern, untouchable now by pity, a figure robed in white, but at its breast it held a wheel of fire. (*LotR*, Tolkien 1995:922)

The key phrase here is "untouchable now by pity": as Frodo's primary tool in his heroism of right-choosing, this manifold failure of pity distorts his heroic right to choice. The language of free will is inverted at Mt Doom to show its crucial failure: "I do not choose now to do what I came to do. I will not do this deed. The Ring is mine!" (*LotR*, Tolkien 1995:924). Here Frodo's legacy of right-choosing serves him; Gollum, whom he had spared, bites off the Ring and falls into the chasm, destroying it and saving his master. In this way right-choosing makes Gollum an agent of eucatastrophe, and allows him to keep his apparently irreconcilable promises to both serve Frodo and seize the Ring. Even in failure, Frodo's choice brings good. Here, eucatastrophe provides Tolkien's *felix culpa*, theoretically relieving the tale of disenchantment in this climax to its spiritual dimensions.

The spiritual nature of Frodo's growth is underlined by his treatment of Saruman back in the Shire:

> I do not wish him to be slain in this evil mood. He was great once, of a kind that we should not dare to raise our hand against. He is fallen, and his cure is beyond us; but I would still spare him, in the hope that he may find it. (*LotR*, Tolkien 1995:996)

Like Milton's Christ in *Paradise Regained*, Frodo returns 'unobserved' to his home; but he does not achieve the same quiet heroism. Christ sacrificially gave his life; Frodo, as Tolkien writes "thought that he had given his life in sacrifice: he expected to die very soon, and one can observe the disquiet growing in him" (Carpenter 2000:327). Frodo cannot be a complete hero; he cannot become a king like Aragorn; like Bilbo he receives no recognition in his own country. Frodo's heroism makes no sense without Christ as a comparative, but Christ has not yet appeared in Middle-earth; to be robbed of an adequate heroic comparison cultivates Frodo's disillusion regarding his own deeds; the Shire is saved, "but not for [him]" (*LotR*, Tolkien 1995:1006). The sense of enchantment reinstated at Mt Doom slides towards disenchantment in Frodo's 'disquiet', just as the literature of Tolkien's time slides from Homer to Owen when story and reality do not mesh.

FALSE HEROISM

It is clear that Tolkien considered heroism carefully; in that consideration he did not ignore concerns, shared with other writers, regarding the effects of literature's heroic depictions. In *The Lord of the Rings* characters are caught between the appeal of *kleos* and the author's decision to write based on *sophrosyne*; the Ring tempts characters with this dichotomy: Boromir sees himself leading an army to overthrow Sauron. Éowyn's love for Aragorn is "only a shadow and a thought: a hope of glory and great deeds, and lands far from the fields of Rohan" (*LotR*, Tolkien 1995:849). This false love of heroism brings neither escape nor consolation – she "goes seeking death" (*LotR*, Tolkien 1995:823). Sam's internal dialogue in 'The Choices of Master Samwise' exemplifies the conflict between Tolkien's heroism of right-choosing and literature's established heroic tradition. On finding Frodo apparently dead Sam considers canonically heroic responses: committing suicide and seeking vengeance. We can assume that these are founded on a reading of literature as Sam makes constant reference to song and story. Deciding to take the Ring he sees a group of Orcs coming towards his master's body. Again, he is afflicted by what he feels is expected of a hero:

> How many can I kill before they get me? They'll see the flame of my sword as soon as I draw it, and they'll get me sooner or later. I wonder if any song will ever mention it: How Samwise fell in the High Pass and made a wall of bodies round his master. No, no song. Of course not, for the Ring'll be found, and there'll be no more songs. I can't help it [...] I can't be their Ring-bearer. Not without Mr. Frodo.
> (*LotR*, Tolkien 1995:718)

Ultimately Sam's choice is not based on literature's dictates but on love for his master. In an interesting turn the height of his heroism, typified by love and service, inspires him to make his own song at the Tower of Cirith Ungol; later he becomes one of the 'chroniclers' of the story itself. Tolkien implies that heroes enchanted by Christian love and 'good' heroic literature become the next generation of artists; Sam's 'visions' (see above) accent his integration with the spiritual realm of Middle-earth. Unlike Frodo, Sam returns to the Shire at peace and enriched. In these senses, he exemplifies Tolkien's ideas of recovery and mimesis. But, despite the apparent culmination of his theory in Sam, it is in Frodo's position that Tolkien finds himself.

THE DISENCHANTED?

The hero-anxiety engendered by the Great War created a literary environment in which traditional concepts of heroism could no longer match the experience of the primary world. But there was still a need for heroes, one that Tolkien answered by exploring the nature of heroism to disperse the prevailing sentiment of disenchantment. To do this, his writings drew from a large linguistic, literary, religious and historical tradition. Tolkien's heroes try to reinstate heroic vision whilst remaining aware of the dangers of their media.

Charles Douie asked if "the prose and poetry of this age [were] to be charged with disillusion and despair?" (Garth 2003:303). While Tolkien's theories sought to show that it did not need to be, his greatest hero, Frodo, is beset by disenchantment within and without the text; in Tolkien's historical perspective and in the imminent departure of the Elves, representing the disenchantment of Middle-earth. Frodo's circumstance – caught between the heroic and the unheroic – is a motif of Tolkien's present, a summation of the Great War's disillusioning effect. In this regard, whilst epitomising so much of Tolkien's anti-disenchantment theory, Frodo is inescapably symptomatic of the conflict which he was framed to address.

ANNA SLACK graduated from the University of Cambridge in July of 2005 with a BA (Hons.) in English Literature, having overturned the rigid canon of the department by submitting a highly successful dissertation on Tolkien's works for her final exams. Anna spent two years editing the tri-annual journal of the Cambridge Tolkien Society, *Anor*, and a year as the society secretary. She helped pioneer and partook in the acclaimed performance of the BBC Radio Adaptation of *The Lord of the Rings* in aid of the National Trust, and was invited to lecture on Tolkien's heroes at the recent conference in Birmingham, Tolkien 2005, where she also performed in various Tolkien-related sketches. She is currently working on a paper for the forthcoming Walking Tree publication *The Silmarillion: 30 Years on*. She is particularly fascinated by eucatastrophe and the application of Tolkien's critical thought to his work, and hopes to return to academia in the future to study the works of Tolkien and Lewis together in this and other contexts as the basis for a PhD.

Bibliography

Adams, Robert M., 1981, 'The Hobbit Habit', in Neil D. Isaacs and Rose A. Zimbardo (eds.), 1981, *Tolkien: New Critical Perspectives*, Lexington, Kentucky: The University Press of Kentucky, 168-175.

Auden, 2004, 'The Quest Hero', in Rose A. Zimbardo and Neil D. Isaacs (eds.), 2004, *Understanding The Lord of the Rings. The Best of Tolkien Criticism*, Boston and New York: Houghton Mifflin, pp. 31-51.

Bentley, Eric, 1947, *A Century of Hero-Worship*, London: R. Hale.

Bettelheim, Bruno, 1976, *The Uses of Enchantment*, London: Thames and Hudson.

Burrow, Colin, 'Heroes: Saviours, Traitors and Supermen' in *The Guardian Review*, 9th October, 2004.

Campbell, Joseph, 1949, *The Hero with A Thousand Faces*, New York: Princeton University Press.

Carlyle, Thomas, 1898, *On Heroes, Hero-Worship and the Heroic in History*, London: Chapman and Hall

Carpenter, Humphrey, 1977, *J.R.R. Tolkien: A Biography*, London: George Allen and Unwin.

---, 1978, *The Inklings: C.S. Lewis, J.R.R. Tolkien, Charles Williams and their Friends*, London: George Allen and Unwin.

--- (edited with the assistance of Christopher Tolkien), 2000, *The Letters of J.R.R. Tolkien*, (first published 1981), Boston and New York: Houghton Mifflin.

Garth, John, 2003, *Tolkien and the Great War: The Threshold of Middle-Earth*, London: HarperCollins.

Gawain-Poet, date unknown, *Gawain and the Green Knight*, (revised edition 1977), edited by Norman Davies, J.R.R.Tolkien and E.V. Gordon, (first published 1925), Oxford, Oxford University Press.

Graves, Robert, 1995, *The Complete Poems of Robert Graves*, edited by Beryl Graves and Dunstan Ward, (first published London: Heinemann 1916), Manchester: Carcanet.

Homer, date unknown, *The Iliad*, (translated from the Greek by E.V.Rieu, 1950), Harmondsworth: Penguin.

Hourihan, Margery, 1997, *Deconstructing the Hero*, London and New York: Routledge.

Hughes-Hallett, Lucy, 2004, *Heroes: Saviours, Traitors and Supermen*, London: HarperCollins.

Isaacs, Neil D. and Rose A. Zimbardo (eds.), 1970, *Tolkien and the Critics*, Notre Dame: University of Notre Dame Press.

--- (eds.), 1981, *Tolkien: New Critical Perspectives*, Lexington, Kentucky: The University Press of Kentucky.

Jordan, Richard Douglas, 1989, *The Quiet Hero: Figures of Temperance in Spenser, Donne, Milton and Joyce*, Washington: Catholic University of America Press

King James Bible, 1611, London: Robert Barker.

Layamon, date unknown, *Brut*, (translated from the Old English by W.R.J Barron and S.C. Weinberg., 1955), Harlow: Longman.

Lewis, Clive Staples, 2004, 'The Dethronement of Power', (originally published in *Time and Tide*, 25 October 1955); republished in Rose A. Zimbardo and Neil D. Isaacs (eds.), 2004, *Understanding The Lord of the Rings. The Best of Tolkien Criticism*, Boston and New York: Houghton Mifflin, pp. 11-15.

Owen, Wilfred, 1933, *The Poems of Wilfred Owen,* edited by Edmund Blunden (first published 1931), London: Chatto and Windus.

Propp, Vladimir, 1968, *Morphology of Folktale*, (first published 1958), Austin: University of Texas Press.

Sale, Roger, 1973, *Modern Heroism: Essays on D.H. Lawrence, William Empson and J.R.R. Tolkien*, Berkeley: University of California Press.

Sassoon, Siegfried, 1961, *Selected Poems of Siegfried Sassoon*, London: Faber and Faber.

Shippey, Tom, 2001, *J.R.R. Tolkien: Author of the Century* London: HarperCollins.

---, 1982, *The Road to Middle-Earth*, London: HarperCollins.

Stallworthy, Jon, 1984, *The Oxford Book of War Poetry*, Oxford: Oxford University Press.

Tolkien, J.R.R., 1995, *The Lord of the Rings*, (first published as one volume 1968), London: HarperCollins.

---, 1999a, *The Hobbit*, (first published 1937), London: HarperCollins.

---, 1999b, *The Silmarillion* (edited by Christopher Tolkien; first published 1977), London: HarperCollins.

---, 2001, *Tree and Leaf*, (first published 1964), London: HarperCollins.

Virgil, *The Aeneid*, (translated from the Latin by David West 1990), Harmondsworth: Penguin.

Wilson, Edmund, 1956, 'Oo, Those Awful Orcs!', in *The Nation* 182, pp.312-14.

Zimbardo, Rose A. and Neil D. Isaacs (eds.), 2004, *Understanding The Lord of the Rings. The Best of Tolkien Criticism*, Boston and New York: Houghton Mifflin.

Hidden Paths of Time:
March 13th and the Riddles of Shelob's Lair

JUDITH KLINGER

Abstract

Experiences of Other Time form an important theme in Tolkien's works. In *The Lord of the Rings*, this theme is of particular significance for the process of transformation that Frodo undergoes in the course of the Ring-Quest, and which eventually takes him across the sea to Valinor. Read in this context, the crisis at Cirith Ungol amounts to a passage through death and a transcendence of finite, linear time, achieved jointly by Frodo and Sam. As a close reading can demonstrate, the presence of Shelob on the boundary of Mordor causes a suspension of linear temporality and allows for a different experience of time: one that opens the view towards the timeless present of Valinor. This essay examines the temporal and narrative complexities of the Cirith Ungol-episode alongside their implications for Frodo's 'road to Faërie'.

"Yet even the most subtle spiders may leave a weak thread."
Gandalf, in *The Lord of the Rings* (Tolkien 1991:278, II.2)[1]

Recent Tolkien scholarship has identified several central themes in J.R.R. Tolkien's literary works that engage in a vivid dialogue with the defining experiences and concerns of the 20th century.[2] Among these is

---

[1] All quotes from *The Lord of the Rings* refer to page numbers of the Harper Collins 1991 one-volume edition (Tolkien 1991). Tolkien's own numbering of books and chapters is retained to facilitate finding the quotes in other editions. Since I am quoting from various works by Tolkien, abbreviations of the more frequently cited titles will be added. – Over various stages of expansion and revision, this article has profited immensely from extended discussions with Lisa Kuppler, whose thoughtful contributions I wish to acknowledge here with much gratitude. Furthermore, I would like to thank Verlyn Flieger for kindly offering comments and advice on an earlier draft.

[2] Cf. the studies by Curry 1997, Flieger 1997, Garth 2003, and Shippey 2002, among others.

the modern fascination with time whose nature was irrevocably redefined by Albert Einstein's Theory of Relativity. In *A Question of Time: J.R.R. Tolkien's Road to Faërie* (1997), Verlyn Flieger demonstrates how Tolkien engaged with contemporary theories of time, but – as the title of Flieger's study already indicates – it becomes equally apparent that Tolkien employed these concepts in a unique way, adapting and modifying them to suit his own understanding of 'time travel'. For that is, in Tolkien's view, one of the remarkable powers of 'fairy-stories': "they open a door on Other Time" (Tolkien 1997:129). As Flieger observes: "this is also a very good assessment of Tolkien's own fiction. His own desire to pass through the door into Other Time, and thus to stand outside his own time and perhaps Time itself, led him to the creation of his own world of Faërie, Middle-earth" (Flieger 1997:2).

In various texts, Tolkien's travelling heroes, too, move through Other Time and Other Space. This is certainly true of Frodo Baggins, who, in *The Lord of the Rings*, finds himself among the few mortals who gain admission into the guarded realm of Lothlórien where time passes differently.[3] Yet Frodo's journey does not amount to an adventurous 'there and back again': At the very end of *The Lord of the Rings*, he leaves Middle-earth altogether and sails along the Straight Road to Valinor. This ultimate passage beyond mortal time provides neither happy ending nor closure, for Frodo's painful departure from the beloved world of the Shire raises vexing questions. One may wonder not only about Frodo's reasons to leave his own world behind, but about the forces and factors enabling him to do so. How could a mere (mortal) hobbit gain access to the Undying Lands at all?[4] In the following, I will examine one

---

[3] Compare Flieger's analysis of the Lothlórien episode in particular (Flieger 1997:89-115). Tolkien's two unfinished novels, *The Lost Road* (1936) and *The Notion Club Papers* (1945), feature 'time travel' by means of visionary dreams and related experiences.

[4] Within Tolkien's mythology, Eärendil's mortal father Tuor appears to be the only precedent (*Silmarillion*, Tolkien 1979:295). In earlier drafts, the Silmarillion tales

particularly pertinent episode and its connections to the theme of the 'road to Faërie' as well as time's complexities in *The Lord of the Rings*.

INTRODUCTION: FRODO'S PASSAGE OUT OF TIME

What happened to Frodo after the end of the Ring-Quest, and why did he leave Middle-earth? The most immediate answer may be found in Frodo's own words. In the grip of haunting memories on October 6th, he says: "There is no real going back. Though I may come to the Shire, it will not seem the same; for I shall not be the same. I am wounded with knife, sting, and tooth, and a long burden. Where shall I find rest?" (Tolkien 1991:1026, VI.7). Changed and injured, Frodo cannot return to the life that he left behind. Yet his injuries also affect him in very different ways, and the 'fit' he suffers on March 13th, the anniversary of his encounter with Shelob at Cirith Ungol, is fraught with ambiguity:

> On the thirteenth of that month Farmer Cotton found Frodo lying on his bed; he was clutching a white gem that hung on a chain about his neck and he seemed half in a dream. 'It is gone for ever,' he said, 'and now all is dark and empty.' But the fit passed, and when Sam got back on the twenty-fifth, Frodo had recovered, and he said nothing about himself. (Tolkien 1991:1062, VI.9)

At first glance, the trauma[5] caused by Shelob appears to be compounded by the Ring's destruction, and Frodo's words may seem to imply that he

---

are framed by the narration of another mortal traveller and mariner (first named Eriol, later Ælfwine) who returned from the Immortal Realm (on the evolution and significance of this narrator cf. Flieger 2005:87ff.). However, Frodo – like Tuor before him and Sam who follows him – does not return from Valinor.

[5] Applying the term 'trauma' to Frodo is somewhat problematic, since it can evoke a specifically psychoanalytical concept. In Freud's terms, an experience becomes traumatic when the psyche is incapable of dealing with the shock of the original event. This results in an uncontrolled, neurotic recurrence of certain stimuli, both

is overcome by a lingering desire for the Ring.[6] However, no unequivocal reference to the Ring can be found in this short passage. In the absence of such a reference, or any identifiable allusion to the Ring (e.g. the catchword 'precious'), the pronoun 'it' at the beginning of Frodo's statement remains tantalizingly ambiguous. The lack of a grammatical reference leaves it to the reader to identify what 'it' may be.

While the words 'gone forever' seem to point towards the loss of the Ring, two elements argue against such a reading. The date of Frodo's illness does not coincide with his final separation from the Ring on March 25th, 1419. In fact, after its destruction in the fires of the Sammath Naur, Frodo mourns neither the Ring's unmaking nor the loss of his finger;[7] and in 1420, the 25th of March is marked by his recovery, not a recurrence of his illness. Frodo's description of his present perceptions – "now all is dark and empty" – is equally incongruous with an interpretation that posits a secret desire for the Ring. Throughout *The Lord of the Rings*, Tolkien employs a coherent set of terms and imagery that defines the threat of Sauron's power: most prominently, an over-

---

emotional and physical, that are connected to the experience. While the general description of 'recurring symptoms' holds true for Frodo, the attendant concept of neurotic fixation cannot be applied to Frodo's responses. Throughout this article, I therefore use 'trauma' in the older, strictly medical sense, as an experience of rupture whose effects range beyond the immediate injury and can cause a larger disturbance (see the entry 'trauma' in Laplanche and Pontalis 1983).

[6] This is indeed how Tolkien himself interpreted Frodo's words in a letter draft written in September 1963: "he was tempted to regret its destruction, and still to desire it" (*Letters*, Tolkien 1995:328). However, as I will demonstrate in this article, textual evidence from *The Lord of the Rings* itself calls this assertion into question. It is furthermore questionable whether Frodo experienced any desire for the One Ring: As I have argued elsewhere (*The Fallacies of Power: Frodo's Resistance to the Ring*; forthcoming), Tolkien's highly nuanced descriptions trace a process by which Frodo learns to distinguish an externally imposed 'desire' from his own motives and intentions. After his wounding at Weathertop, Frodo is therefore able to maintain a clear defence against the Ring's manipulations, and the term 'desire' is never again applied to his relationship with this extraordinary burden.

[7] In fact, his words to Sam express nothing but relief: "For the Quest is achieved, and now all is over. I am glad you are here with me. Here at the end of all things, Sam" (Tolkien 1991:983, VI.3).

whelming darkness that can even manifest as a "window into nothing" (Tolkien 1991:383, II.7).[8] Yet if that is the case, how can the very ruin of this power be experienced as darkness and emptiness in turn? Frodo's words suggest the absence of a light that he longs for – yet the Ring never appears as a source of light, except as a horrifying "wheel of fire" (Tolkien 1991:954, VI.2; 979, VI.3).

On the other hand, Frodo's perception that "all is dark and empty" corresponds very well with the haunting experience of passing through Shelob's Lair. Not only is the Lair's darkness so voracious that it threatens the very memory of light, Shelob – as a descendant of Ungoliant – is herself a creature of the outer Void,[9] which certainly resonates with Frodo's sense of emptiness. A close reading of these lines thus uncloses a deliberate ambiguity that Tolkien may have employed to prompt the very questions this article seeks to explore: How exactly do Frodo's experiences of October 6th and March 13th affect him, and why are they so deeply traumatizing? How are they connected to his final departure from Middle-earth?

The original events of October 6th provide a fairly clear answer. At Weathertop, Frodo is stabbed with the poisonous Morgul-blade that could have transformed his entire being, subjecting him completely to the power of the Nazgûl and Sauron, in the altered state of a 'wraith', as Gandalf explains in Rivendell: "They tried to pierce your heart with a Morgul-knife which remains in the wound. If they had succeeded, you would have become like they are, only weaker and under their command.

---

[8] Compare the striking description of Frodo's vision of the Eye in Galadriel's Mirror: "But suddenly the Mirror went altogether dark, as dark as if a hole had opened in the world of sight, and Frodo looked into emptiness. [...] The Eye was rimmed with fire, but was itself glazed, yellow as a cat's, watchful and intent, and the black slit of its pupil opened on a pit, a window into nothing" (Tolkien 1991:383, II.7).

[9] Cf. the description of the Lair in Tolkien (1991:745, IV.9), and the characterization of Ungoliant in *The Silmarillion* (Tolkien 1979:85-86), both discussed later in this article.

You would have become a wraith under the dominion of the Dark Lord" (Tolkien 1991:238, II.1). That such an injury can result in a painful 'memory of darkness' is easily conceivable.

However, the consequences of this wounding also exceed the purely traumatic. As he watches Frodo in Rivendell, Gandalf perceives "a faint change just a hint as it were of transparency, about him, and especially about the left hand that lay outside upon the coverlet" (Tolkien 1991:239, II.1). The wizard's subsequent musings reveal that the transformation triggered by the Morgul-blade cannot be undone, yet the ultimate result may subvert all evil intentions: "He is not half through yet, and to what he will come in the end not even Elrond can foretell. Not to evil, I think. He may become like a glass filled with a clear light for eyes to see that can" (ibid). Sam's perception of the light that shines through Frodo, later in the Quest, substantiates Gandalf's belief that the injury's lingering effects won't lead to evil. It is therefore important to note that Frodo's wounds are ruptures in a twofold sense: Their immediately debilitating effects are complemented by a far-reaching process of transformation, implied as early as Rivendell. While this process may be equally unsettling for Frodo, it is also set apart from destructive intents and effects.

The questions I have raised above are far more difficult to answer with regards to Shelob and the events of March 13th. If this experience, too, results in a transformation that exceeds the aggressor's original intent, this aspect is never made explicit in *The Lord of the Rings*. In this article, I will explore the nature of the original trauma and its connection to the painful transformation that eventually makes it impossible for Frodo to remain in the Shire. My reading centres on the idea that Shelob, a creature whose origins lie beyond Arda, causes a *temporal distortion* within the time continuum of Middle-earth.

I will start out by demonstrating that Frodo and Sam experienced complex lapses and contortions of time in the course of their passing through the Lair and into Mordor (1). A discussion of the implications, of Shelob's nature specifically (2), and the significance of the Mordor boundary (3), will be followed by a broader analysis of the concepts of time that come into play (4). In the last sections, I will propose a reading of the Cirith Ungol episode as a trial that both Frodo and Sam undergo (5), on which my conclusions about the meaning of March 13th (6) are based. With these considerations, I hope to provide a framework that allows for a more comprehensive understanding of Frodo's departure from Middle-earth and the transformative process underlying his injuries.

1 SLIPPING TIME, CONFUSED MAPS: 'THIS WAS TOMORROW'

That Frodo and Sam lose track of time as they approach Shelob's Lair is immediately visible from Tolkien's description. At a closer look, an attendant confusion emerges that seems to affect the author himself. Not only is it difficult to calculate the time that the hobbits spend in the area of Cirith Ungol, it seems as if two whole days, if not more, are unaccountably lost in the events. This observation suggests two possible explanations: The discrepancies could either be due to Frodo's and Sam's subjective confusion, or Tolkien himself erred in his calculation of their progress. After discussing the textual evidence, I will argue that neither explanation is satisfactory. I contend that the events of Cirith Ungol involve an objective distortion, caused by Shelob who devours life, light, and time.

In the following analysis, I will draw on Tolkien's drafts and notes for the relevant chapters, edited by Christopher Tolkien and published in *The History of Middle-earth*. These materials yield valuable insights into the process by which the Cirith Ungol episode gained its final shape. More importantly, they illuminate the semantic and conceptual framework underpinning this episode and thus provide important clues for the unriddling of the published text.

In *The Two Towers*, the first indication of temporal disorientation can be found when Gollum returns to the Stairs where Frodo and Sam have fallen asleep. His answer to Sam's question amounts to a temporal paradox: "'What's the time? Is it today or tomorrow?' 'It's tomorrow,' said Gollum, 'or this was tomorrow when hobbits went to sleep [...]'" (Tolkien 1991:742, IV.8). If it 'was tomorrow' when Sam and Frodo fell asleep, what happened to 'today'? Between past (*was*) and future (*tomorrow*) the present (*today*) is suddenly missing. That Gollum is not merely speaking in riddles (perhaps with the intention of disguising his treacherous activities) but refers to a factual anomaly can be shown by a look at the chronology. In her *The Atlas of Middle-earth*, Karen Wynn Fonstad provides a detailed calendar showing the distances that Frodo and Sam covered.[10] Her calculation features two severe temporal lapses (Fonstad 1991:160): On March 11th, the hobbits supposedly "slept all day and night" on the Stairs of Cirith Ungol. Secondly, 24-30 hours appear to have elapsed between entering the Lair (on March 12th) and Frodo's capture by the orcs in the evening of March 13th.

Both results are necessarily baffling. Even though Frodo and Sam are exhausted after their strenuous climb, nothing in Tolkien's description suggests that they spend twenty-four hours in unbroken slumber on the Stairs. External circumstances hardly allow for such an extended rest: The hobbits take cover from the cold wind "in a dark crevice between two great piers of rock" (Tolkien 1991:738, IV.8), certainly a most

---

[10] This is Fonstad's complete account of the pertinent days (Fonstad 1991:160): "M[arch] 11: Slept all day and night. – Top of Winding Stair. M. 12: Day and night of M. 12, and day of M. 13 – Shelob's Lair. M. 13: Capture by Orcs at dusk. M. 14: Tower of Cirith Ungol. M. 15: Escape from Tower. Walk 5 a.m. to dusk, several halts." Compare the corresponding dates given in Appendix B for March 1419 (Tolkien 1991:1130): "10: The Dawnless Day [...]. Frodo passes the Cross-roads, and sees the Morgul-host set forth. 11: Gollum visits Shelob, but seeing Frodo asleep nearly repents [...]. 12: Gollum leads Frodo into Shelob's lair [...]. 13: Frodo captured by the Orcs of Cirith Ungol [...]. 14: Samwise finds Frodo in the Tower [...]. 15: [...] Frodo and Samwise escape and begin their journey north along the Morgai."

uncomfortable place. The positions that Gollum finds them in when he returns also suggest that Sam has only recently fallen asleep.[11] Yet the chronology set forth in Appendix B: *The Tale of Years* allows only for the conclusion that the hobbits indeed slept a whole day. The discrepancy between description and calendar may give rise to the suspicion that Tolkien aligned events to the established timeline in retrospect, thereby 'stretching' certain uneventful periods, perhaps beyond credibility.[12] However, examination of the second lapse on March 12/13 can demonstrate that the confusion runs deeper than that.

How much time do Frodo and Sam actually spend inside the Lair? They enter early on March 12th and do not emerge again until the evening of the following day ("the last hours of a sombre day were passing"; Tolkien 1991:750, IV.9), hence Fonstad calculates that 24 to 30 hours must have passed. In accordance with this calculation, the main tunnel through which the hobbits pass is about 12-14 miles long on her map (Fonstad 1991:143). Yet the map of the Lair featured in *Journeys of Frodo* by Barbara Strachey shows a tunnel of only a good mile's length (Strachey 1984, maps 37-38): a rendering that corresponds directly with Tolkien's own sketch (*HoME* 8, Tolkien 1997a:201). The contradiction between these maps is directly related to the inexplicable time lapse. In trying to match the spatial dimensions to the calculated time, Fonstad dilates distances enormously. Strachey makes no attempt to accommodate the temporal dilation geographically and follows Tolkien's own

---

[11] Cf. Tolkien (1991:741, IV.8): "Sam sat propped against the stone, his head dropping sideways and his breathing heavy. In his lap lay Frodo's head, drowned deep in sleep; upon his white forehead lay one of Sam's brown hands, and the other lay softly upon his master's breast."

[12] The published *Tale of Years* with its detailed account of events during and after the Quest was written in 1954/55, immediately before *The Return of the King* was published. An earlier version that Tolkien had long intended for publication does not feature a detailed account of Frodo and Sam's doings from March 10 to 15 (cf. *HoME* 12, Tolkien 1997b:226, 242).

description instead: "Minas Morghul to top of Kirith Ungol (and pass below the tower) 15 miles on flat" (*HoME* 9, Tolkien 2002c:10).

While Tolkien's own map of the Lair is detailed and clear, another peculiarity must be noted: Instead of placing east on the right and west on the left side of the page, as with all other maps, Tolkien reversed the map's orientation. More confusing, however, is the fact that north and south retain their usual positions. In other words, the map, being thus both mirrored *and* inverted, cannot be set right by simply flipping it over. Clearly, there are related confusions (or distortions) of time *and* space involved. What remains to be determined is the source of this confusion.

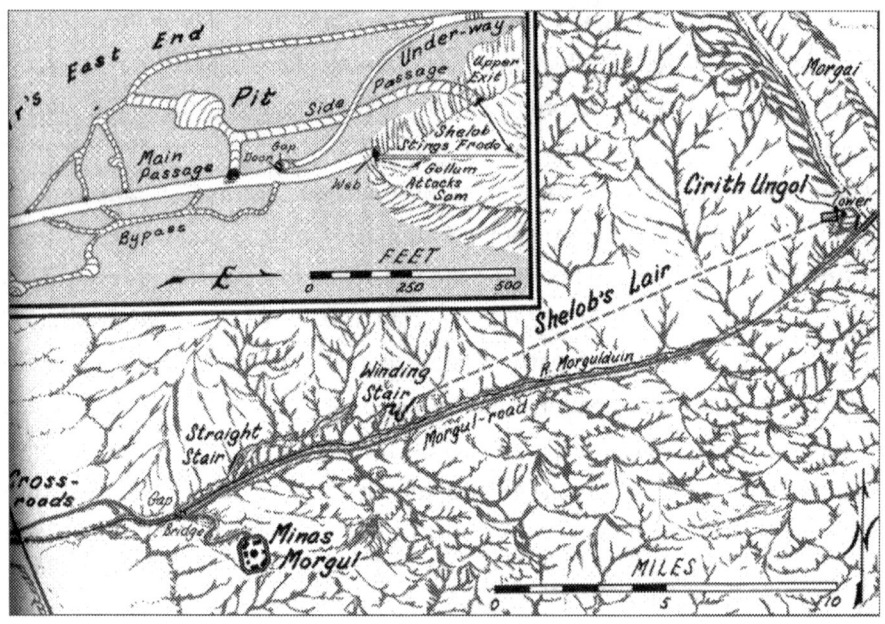

Illustration 1: Fonstad's map of Cirith Ungol (Fonstad 1991:143)

Hidden Paths of Time: March 13th and the Riddles of Shelob's Lair   153

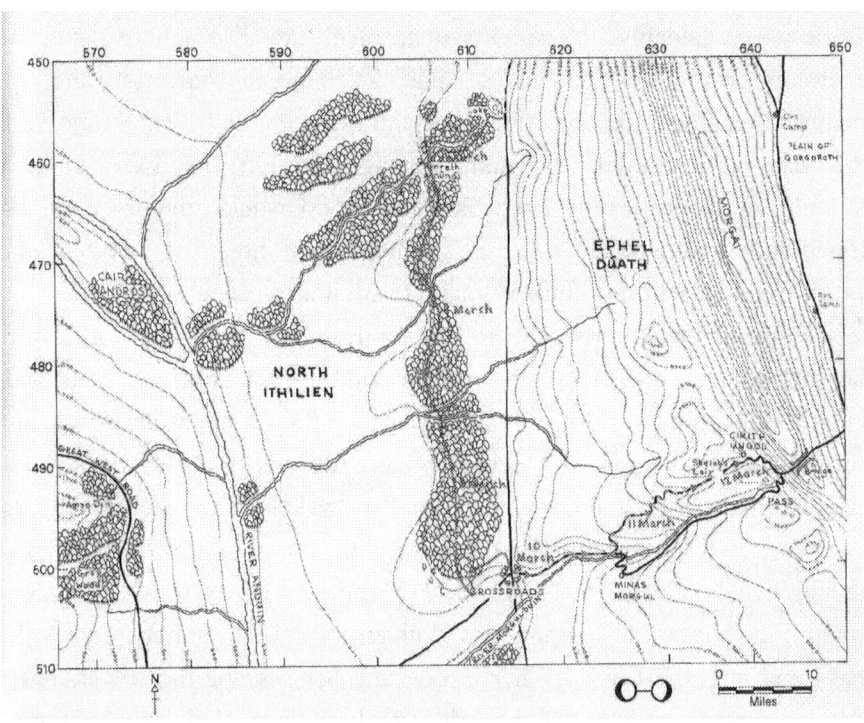

Illustration 2: Strachey's map of Cirith Ungol (Strachey 1984: map 37)

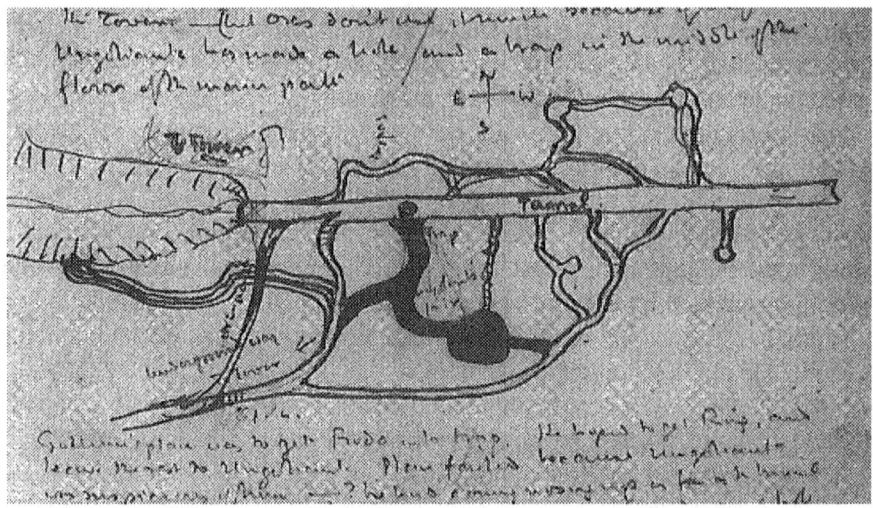

Illustration 3: Tolkien's map of the Lair (*HoME* 8, Tolkien 1997a:201)

Quite understandably, the hobbits themselves are disoriented inside the Lair and soon lose every sense of time. Yet both the narration and Appendix B establish the objective dates and times for their entry and exit. According to Tolkien, the main passage through the Lair is fairly straight and about a mile long: Sam and Frodo would have kept an astoundingly slow average pace of 53 meters per hour (or about a yard every minute), had they indeed spent 24-30 hours inside.

During the events that follow their escape from the Lair, both hobbits lose consciousness for certain periods which complicates all calculations. Sam passes out after discovering Frodo's apparent death and falls unconscious again by the Undergate. However, the text does establish external dates at intervals: When Sam wakes up by the Undergate, "it was drawing to noon upon the fourteenth day of March in the Shire-reckoning" (Tolkien 1991:932, VI.1). From this point onwards, a continuous description of his progress is given: out of the tunnels, across the pass, and into the tower. When Frodo and Sam escape the tower, hurry down the road and leap off the bridge to hide themselves, the text provides another temporal marker: "Day was coming again in the world outside, and far beyond the glooms of Mordor the Sun was climbing over the eastern rim of Middle-earth" (Tolkien 1991:952, VI.2). It is now the morning of March 15th. In Fonstad's calculation, based on Appendix B, 17 hours have elapsed between the moment when Sam regained consciousness and the hobbits' escape from the tower. Once again, Tolkien's descriptions suggest a much shorter span. While Sam may move cautiously at times, nothing explains how it could have taken him up to ten hours to find Frodo in the tower,[13] and it is equally unclear how their fairly quick escape could account for the remaining seven hours.

---

[13] At their reunion, Sam guesses that "more than a day" has passed since Frodo's capture: If that is correct, it would then be late in the evening of the 14th, even though Sam left the tunnels at noon. Not long after this remark from Sam – at most, two hours may have passed – they leave the tower, but a short while afterwards the reader is informed that day is already breaking.

This brief survey shows that the temporal discrepancies cannot be ascribed to Sam's and Frodo's subjective confusion. If there is an error involved, Tolkien himself would have to be at fault. In his comments on the drafts for these chapters, Christopher Tolkien calls the entire Cirith Ungol section an "extraordinarily dismembered text" (*HoME* 8, Tolkien 1997a:196): His father had difficulties with establishing not only the chronology of events but the geography surrounding Shelob's Lair as well. However, the published drafts and notes also show that Tolkien was quite aware of these problems and tried to synchronize the Frodo-Sam thread to the events in Gondor. As he laboured to establish a coherent chronology, the dates he applied to Cirith Ungol shifted from one draft to the next (cf. *HoME* 9, Tolkien 2002c:7ff.), and a related 'error' occurs in the draft of *The Grey Havens*. Here, the date of Frodo's illness is March 12th (*HoME* 9, Tolkien 2002c:110). Christopher Tolkien notes that this date was 'corrected' in the next typescript, yet only Appendix B unequivocally establishes March 13th as the date of Shelob's attack on Frodo. It seems that, despite all his efforts to establish a reliable chronology, Tolkien was still uncertain – but why?

On May 14th, 1944 (while he was working on the Cirith Ungol chapters), he wrote to Christopher that he was having "trouble with the moon": "By which I mean that I found my moons in the crucial days between Frodo's flight and the present situation (arrival at Minas Morgul) were doing impossible things, rising in one part of the country and simultaneously setting in another" (Carpenter 2002:264).[14] Tolkien's inability to control the moon seems directly related to something Gollum says in a 'Journey to the Cross-roads' draft: "'There comes the White Face,' said Gollum. 'We doesn't like it. And Yellow Face is coming soon, sss. Two faces in the sky together, at once, not a

---

[14] This section is not included in the edition of Tolkien's letters (cf. *Letters*, Tolkien 1995:80-81).

good sign. And we've got some way to go.'" (*HoME* 8, Tolkien 1997a:180). This passage did not make it into the published version of the chapter, but it indicates that there is more involved than an author's failure to devise a consistent timeline matched by coherent maps. The simultaneous presence of the sun and the moon evokes an uncertainty about time: How can the moon rise when the sun is about to do the same?[15] An impossible conjunction foreshadows the temporal distortions of Cirith Ungol.

2 SPELLS AND COUNTER-SPELLS: 'A SHADOW CAST BY NO LIGHT'

If the passage through Shelob's Lair does indeed involve an experience of discrepant times, a parallel can be found in the fellowship's passage through Lothlórien. As the travellers realize upon leaving the Golden Wood, time runs differently in Galadriel's realm. In fact, it is the unexpected appearance of the new moon that prompts Sam to wonder about the discrepancy (cf. Tolkien 1991:408-09, II.9). While I will discuss the specific understanding of time underlying *The Lord of the Rings* in section 4, the Lórien episode establishes that the presence of higher or immortal powers results in a complex 'layering' of temporal experience in Middle-earth. Can a similar power be attributed to Shelob, and if the spell that she weaves truly affects time, how can that effect be defined precisely?

In an early note, Tolkien suggested that the spiders at the pass would put a "spell of sleep" on Frodo (*HoME* 7, Tolkien 1993:209), but the spell emerging from the final rendering of the story is of a far more

---

[15] Close to new moon, the moon may indeed rise quite late, within one or two hours of dawn. However, the moon was full two nights before the muster at Edoras, on March 8th (compare Tolkien 1991:568, III.8: "they bore his summons also, bidding all men, young and old, to come in haste to Edoras. There the Lord of the Mark would hold an assembly of all that could bear arms, on the second day after the full moon"); Gollum's apprehensions are voiced on the 8th, and the draft (while adhering to different dates) refers to a moon that has barely passed fullness as well.

complex nature. If time seems to drag for Frodo and Sam in and around the Lair, the external chronology reveals a dilation of time, inverting the contraction experienced in Lórien.

As weavers of the 'thread of mortal life', spiders are connected to a complex mythological tradition that links time with fate.[16] And Shelob is no ordinary spider: In the published text, she is identified as a descendant of Ungoliant, yet in Tolkien's earlier drafts Shelob *was* Ungoliant (cf. *HoME* 8, Tolkien 1997a:196ff.), a creature which, according to *The Silmarillion*, entered the world "from the darkness that lies about Arda", the Timeless Void beyond the space and time of Creation. Ungoliant hungered only to "feed her emptiness", "sucked up all light that she could find, and spun it forth in dark nets of strangling gloom" (*Silmarillion*, Tolkien 1979:85, 86). As Melkor's ally against the Valar, she devoured the light of the Two Trees, the original sources of a division between day and night. The consequences resemble the descriptions of Shelob's Lair, and the pursuing Valar are blinded:

> the Darkness that followed was more than loss of light. In that hour was made a Darkness that seemed not lack but a thing with being of its own: for it was indeed made by malice out of Light, and it had power to pierce the eye, and to enter heart and mind, and strangle the very will.
> (*Silmarillion*, Tolkien 1979:89)

---

[16] The three 'Fates' (Moirae) of antiquity already represent the three dimensions of time; one of them, Klotho, is identified as a weaver. Equally important are the three Norns of Norse mythology (Urd, Verdandi and Skuld, the 'wyrd sisters'), whose names represent past/fate, present/being and future/necessity. In his elaborate account of the various traditions, Grimm cites several sources depicting the Norns as weavers (cf. Grimm 1981:335ff.). – An immediate connection between time and weaving, or the spinning of threads, can be found among the earliest texts of Tolkien's own mythology: In *The Book of Lost Tales*, three (male) weavers present Manwë with invisible ropes that bind the newly created sun and moon to their course and which represent Time as days, months and years (cf. *HoME* 1, Tolkien 2002a:217-19).

Ungoliant cloaked herself in "Unlight, in which things seemed to be no more, and which eyes could not pierce, for it was void" (*Silmarillion*, Tolkien 1979:86). In *The Lord of the Rings*, two complementary aspects of the Unlight-from-Void emerge, the first of which occurs in the description of Minas Morgul:

> Not the imprisoned moonlight welling through the marble walls of Minas Ithil long ago, Tower of the Moon, fair and radiant in the hollow of the hills. Paler indeed than the moon ailing in some slow eclipse was the light of it now, wavering and blowing like a noisome exhalation of decay, a corpse-light, a light that illuminated nothing.
> (Tolkien 1991:730, IV.8)

As a complement to this 'corpse-light' we find a 'shadow cast by no light' when Frodo and Sam discover Shelob's cobwebs that block the tunnel mouth: "Holding aloft the Phial Frodo looked and before him he saw a greyness which the radiance of the star-glass did not pierce and did not illuminate, as if it were a shadow that being cast by no light, no light could dissipate" (Tolkien 1991:749, IV.9).[17]

The idea that Shelob's 'unlight' may also define her relationship with time is, in fact, suggested by Sam's discovery on the Stairs. An unbroken continuum of light connects Beren's quest for the Silmaril to the voyage of Eärendil and finally to the star-glass that Galadriel gave to Frodo.[18] In Sam's own words, he and Frodo find themselves within the

---

[17] The draft version underlines this effect: "Before them was a greyness which the light did not penetrate. Dull and heavy it *absorbed* the light" (*HoME* 8, Tolkien 1997a:194).

[18] In *Splintered Light: Logos and Language in Tolkien's World* (2002), Verlyn Flieger sets forth an interpretation that centres on the continuous 'splintering' of Arda's original Light into smaller and smaller fragments in the course of the world's history. While the idea of a 'long defeat' is certainly crucial to Tolkien's Middle-earth texts, and the subsequent ages of Arda are marked by an increasing distance between Aman and the world of mortals, I would argue that the 'splinter-

same unending 'tale', but what he describes is a history written in light, a history of time itself. A first measure of time entered creation with the Two Trees of Valinor, and their mingled light is reflected by Fëanor's Silmarils, one of which eventually became the star of Eärendil. If we envision the chain of salvaged light implied here – the Two Trees > Fëanor's Silmarils > the Star of Eärendil > Galadriel's Phial – it amounts to an extremely condensed account of the world's history that reaches from the initial radiance of Valinor to the shadow Sauron's renewed threat casts across Middle-earth at the end of the Third Age. Yet Frodo's Phial reflects from afar not only the light of Valinor but the beginning of reckoned time,[19] and it is the Phial, too, which can hold Shelob's consuming darkness at bay.

---

ing' metaphor simplifies the process Tolkien portrayed. In *The Lord of the Rings*, 'breaking' light into fragments is specifically associated with Saruman's fall from wisdom, as Gandalf relates it to Elrond's council (cf. Tolkien 1991:276, II.2). In Galadriel's Phial, on the other hand, "is caught the light of Eärendil's star, set amid the waters of my fountain" (Tolkien 1991:397, II.8). This description implies a process of reflection by which the light's essence is captured, although conveyed into a smaller vessel. Secondly, the reference to the fountain alludes to a concept of light as a *liquid* element which the Two Trees spill as 'rain' and 'dew' and that Varda "hoarded in great vats like shining lakes" (*Silmarillion*, Tolkien 1979:44). The same concept emerges in even more striking terms from Tolkien's earliest drafts in *The Book of Lost Tales*. E.g. *HoME* 1 (Tolkien 2002a:69): "Those were the days of Gloaming (Lomendánar), for light there was, silver and golden, but it was not gathered together but flowed and quivered in uneven streams about the airs, or at times fell gently to the earth in glittering rain and ran like water on the ground." The liquid nature of the light evidently implies organic segregation rather than fracturing. That the Phial contains the self-same light is emphasized when Frodo first wields it against Shelob: "it began to burn [...] as though Eärendil had himself come down from the high sunset paths with the last Silmaril upon his brow" (Tolkien 1991:747, IV.9).

[19] *Silmarillion* (Tolkien 1979:44): "Thus began the Days of the Bliss of Valinor, and thus began also the Count of Time." Compare Tolkien's detailed account in the *Annals of Aman* (*HoME* 10, Tolkien 2002d:50): "Time indeed began with the beginning of Eä, and in that beginning the Valar came into the world. But the measurement which the Valar made of the ages of their labours is not known to any of the Children of Ilúvatar, until the first flowering of Telperion in Valinor. Thereafter the Valar counted time by the ages of Valinor, whereof each age contained *one hundred* of the Years of the Valar, but each such year was longer than are *nine* years under the sun."

At this point, it is necessary to examine the different forces that come into play during the hobbits' confrontation with Shelob, and to explore the time-related implications of this episode. The descriptions that refer to temporal distortions in the Cirith Ungol chapters are too numerous to quote them all, but a few examples can serve to highlight the various aspects.

Within proximity of Minas Morgul, the effect is already noticeable: "time seemed to slow its pace, so that between the raising of a foot and the setting of it down minutes of loathing passed" (Tolkien 1991:730-31, IV.8).[20] Temporal orientation slips when the hobbits finally rest on the Stairs (Sam says, "I don't know what time of day or night it is, but we've kept going for hours and hours"; Tolkien 1991:738, IV.8) and becomes the dominant experience inside the Lair:

> They walked as it were in a black vapour wrought of veritable darkness itself that, as it was breathed, brought blindness not only to the eyes but to the mind, so that even the memory of colours and of forms and of any light faded out of thought. Night always had been, and always would be, and night was all. [...] One hour, two hours, three hours: how many had they passed in this lightless hole? Hours – days, weeks rather. (Tolkien 1991:745, IV.9)

Later in the events, when Sam regains consciousness by the Undergate, this profound temporal dislocation is reiterated in striking terms:

> He wondered what the time was. Somewhere between one day and the next, he supposed; but even of the days he had quite lost count. He was in a land of dark-

---

[20] This effect cannot be ascribed to the proximity of the Nazgûl, since there is no evidence elsewhere in the text suggesting that they alter the mortal experience of time.

ness where *the days of the world seemed forgotten*, and where all who entered were forgotten too. (Tolkien 1991:931, VI.1; emphasis added)

While Sam's subjective confusion is expectable, the narrator comment emphasizes that the Lair is disconnected from the world beyond it. Within, the ordinary temporal continuum loses effect. Shelob's 'webs of shadow' and the darkness that she 'vomits' paralyze the senses, her power consumes memory and all ability to move forward – in other words, the dimensions of past and future. Inside her Lair, she creates a space of perpetual lightlessness and oblivion, accompanied by a suffocating silence.[21] Ultimately, her victims are frozen in a timeless moment, suspended between past and future, life and death: That is, in essence, the effect of her poison as well.

However, as Frodo and Sam's escape from the Lair demonstrates, certain counter-forces can temporarily disable the spell of Shelob: first and foremost memory, and the memory of light specifically. The first turning point is reached when Sam recalls the light of Lórien and Galadriel's gift to Frodo (Tolkien 1991:746-47, IV.9). As I have argued above, the Phial can thwart Shelob's power not only because it reflects the original light of Valinor, but also as a manifestation of history, or fulfilled time.

That memory itself is important becomes apparent at various points. Frodo manages to shake off the paralyzing sense of loss near

---

[21] The difficulty of speaking in the smothering silence of the Lair that dulls and swallows every sound is invoked again and again. Even on the Stairs of Cirith Ungol, as Frodo laughs out loud, it seems to Sam that "all the stones were listening and the tall rocks leaning over them" (Tolkien 1991:740, IV.8). Inside the Lair, "sound falls dead" (Tolkien 1991:744-45, IV.9), and only with effort do Frodo and Sam manage to speak ("in a hoarse breath without voice"; Tolkien 1991:746, IV.9). When Frodo tries to call for Gollum, "his voice croaked, and the name fell dead almost as it left his lips. There was no answer, not an echo, not even a tremor of the air" (ibid). Only when Sam reminds Frodo of the Phial "the life and urgency came back into his voice", whereas Frodo speaks "as one answering out of sleep" (Tolkien 1991:747, IV.9).

Minas Morgul at the sound of Sam's voice, which in turn brings a memory of Shire mornings ("Then at a great distance, as if it came out of memories of the Shire, some sunlit early morning, when the day called and doors were opening, he heard Sam's voice speaking"; Tolkien 1991:734, IV.8). Sam, on the other hand, remembers Lórien and Galadriel at crucial moments, not only inside the Lair, but also as he confronts Shelob: "a thought came to him, as if some remote voice had spoken". Upon touching the Phial,

> he heard voices far off but clear: the crying of the Elves as they walked under the stars in the beloved shadows of the Shire, and the music of the Elves as it came through his sleep in the Hall of Fire in the house of Elrond. *Gilthoniel A Elbereth!* And then his tongue was loosed and his voice cried in a language which he did not know. (Tolkien 1991:756, IV.10)

The memories invoked here connect the Shire, the hobbits' first meeting with Elves, Rivendell and Lórien. Recollections of voice and song materialize as other voices seem to speak through Frodo and Sam, in languages they do not understand.

Another song, the one that comes to Sam as he sits dejected in the tower of Cirith Ungol and feels "the darkness cover him like a tide" (Tolkien 1991:943, VI.1), acts as a counter-force to threatening paralysis as well and brings about Frodo and Sam's reunion. It combines memories of the Shire with sudden inspiration, strengthening Sam's voice, while the song's content restores awareness of a world beyond the tower and the border region, a world of light untouchable by darkness. Tolkien's earlier version of Sam's song makes the loss of time and memory more explicit:

> But here I sit alone and think
> of days when grass was green,
> and earth was brown, and I was young:

> *they might have never been.*
> *For they are past, for ever lost,*
> and here the shadows lie
> deep upon my heavy heart
> and hope and daylight die.
> (*HoME* 9, Tolkien 2002c:27; emphasis added)

Another line in this version intensifies the contrast between remembering the past or the world outside and the place where Sam now finds himself, once again assailed by the heavy darkness of oblivion: "And now *beyond the world* I sit | and know not where you lie" (*HoME* 9, Tolkien 2002c:27; emphasis added). This description not only locates the tower outside the known continuum of space and time, it is also reminiscent of the Void beyond Arda in *The Silmarillion*, Ungoliant's original abode.[22]

It seems, then, that the tower of Cirith Ungol is situated within the area affected by temporal distortions, and the description of the Silent Watchers in particular suggests this connection. The three heads that are turned into different directions correspond with a traditional representation of the three ages of men and the three dimensions of time that became especially popular in Renaissance art.[23]

---

[22] Compare to this Aragorn's description of being inside Lórien: "There time flowed swiftly by us, as for the Elves. The old moon passed, and a new moon waxed and waned in *the world outside*" (Tolkien 1991:409, II.9; emphasis added).

[23] On the pictorial tradition cf. Erwin Panofsky's essay on Titian's 'Allegory of Prudence' (Panofsky 1955). Panofsky traces the motif of the triple-headed beast back to ancient Egypt and points out that Macrobius first interpreted this figure as a representation of time in the 5th century A.D. – In *The Lord of the Rings*, the ringing of a bell in the tower when the Watchers' barrier is broken seems to allude to the passing of time, too. Furthermore, the three Watchers are reminiscent of the three Norns of Norse mythology, themselves representatives of the three dimensions of time (compare footnote 16).

Illustration 4: The three heads of time at the church of St. Gervais & Protais, Paris (16th cent.) in Gaignebet and Lajoux (1985:67, plate 5)

Illustration 5: *Allegory of Prudence* by Titian, London: National Gallery (16th cent.) in Panofsky (1955: plate 28)

The Watchers' appearance clearly follows this pattern: "Each had three joined bodies, and three heads facing outward, and inward, and across the gateway" (Tolkien 1991:936, VI.1). The barrier they create is compared explicitly to Shelob's cobwebs when Sam tries to get through: "But just as he was about to pass under its great arch he felt a shock: as if he had run into some web like Shelob's, only invisible" (ibid). As they try to leave the tower, Frodo and Sam both experience a weariness that closely resembles that of the Lair's tunnels: "Before they even reached the archway they were brought to a stand. To move an inch further was a pain and weariness to will and limb" (Tolkien 1991:949, VI.1). When they break through, the similarity to breaching Shelob's web is once again invoked: "The will of the Watchers was broken with a suddenness like the snapping of a cord" (Tolkien 1991:950, VI.1). Minas Morgul has similar Watchers, as Gorbag mentions (cf. Tolkien 1991:766, IV.10), and the description of the architecture itself suggests a connection with the Lair: The windows of Minas Morgul are "like countless black holes looking inward into nothing" (Tolkien 1991:730, IV.8).

All taken together, the implications are that the temporal distortion affects the entire area from Minas Morgul to the tower of Cirith

Ungol, which is directly connected to the Lair by way of the winding tunnel.[24] Shelob herself not only occupies the space between these two strongholds but can be identified as the very centre and source of this disturbance. Her devouring darkness paralyzes mind and motion and could be likened to a funnel that absorbs time, light, memory and voice. The decayed light of Minas Morgul and the light-absorbing greyness of Shelob's web both represent the temporal distortion, or the slowing of

---

[24] This raises the question whether the orcs who pass through the tunnels on occasion remain unaffected by the distortion, and if so, why. To be sure, none of the orc characters explicitly mentions anything of the kind, but the scant textual evidence yields a few hints nonetheless. When Shagrat's and Gorbag's companies meet, Gorbag's orc band has passed through the Lair after being "ordered out" on the day following the Wraith-king's departure from Minas Morgul (Tolkien 1991:766, IV.10). According to Appendix B, the host departed on March 10 (Tolkien 1991:1130), so that Gorbag's group would have set out on March 11; the conversation between Gorbag and Shagrat then takes place on March 13. How the Minas Morgul orcs spent the two previous days (March 11-12) is not discussed any further, but one wonders why they did not overtake Sam and Frodo on the Stairs, where the hobbits allegedly slept for 24 hours. Yet the matter is still more complicated: Gorbag mentions that, although the Silent Watchers of Minas Morgul were "uneasy more than two days ago" (Tolkien 1991:766, IV.10), marching orders were delayed for another day to accommodate the Wraith-king's departure to war. If "more than two days ago" can refer to a span somewhere between two and three days (excluding the present day), and time is reckoned backwards from the moment of the conversation in the evening hours of March 13, the Watchers' uneasiness could not have set in any earlier than March 10. But if the Wraith-king departed a day after this uneasiness began, he would have left on the 11th (not the 10th), with Gorbag following on the 12th. While this would explain why the orc band did not catch up with Frodo, Sam, and Gollum, it also unsettles the connections between dates and events established in Appendix B. The shift one encounters when trying to date Gorbag's departure from Minas Morgul then seems to imply that at least one day cannot be accounted for. A similar uncertainty emerges from Shagrat's comment that Gollum was seen near the pass "a day before all this racket [...] [e]arly last night" (Tolkien 1991:766, IV.10). Since the 'racket' occurred on the 13th, Gollum's secret visit to Shelob would have taken place on the 12th, whereas Appendix B dates it to March 11. If Shagrat's simpler observation is correct (and Shagrat, unlike Gorbag, did not enter the tunnels before Frodo was discovered), the only possible conclusion is that the hobbits entered the Lair on the 13th rather than the 12th, as Appendix B states (and the narration implies). There seems to be no way to resolve these discrepancies, but they once more point back to a crucial loss of time between March 11 and 12 and confirm that the temporal anomalies in this episode reach beyond Frodo's and Sam's purely subjective experience.

time, whereas the Phial counters it and sets time in motion again, allowing progress.

Another description in the drafts illuminates this effect. When Frodo raises the Phial "the darkness receded from it and it shone in a globe of space enclosed with utter blackness" (*HoME* 8, Tolkien 1997a:203).[25] Instead of penetrating Shelob's Night, the Phial's light creates a separate temporal sphere (rather like a drop of oil in water) within which the hobbits can break the paralysis and move forward.[26] Memories of light, of Elven voices and song supply the counter-forces that enable Frodo and Sam's flight from the tunnels and the tower. As a carrier of living history,[27] the temporal, connecting light of the star-glass acts as a counter-spell against the draining void of Shelob.

3 CROSSING THE BOUNDARY: 'THE VERY GATE OF PARTING'

The Cirith Ungol chapters are marked not only by a struggle of light and memory against darkness and oblivion, but also by a complicated choreography of movements. Several times Frodo and Sam (and, later on, Sam alone) are brought to apparent dead ends where continued progress seems impossible.[28] Twice (by the blocked tunnel and at the tunnel mouth) this

---

[25] In the published version: "The darkness receded from it until it seemed to shine in the centre of a globe of airy crystal, and the hand that held it sparkled with white fire" (Tolkien 1991:747, IV.9).

[26] This image also echoes the first vision of the created world as the Ainur perceive it in *The Silmarillion* (Tolkien 1979:18): "they saw a new World made visible before them, and it was globed amid the Void, and it was sustained therein, but was not of it."

[27] In this context, it is interesting to note that the Silmarils (hence Eärendil and the Phial) reflect the *mingled* light of the Two Trees in Valinor before their destruction. This mingling happens twice a day, corresponding to dawn and dusk but also to the conjunction that Gollum feared in the draft version: the simultaneous presence of the yellow and the white face, or sun and moon.

[28] The hobbits reach the first dead end in the blocked tunnel where they encounter Shelob (as the reader discovers later, the tunnel is barred by an outer gate but leads to the tower). They are stopped a second time by the web covering the tunnel mouth. When Sam follows the orcs who have taken Frodo, he is brought to a halt

paralysis is broken, and in both cases the light of the Phial enables sudden bursts of speed. Yet progress and motion are riddled by further complications: On the one hand, Frodo and Sam move at different paces once they leave the Lair; on the other, Sam finds himself caught in a repetitive back-and-forth movement between the blocked tunnel and the pass, but each new loop also takes him closer to the boundary of Mordor, situated at the apex of the pass.[29]

Inside the Lair, Sam's memory of light permits Frodo to wield the Phial against Shelob, and the hobbits' combined efforts bring about their unprecedented escape. But when Frodo and Sam are separated, within view of the border, disaster ensues. Beyond the chain of events precipitating this crisis, the boundary itself is fraught with significance. On the Stairs of Cirith Ungol, Frodo has a curious premonition: "All his mind was bent on getting through or over this impenetrable wall and guard. If once he could do that impossible thing, then somehow the errand would be accomplished" (Tolkien 1991:738, IV.8). It is hardly logical that Frodo accords such importance to the mere crossing of the border, since he must afterwards still walk across Mordor and reach Mount Doom, within sight of Barad-dûr. However, the same notion drives him to a wild run when he and Sam escape the tunnels: "A short race, a sprinter's course and he would be through!" And:

> 'The pass, Sam!' he cried, not heeding the shrillness of his voice, that released from the choking airs of the tunnel rang out now high and wild. 'The pass!

---

[29] first by the blocked tunnel (the outer gate, over which he climbs eventually) and then by the gate directly under the tower (the Undergate). He slows down on the pass, is subsequently stopped again by the Watchers and arrives at a final dead end inside the tower where he does not discover the trap-door in the roof until Frodo responds to his song.
Sam first chases after Gollum, then finds and tries to leave Frodo, turns back again to follow the orcs, until he finally emerges from the tunnels again to take the path that leads to the tower (compare illustration 6).

Run, run, and we'll be through – through before any one can stop us!' (Tolkien 1991:750, IV.9)

The draft version adds a very remarkable element: "A sudden madness (?) on Frodo [...]. Run! ..... Sam, he said. *The door, the path*. Now for it, before any can stay us." (*HoME* 8, Tolkien 1997a:208; emphasis added). Here, Frodo perceives a path and a door, not merely a passage into Mordor: an intuition that points far beyond a description of the actual geography and which I will examine more closely in the final section of this article. As mysterious as the implications are, it is Frodo's 'mad' perception of a 'door' that sends him forward in a rush, only to be cruelly stopped by Shelob and paralyzed in a state of living death. While neither 'door' nor 'path' is mentioned in the published text, the conceptual framework remains effective and shapes Frodo's response.[30]

Sam has an equally strong yet opposite reaction to the prospect of crossing this border. During his first attempt to climb the pass, he is halted by his unquenchable desire to remain with Frodo. Yet when he sets out to the tower a second time, aware that Frodo is still alive, he slows down once again and stops to sit near the top rather than hurrying on: "He felt that if once he went beyond the crown of the pass and took one step veritably down into the land of Mordor, that step would be irrevocable. He could never come back" (Tolkien 1991:932, VI.1). This response is not any more reasonable than Frodo's initial reaction and later proved to be unwarranted, since Sam returns from their journey through Mordor. However, his misgivings about crossing this ultimate boundary are reflected in his perception of Frodo who seems to be gripped by a "fey mood" as he runs towards the pass. The word 'fey' – glossed as

---

[30] There is, however, a description of the pass as a 'high gate' in the published text, when the hobbits walk through the Lair: "But after a time their senses became duller, [...] and they kept on, groping, walking, on and on, mainly by the force of the will with which they had entered, will to go through and desire *to come at last to the high gate beyond*" (Tolkien 1991:745, IV.9; emphasis added).

"death-bound" in *The Lays of Beleriand* (*HoME* 3, Tolkien 2002b:369) – specifies Sam's foreboding: Crossing the border leads to death rather than achievement of the Quest. Once again, the draft version translates an intuitive reaction into the mystifying perception of a door, as Sam struggles to drag himself away from Frodo's 'dead' body:

> He hadn't gone far when he looked back and through his tears saw the little dark patch where all his life had fallen in ruin. Again he turned and went on, and now he was come almost to the V [i.e. the Cleft]. So *the very gate of parting*.
> (*HoME* 8, Tolkien 1997a:211; emphasis added)

If the pass is a 'door' or a 'gate', its meaning is defined by a coincidence of opposites. It may signify a fulfilled future (Frodo's hope) or an absolute ending and death (Sam's fear). The hobbits' discrepant emotional responses are reflected by their sharply diverging paces that cause their actual separation. While Frodo breaks into a wild run within sight of the pass, Sam lags behind and from this moment onward seems to struggle constantly against a crucial moment's delay. The results of their contradictory impulses are paradoxical, however. Frodo, who wanted to run, ultimately remains stationary and is carried across the boundary, whereas Sam, who is nearly paralyzed facing it, crosses under his own power.

What then does it mean that the pass becomes a 'parting gate' between life and death, a dividing line between time continued (hope for the future) and time ending (fear of death)? Furthermore, how is this related to the temporal distortion described above? Without doubt, the hobbits' crossing into Mordor forms one of the most critical moments in the entire Quest. What would have happened after all, if Frodo and Sam had left the Lair together, unharmed by Shelob? The only available road passes directly underneath the guarded walls of the tower, and later events reveal that the orcs stationed there and at Minas Morgul had been alerted to watch for trespassers. As these details are successively disclosed, it becomes impossible to envision how Frodo and Sam might have passed safely together.

Trapped between the two orc-bands, surely at least one of them would have been captured, and even if the other had escaped,[31] he would likely have done so by making use of the Ring, thus immediately revealing himself to Sauron's searching eye.[32] Unknown to them, Frodo and Sam face an insurmountable obstacle as they approach the boundary, and subsequently disclosed facts prove the clairvoyance of their premonitions. But their conflicting responses to the boundary also articulate different versions of the future: Within the future Frodo anticipates, that truly 'impossible thing' – bypassing certain disaster – is accomplished, whereas Sam perceives the enormous likelihood of death that awaits them.

In the border region, the interplay of possibilities, chance encounters and covert paths that have governed the hobbits' progress so far is reduced to binary opposites. Overwhelming darkness stands against piercing light, oblivion against memory, suffocating silence against remembered voices and songs, death against life. The boundary of Mordor itself is fraught with the fundamental conflict of hope and fear, of continuation and termination. Either the hobbits will be killed and the Ring lost to Sauron's forces, or they will miraculously manage to escape and continue the Quest. Yet from this conflict of mutually exclusive opposites, a third and unforseeable alternative emerges, and it takes the shape of a paradox. On the very boundary of Mordor, the Ring-bearer is both

---

[31] In his earliest notes for the Cirith Ungol chapters, Tolkien considered the possibility that Sam might die sacrificing himself, so that Frodo could escape with the Ring (cf. *HoME* 7, Tolkien 1993:209). In a first more extensive draft, Sam makes such an offer, but Frodo refuses (*HoME* 7, Tolkien 1993:335).

[32] Prompted by a sense of warning, Sam takes off the Ring at the very moment of crossing the border: "He took off the Ring, moved it may be by some deep premonition of danger" (Tolkien 1991:933, VI.1).

dead and alive, accompanied by the Ring yet no longer in possession of it.

It may seem like an irony of fate or a wildly fortuitous coincidence that Shelob's sting and Frodo's apparent death generate such an unexpected sequence of events: one that allows Frodo and Sam to survive together and carry the Ring to Mount Doom. But the crossroads motif preluding the Cirith Ungol chapters also implies that the choices Sam and Frodo make between stark alternatives will now decide the Quest. The motif recurs inside the tunnels, where the hobbits find themselves deserted by Gollum and the narrator comment emphasizes the utter importance of choosing the right path:

> The tunnel forked, or so it seemed, and in the dark they could not tell which was the wider way, or which kept nearer to the straight. Which should they take, the left, or the right? They knew of nothing to guide them, yet a false choice would almost certainly be fatal.
> (Tolkien 1991:746, IV.9)[33]

Two factors within the pitched conflict effect the unpredictable reversal: Shelob's interference on the one hand, and Sam's choices on the other. Shelob can play the role of a 'wild card' because she occupies a unique position within the conflict that divides Middle-earth. An evil force in her own right, she is not a servant of Sauron, and the Ring means nothing to her.[34] As a creature whose origins lie beyond Arda, she disrupts the

---

[33] In one of the draft versions, Frodo and Sam make use of the Phial before encountering Shelob, and its light aids their decision about the path they should take: "But before them within the radius of its light were two openings. Now their doubt was resolved" (*HoME* 8, Tolkien 1997a:203).

[34] The narrator comment points out that Sauron erroneously thinks of Shelob as his pet ("his cat he calls her, but she owns him not"; Tolkien 1991:751, IV.9). – Within the darkness of the Lair, the Ring's powers cannot be of any use, and Gollum hopes to gain the Ring once Shelob has devoured the hobbits: "But her lust was not his

ordinary continuum of time to which she does not belong. The topography of Cirith Ungol, and the deployment of the hobbits' enemies behind and before them, predict a chain of events that can only lead to their capture and death. Yet Shelob unsettles the linear progression of time and the logical sequence of causes and effects. By creating a temporal distortion, she also provides the conditions that allow for an unexpected resolution. As the following course of events shows, this ultimately fortunate outcome depends entirely on Sam's choices.

Sam's entrapment at this moment of desperate crisis is twofold: Emotionally, he struggles with the apparent reality of Frodo's death and his own desire to remain at Frodo's side; within the spider-web of warped time, he struggles to discover the right path that will take him back to Frodo. Ultimately, Sam succeeds at overcoming the separation imposed by death, both literally and figuratively.

The very literal aspect of this trial is directly reflected in the repeated back-and-forth of his movements, exacerbated in turn by distortions of time and space. As the hobbits emerge from the tunnel, Sam experiences a sudden heaviness that makes it impossible for him to catch up with Frodo who seems to move impossibly fast:

> a fear was growing on him, a menace which he could not see; and such a weight did it become that it was a burden to him to run, and his feet seemed leaden [...]. His master was gaining on him; already he was some twenty strides ahead, flitting on like a shadow; soon he would be lost to sight in that grey world.
> (Tolkien 1991:752, IV.9)

---

lust. Little she knew of or cared for towers, or rings, or anything devised by mind or hand" (ibid).

A similar temporal dilation stands out when the group of orcs appears and Sam puts on the Ring: "The world changed, and a single moment of time was filled with an hour of thought" (Tolkien 1991:761, IV.10). Time and distance seem to expand as Sam follows the retreating orcs into the tunnels: "his legs would not carry him as he wished. He was too slow. The path seemed miles long" (Tolkien 1991:763, IV.10). While Sam's growing exhaustion slows his pace, the confusing meanders of the tunnels and the Ring's influence contribute to his disorientation: "he thought he was catching the two Orcs up: their voices were growing nearer again. [...] And with that he raced round the last corner, only to find that by some trick of the tunnel, or of the hearing which the Ring gave him, he had misjudged the distance" (Tolkien 1991:769, IV.10). If orientation slips inside the Lair, the Ring compounds these effects by lending Sam unnaturally

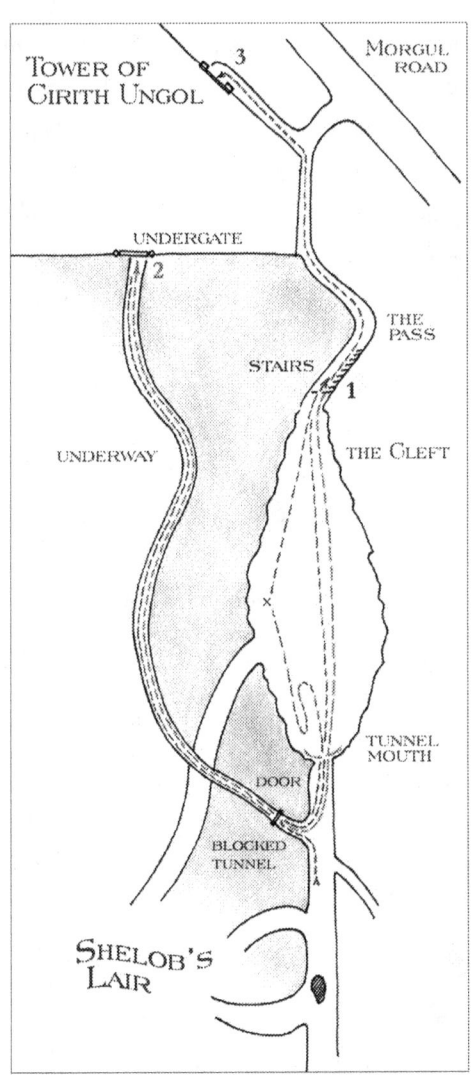

Illustration 6: Sam's paths at Cirith Ungol (illustration by Judith Klinger)

sharp hearing.[35] But it also burdens Sam and intensifies the dragging weariness caused by the timeless dark of the Lair, so that he arrives at the Undergate a fraction too late.[36]

References to the crucial temporal gap that separates Sam from Frodo are numerous: "He spun round, and rushed wildly up the path, calling and calling his master's name. He was too late" (Tolkien 1991:754, IV.9). Although he urges himself on inside the tunnels – "'Come on, Sam!' he said, 'or you'll be too late again!'" (Tolkien 1991:763, IV.10) – he comes to the Undergate only to have it slammed shut in his face. When Sam regains consciousness, he knows at once that "time was desperately precious" (Tolkien 1991:931, VI.1); inside the tower, he is nearly overwhelmed by the anxiety of failing to reach Frodo in time ("He felt that even minutes were precious, but one by one they escaped; and he could do nothing"; Tolkien 1991:942, VI.1). Clearly, the crux of Sam's choices is intrinsically connected to the temporal complexities of this episode.

According to the draft, Frodo and Sam perceive a 'door' or a 'gate' of irreconcilable possibilities that opens before them as they ap-

---

[35] Something very similar happens when Sam approaches the pass a second time, now headed for the tower of Cirith Ungol: "harsh and clear, and very close it seemed, he heard cries and the clash of metal [...]. He was glad of the Ring, for here was yet another company of orcs on the march. Or so at first he thought. Then suddenly he realized that it was not so, his hearing had deceived him: the orc-cries came from the tower, whose topmost horn was now right above him, on the left hand of the Cleft" (Tolkien 1991:933, VI.1).

[36] When he finally rouses himself from his swoon by the Undergate and turns back, Sam is confused about the dimensions of time *and* space: "Slowly he groped his way back in the dark along the tunnel [...] and as he went he tried to fit together the events since Frodo and he had left the Cross-roads. He wondered what the time was. Somewhere between one day and the next, he supposed; but even of the days he had quite lost count. He was in a land of darkness where the days of the world seemed forgotten, and where all who entered were forgotten too. [...] He waved his hand vaguely in the air before him; but he was in fact now facing southwards, as he came back to Shelob's tunnel, not west. Out westward in the world it was drawing to noon upon the fourteenth day of March in the Shire-reckoning" (Tolkien 1991:931, VI.1).

proach the boundary of Mordor. Consistent with the published version, this perception points to veritable crossroads of discrepant futures: Time itself 'forks' where Shelob spins her webs of 'unlight', and the linear continuum disintegrates where it borders on 'untime'.

4 OBSERVATIONS OF LAYERED TIME:
'RICH ARE THE HOURS, THOUGH SHORT THEY SEEM'

Within Tolkien's Middle-earth texts, time can never be fully separated from those who experience it, who sustain or direct it. Rather than forming an abstract continuum, detached from the awareness of sentient beings, time in Arda does not lend itself to a universal, unchanging experience. While the result is a complex layering I can merely outline here, a doubleness of time forms the foundation of these complexities, as the cosmogenic myth of *The Silmarillion* shows most clearly.

Creation unfolds from the original music of the Ainur: Once the labours of the Valar have given shape to Arda, history begins and with it a linear continuum of time emerges.[37] The Song of Creation already contains the entirety of time and space, however, and remains present as an atemporal matrix. The Valar may at certain points access the Song and discover in it events that have meanwhile come to pass;[38] immortals and

---

[37] Cf. *Silmarillion* (Tolkien 1979:22): "they had entered in at the beginning of Time". In the context of this article, my description of 'history' as conceptualized in *The Silmarillion* must be necessarily brief and simplified. Closer examination would show that Time, once initiated, runs at different 'paces' during the subsequent ages of the world, accompanied by a continuous redistribution of the original light of Valinor, first embodied in the two lamps raised in the north and south of the world and then by the Two Trees of Valinor (cf. *Silmarillion*, Tolkien 1979:39ff.). The progression of history is furthermore articulated in the hiding and withdrawing of Valinor from Middle-earth over various stages, so that different experiences of time are also directly connected to the relative proximity of Valinor and its reflected light.

[38] Compare, for instance, the account of the creation of Ents and Eagles: Only in hindsight do Manwë and Yavanna discover their presence in the Song (*Silmarillion*, Tolkien 1979:53). The Ainur generally possess foresight because they remember the words of Ilúvatar and the Song (cf. *Silmarillion*, Tolkien 1979:28).

even mortals may catch remote echoes of the original music, though they do not understand what they hear.[39] Time in Arda is thus shaped by the co-existence of the lingering Song – a timeless present filled with everything that was, is, or will be – and the passage of history, a linear unfolding of this rich potential.[40]

Despite its basic linearity within creation, time is by no means the same in every region of Middle-earth, nor is temporality experienced in the same way by all its inhabitants. As the fellowship's discussion of their sojourn in Lothlórien illustrates, a fundamental difference exists between the perceptions of mortals and immortals:

> Legolas stirred in his boat. 'Nay, time does not tarry ever,' he said; 'but change and growth is not in all things and places alike. For the Elves the world moves, and it moves both very swift and very slow. Swift, because they themselves change little, and all else fleets by: it is a grief to them. Slow, because they do not count the running years, not for themselves. The passing seasons are but ripples ever repeated in the long long stream. Yet beneath the Sun all things must wear to an end at last.'
> (Tolkien 1991:408-09, II.9)

As immortals in a world already dominated by mortals, Elves experience a doubleness that reflects the primary doubling of time on a less com-

---

[39] *Silmarillion* (Tolkien 1979:20): "And it is said by the Eldar that in water there lives yet the echo of the Music of the Ainur more than in any substance else that is in this Earth; and many of the Children of Ilúvatar hearken still unsated to the voices of the Sea, and yet know not for what they listen."

[40] At various points, *The Silmarillion* indicates that history will ultimately complete itself in a vast circle (Tolkien 1979:21: "the circles of time"). Together with all immortals, the Valar are irrevocably bound to the created world "while it lasts", whereas mortals alone may pass beyond the temporal sphere of Arda (*Silmarillion*, Tolkien 1979:319; cf. 21: "But this condition Ilúvatar made, [...] that their [i.e. the Valar's] power should thenceforward be contained and bounded in the World, to be within it for ever, until it is complete.").

prehensive level. Lórien itself appears to form an enclave where the immortal 'pace' of time holds sway, sustained by Galadriel's powers. As Verlyn Flieger writes in *A Question of Time*: "The Elves are living in a greatly slowed, if not altogether arrested, time, one in which past and present coexist" (Flieger 1997:109).

However, Cerin Amroth and the Mirror of Galadriel, embodiments of the 'magic' that defines Lórien's position in time, reveal that the Elven enclave allows for a different view of the future as well. At Cerin Amroth, Frodo not only "felt that he was in a timeless land that did not fade or change or fall into forgetfulness", he also anticipates that his own presence will linger within this timelessness even after he has left: "When he had gone and passed again into the outer world, still Frodo the wanderer from the Shire would walk there, upon the grass among elanor and niphredil in fair Lothlórien" (Tolkien 1991:370, II.6). Viewed from the place that Frodo occupies in the present, the future segregates into two distinct spheres. The platform he climbs together with Sam and Haldir allows for a perception of the world beyond Lórien and his own future path.[41] Yet while he and his companions will eventually return into the linear stream of events, the future of Cerin Amroth will also retain his presence as manifest memory.

This complex view of the future again points to a co-existence of linear history and a timeless present, here unfolded in spatial terms as well. Cerin Amroth enables a perception of the essential world as it was present at the moment of creation, and this unique possibility reveals itself to Frodo's mortal sight as an unknown light, pervading and transforming every shape and colour:

---

[41] Tolkien (1991:370, II.6): "Then he looked eastward and saw all the land of Lórien running down to the pale gleam of Anduin, the Great River. He lifted his eyes across the river and all the light went out, and he was back again in the world he knew." Galadriel's Mirror in turn shows "things that were, and things that are, things that yet may be" (Tolkien 1991:381, II.7).

> A light was upon it for which his language had no name. All that he saw was shapely, but the shapes seemed at once clear cut, as if they had been first conceived and drawn at the uncovering of his eyes, and ancient as if they had endured for ever. He saw no colour but those he knew, gold and white and blue and green, but they were fresh and poignant, as if he had at that moment first perceived them and made for them names new and wonderful.
> (Tolkien 1991:369, II.6)

Sam articulates a similar awareness in radically different terms when he remarks "I feel as if I was inside a song" (ibid) – indeed a very accurate description of the temporality of Cerin Amroth which is, perhaps, the one remaining site in Middle-earth where one can appreciate fully, beyond the 'changing', 'forgetting' and 'fading' that linearity effects, what it means to be 'inside' the Song of Creation. Both literally and figuratively, Cerin Amroth allows for an elevated viewpoint from which both past and future may be perceived, while its timeless present can contain both.

In her study on time-concepts in Tolkien's works, Verlyn Flieger points out that Tolkien was influenced by contemporary theories that describe time in terms of distinct fields of observation.[42] Within this framework, the range of observation, or the mind's focus of attention, determines the individual's position in time. A related concept is expounded in Tolkien's unfinished novel *The Notion Club Papers* (written during the long hiatus in his work on *The Lord of the Rings*, after the Cirith Ungol chapters had been completed). One of the chief characters develops a theory of 'time travel' within dreams, where the mind is free

---

[42] Most notably the theories of J.W. Dunne (*An Experiment with Time*, London 1927); compare Flieger (1997:38ff. and 104ff.).

to shift its attention to points of observation in the past or future.[43] Similar notions emerge from *The Lord of the Rings*, where dreams may accurately capture remote or future events, and alternate temporal fields of observation are available to the waking mind.[44]

That time cannot be separated from the individual's perception is implied in Legolas' description as well: "His explanation introduces experience as a valid measure of time. The issue is not *whether* time counts, but *how* it counts" (Flieger 1997:99).[45] The twofold experience of time that Legolas describes appears to be typical for immortals in the mortal world, yet the fellowship's passage through Lórien shows that it may also be accessible to mortals under specific conditions. The passage through Shelob's Lair amounts to a comparable experience of discrepant times, yet Frodo's and Sam's diverging responses furthermore constitute different 'fields' or layers within the temporal disturbance.

As Verlyn Flieger shows in her meticulous discussion of the Lórien chapters in their various stages of drafting, Tolkien experimented with

---

[43] Cf. *The Notion Club Papers*: Part One. *HoME* 9 (Tolkien 2002c:175-76): "[I]n dream a mind can, and sometimes does, move in Time: I mean, can observe a time other than that occupied by the sleeping body during the dream [...]. But I mean *moving* not by memory, or by calculation, or by invention, as the waking mind can be said to *move*; but as a perceiver of the external, of something new that is not yet in the mind. For if you can see, in other times than the time of dreaming, what you never saw in waking life, so that it is not in your memory – seeing the future, for instance, would be a clear case, and it cannot be doubted that that occurs – then obviously there is a possibility of real first-hand seeing of what is 'not there', not where your body is [...]. And this *movement*, or transference of observation: it is clearly not limited to Other Time; it can occur in Other Space, or in both." Further on *The Notion Club Papers* cf. Flieger (1997:117ff.).

[44] Analysing Tolkien's "Chart illustrating 'Two Times'" that depicts the constellation of discrepant times in Lórien, Flieger concludes: "Both Men and Elves, then, become parts of the series [of observer positions] and parts as well of the wider field of attention that encompasses the whole field of time" (Flieger 1997:105). Aragorn explains it as a sharing of the Elves' temporal perspective: "But so it is, Sam: in that land you lost your count. There time flowed swiftly by us, as for the Elves. The old moon passed, and a new moon waxed and waned in the world outside, while we tarried there" (Tolkien 1991:409, II.9).

[45] For a more detailed analysis of the fellowship's discussion see Flieger (1997:89ff.).

different approaches and chronologies, only to arrive at an inconclusive solution (cf. Flieger 1997:100ff.). On the one hand, the *Tale of Years* firmly anchors the fellowship's passage through Lórien in a continuous chronology with exact dates; on the other, the companions' exchange on the river highlights their experience of 'Other Time' yet falls short of presenting a coherent concept. As Flieger notes, Tolkien "consciously avoided pinning the significance on paper and chose to make implicit rather than explicit what his theme portended" (Flieger 1997:107). This strategy leaves it to the reader to unriddle the implications and connect them to the themes of (im)mortality, memory and change.

The same, I believe, applies to the Cirith Ungol chapters, another episode that went through complicated stages of composition and revision. The most notable difference between Lórien and Cirith Ungol is, of course, that the temporal discrepancies are nowhere explicitly discussed in the latter episode. After their escape from the tower, Frodo and Sam are permanently 'out of their reckoning'. Neither of them can know exactly how much time passed during their respective periods of unconsciousness, and without the light of sun and moon that Sauron's artificial gloom obscures, the passage of time becomes vague. That the temporal lapses of Cirith Ungol become tangible through the hobbits' responses rather than being explicitly debated suggests that the significance of this episode exceeds the temporal disturbance which serves only as its launching point.

To grasp the underlying themes and meanings, it is necessary to establish the differences between Lórien and Cirith Ungol. Compared to the time-span that has passed in the mortal world, the hours lived in Lórien are "short" but "rich", as Frodo says. If a whole month of linear time is experienced as mere days, the quantifiable discrepancy may be described as a *condensing* of time, yet time also takes on another quality. Frodo feels that he has "stepped through a high window that looked on a vanished world" (Tolkien 1991:369, II.6). Sam describes it as "wonderfully quiet" (Tolkien 1991:380, II.7), and at the very heart of this quiet lies Cerin Amroth with its unnamed light. The experience conveyed for the most part through Frodo's and Sam's responses is not one of nostalgia for a past that has faded elsewhere,[46] but one of wonder and a piercing directness that defies all known concepts and terms and amounts to a vibrant awareness of life itself:

> Frodo [...] laid his hand upon the tree beside the ladder: never before had he been so suddenly and so keenly aware of the feel and texture of a tree's skin and of the life within it. He felt a delight in wood and the touch of it, neither as forester nor as carpenter; it was the delight of the living tree itself.
> (Tolkien 1991:370, II.6)[47]

For Aragorn, who relives his most treasured memories to the point where "the grim years were removed from his face" (Tolkien 1991:371, II.6), Cerin Amroth may be described as a window onto the past and a site where the past is rendered present.[48] That Frodo, within the circle of white trees, hears "far off great seas upon beaches that had long ago been washed away" (Tolkien 1991:370, II.6), combines awareness of a vanished age with an allusion to the future that already pervades Frodo's dreams and will eventually take him across the sea. The different quality

---

[46] While I agree with Flieger's perception of Tolkien's profound ambivalence towards the necessity of change, the descriptions of Cerin Amroth in particular transcend "nostalgia for what has passed or is passing", nor does this particular episode illustrate the "dangers of trying to arrest time" (Flieger 1997:111 and 114, cf. 108ff.).

[47] Later on, as he and Frodo discuss the nature of Elven 'magic', Sam observes a shaping process that joins the Elves to their world, echoing Frodo's experience in more general terms ("Whether they've made the land, or the land's made them, it's hard to say, if you take my meaning"; Tolkien 1991:380, II.7).

[48] Yet here, too, the description moves beyond nostalgia and amounts to an *embodiment* of past experience: "For the grim years were removed from the face of Aragorn, and he seemed clothed in white, a young lord tall and fair" (Tolkien 1991:371, II.6).

of time experienced here is twofold: The full present allows for an immediate experience of life in essence and at once opens up the view towards past and future that converge in the present. This wider view of time constitutes an enlarged field of observation peculiar to Lórien.

In certain respects, the temporal disturbance in and around Shelob's Lair can be described as the diametrical opposite. Linear time is dilated or 'stretched' enormously, yet entire days can be drained without leaving a trace in actual experience. If Lórien time is 'rich' and full, then time in the Lair is depleted.[49] Instead of expanding to encompass a wider view, memory, thought and sensation are constricted and quenched in suffocating darkness. An intrusion of the outer Void on the temporal world ultimately results in boundless, insensate night, or 'untime'. That Frodo and Sam battle this onslaught with recourse to Galadriel's gift of light, to memory of Elvish voices and songs, illustrates to what an extent the two episodes operate as mirrored counterparts within the larger narrative structure.[50] The hobbits' 'speaking in tongues' can then be understood as an actualization of the past, similar to the presence of the past in the timelessness of Cerin Amroth. Frodo's and Sam's intuitive invocations of Eärendil and Elbereth collapse enormous expanses of

---

[49] Rather tellingly, mortal superstition can construe a likeness between the very different powers at work in Lórien and Shelob's Lair. In *Cirion and Eorl*, Eorl says of Galadriel that she "weaves webs that no mortal can pass" (*Unfinished Tales*, Tolkien 1998:398).

[50] This juxtaposition is subtly underlined by contrasting imagery. While Frodo's experience of 'Other Time' in Lórien occurs within the circle of *white trees* at Cerin Amroth, a circle of *black trees* at the Cross-roads marks his entry into the sphere of Shelob. Compare Tolkien (1991:729, IV.7): "At length they reached the trees, and found that they stood in a great roofless ring, open in the middle to the sombre sky; and the spaces between their immense boles were like the great dark arches of some ruined hall. In the very centre four ways met [...]. Standing there for a moment filled with dread Frodo became aware that a light was shining; he saw it glowing on Sam's face beside him. Turning towards it, he saw, beyond an arch of boughs, the road to Osgiliath running almost as straight as a stretched ribbon down, down, into the West." That Frodo catches a first glimpse of the light on Sam's face, which then prompts him to turn West, mirrors Sam's perception of Frodo's face by the Phial's light, at the pass of Cirith Ungol (see section 5 below).

space and time, just as the Phial embodies the lingering presence of the light of Aman (Valinor). Indeed, these invocations are themselves directed at creators, mediators and carriers of this unquenchable light: Elbereth the 'Starkindler' (*gilthoniel*) and Eärendil 'the brightest of stars' (*elenion ancalima*).

These invocations also manifest differences that can be connected to the hobbits' diverging experiences of time and their respective 'observer positions'. Frodo's cry to Eärendil is voiced in Quenya, the Elven language that developed in Valinor, whereas Sam's call to Elbereth is Sindarin, the language that evolved in Middle-earth after the Noldor were exiled. In the most elaborate version of the latter invocation, Sam adds the line *le nallon sí di'nguruthos*: "to thee I cry here beneath death-horror."[51] His entreaty thus articulates the perspective of mortality and finite, linear time already described in section 3, and harks back to his encounters with Elves in the Shire and Rivendell. Frodo, on the other hand, repeats a cry from "the deeps of time" (Tolkien 1991:747, IV.9)[52] and invokes the one remaining Silmaril, of which Melian once said: "the Light of Aman and the fate of Arda lie locked now in these things" (*Silmarillion*, Tolkien 1979:152). Frodo's notion on the Stairs that once he achieves "that impossible thing, then somehow the errand would be accomplished", and the 'door' that prompts his wild run, point to a widened field of observation that contains inklings of the future. Such a wider view of time arises in direct defiance of Shelob's consuming darkness, and, as the following events show, can only be sustained by the

---

[51] The 'hymn to Elbereth' appears in three different variants (in Tolkien 1991:92-93, I.3; 254, II.1, and again in 1066, VI.9). While Sam's invocation retains the description of Elbereth as 'far-gazer' (*palan-diriel*) from the Rivendell version, the line just quoted is his only 'original' addition (cf. *Letters*, Tolkien 1995:278).

[52] Tolkien (1991:747, IV.9): "She that walked in the darkness had heard the Elves cry that cry far back in the deeps of time, and she had not heeded it, and it did not daunt her now." In *The Silmarillion*, the whole of Arda is located in the 'deeps of time': "Ilúvatar chose a place for their habitation in the Deeps of Time and in the midst of innumerable stars" (*Silmarillion*, Tolkien 1979:19).

actualized memory of light and song. Sam's perceptions, on the other hand, are at first trapped in foreboding of an inescapable end: a response elicited by Shelob's overwhelming power and reinforced by the danger of death on the border of Mordor.

The hobbits' diverging presentiments also point to competing possibilities, neither of which is complete on its own. As I have suggested above, linear time 'forks' at Cirith Ungol, so that the border becomes a 'gate of parting', separating one possible future from the other. Shelob's sting manifests this doubleness as a paradoxical co-existence of mutually exclusive futures, since Frodo is at once dead and alive. Indeed, both possibilities supersede each other in Sam's awareness as well. At Cirith Ungol, he believes Frodo to be dead, but subsequent events prove that his original interpretation of the glimpse he caught in Galadriel's Mirror came closer to the final truth: "he thought he saw Frodo with a pale face lying fast asleep under a great dark cliff" (Tolkien 1991:381, II.7). Under the influence of Shelob's poison, Frodo is suspended between life and death, but this suspension also preludes the competing futures: If Sam cannot manage to reach and rescue him in time, then Frodo will most assuredly be lost.[53]

The paradox of Frodo's dead-alive state and the ramifications of alternate possibilities cannot fail to bring more recent time-theories to mind, the thought experiment known as 'Schroedinger's Cat' in particular. Placed in an opaque box and exposed to the release of a poison

---

[53] Interestingly, the confrontation between the Mouth of Sauron and the Captains of the West at the Black Gate results in an experience of arrested time when the hobbits' possessions that were seized at Cirith Ungol are displayed: "The Messenger [...] held up first the short sword that Sam had carried, and next a grey cloak with an elven-brooch, and last the coat of mithril-mail that Frodo had worn wrapped in his tattered garments. A blackness came before their eyes, and it seemed to them in a moment of silence that the world stood still." It amounts to a travesty of the actual significance of Sam's choices when the Messenger falsely suggests that Gandalf's choice will decide over Frodo's life: "For Sauron does not love spies, and what his fate shall be depends now on your choice" (Tolkien 1991:923, 924, V.10).

on a quantum level, the cat is at once dead and alive, depending on an observer's access to the box.[54] Based on related speculations and quantum theory, "the 'many worlds' theory [...] proposes that for every quantum event which could resolve itself in more than one way there is a bifurcation of the world into parallel universes."[55] The Cirith Ungol episode may seem to echo such a concept in its constellation of parallel futures. Certainly time around Shelob's Lair resembles a web of slippery, criss-crossing threads, and the challenge Frodo and Sam face is that of discovering the path that will allow them to escape together and alive, with the Ring: the path that will, in other words, lead them towards the desired, if perhaps least likely, future.

It may be useful to draw on the 'many worlds' concept to the extent that it challenges the simplified understanding of time as irreversibly linear. However, Tolkien's framework cannot be described as a correlation of abstract temporal dimensions with accidental observer positions. Frodo's and Sam's actions are shaped by their encounters with immortals and their experience of 'Other Time'. The final resolution of this conflict is inseparable from the individual's choice, purpose and perception.

---

[54] "A living cat is placed in a box into which poison can be released by a quantum event, e.g., sending a photon through a half-silvered mirror. So there are equal possibilities that the cat is either dead or alive. As a quantum phenomenon, the photon is in superposition, and so both passes through, and does not pass through, the half silvered mirror. But according to the Copenhagen interpretation, until a conscious being opens the box to observe, the cat is both dead *and* alive." Stuart Hameroff: 'Consciousness Connects Our Brains to the Fundamental Level of the Universe', 14 May 2001 on KurzweilAI.net. Accessed 25 April 2005 <http://www.kurzweilai.net/meme/frame.html?main=/articles/art0183.html?m%3D3>.

[55] Mike King: 'The New Metaphysics and the Deep Structure of Creativity and Cognition', Proceedings of the 3rd Creativity and Cognition Conference, Loughborough University. New York: ACM Press, 1999, 93-100. Accessed 25 April 2005 <http://www.jnani.org/mrking/writings/earts/cc399.html>.

5 IN NEITHER LIGHT NOR DARKNESS: 'THAT IMPOSSIBLE THING'

Closer to Tolkien's mind than quantum theory, a folklore motif found in legends and fairytales of many cultures can yield a new perspective on the Cirith Ungol puzzle. Occasionally described as a 'riddle test', this popular motif combines an impossible task with an unexpected and most ingenious solution. The version I will quote here retains elements from the northern European mythologies and eventually made its way into nursery stories. Its heroine is Holle, also known as Holda or Hulda, a being of supernatural powers and specifically associated with weaving and the weather.

> Holler, King of Winter and Frost, [...] tested her with a riddle to be sure of Holle's worthiness. She had to come to his palace neither naked nor clothed, neither riding nor walking, neither alone nor with companions, in neither light nor darkness. Holle answered by arriving wrapped in a fishing net, sitting on a donkey with one toe dragging on the ground, surrounded by twenty-four wolves at twilight.[56]

The challenge seems to demand the impossible, since all conditions are phrased as mutually exclusive opposites. The surprising solution then transcends this binary structure by introducing a third alternative that combines apparently irreconcilable elements. Viewed in this context, Frodo's passage into Mordor could easily be construed as the solution to a similar challenge: The Ring-bearer crosses the border neither dead nor alive, neither alone nor accompanied, neither with nor without the Ring, and, indeed, in neither light nor darkness. Yet crucial differences imme-

---

[56] Sandra Kleinschmitt, 'Holle', accessed 16 April 2005 <http://www.pantheon.org/articles/h/holle.html>. Further on the character of Holle/Holda see Grimm (1981:220ff.).

diately stand out. There is, of course, no articulated challenge or riddle and hence no ingenuity involved in the solution. And, although Frodo's crossing may be described as a most unpredictable turn of events, the active part of achieving this improbable future falls to Sam.

When Sam discovers Frodo's 'death', the blackness that has threatened his awareness since their passage through the tunnels engulfs him as though the world itself had "fallen into ruin".[57] As Sam's consciousness shuts itself down, his emotional and physical responses bear out the reality of an absolute ending. Once he rouses himself again, the insight that he is now responsible for the Quest's future success takes shape almost instantly, yet Sam continues to struggle with the overwhelming finality of Frodo's apparent death.

The crux of his inner battle is not the rationale and purpose of the Ring-Quest but the meaning of death itself. At first, his despair translates into an impulse for vengeance ("If once he could go, his anger would bear him down all the roads of the world, pursuing, until he had him at last: Gollum. Then Gollum would die in a corner"; Tolkien 1991:759, IV.10). Sam rejects this impulse at once, and his subsequent thoughts centre on being dead together with Frodo, culminating in suicidal intent ("He looked on the bright point of the sword. He thought of the places behind where there was a black brink and an empty fall into nothingness"; ibid). This option, too, is rejected as an illusory escape and a denial of grief. Subsequently, Sam's growing resolve to attempt the completion of the Quest on his own is accompanied by a transforming perception of death.

---

[57] Tolkien (1991:758, IV.10): "And then black despair came down on him, and Sam bowed to the ground, and drew his grey hood over his head, and night came into his heart, and he knew no more. When at last the blackness passed, Sam looked up and shadows were about him; but for how many minutes or hours the world had gone dragging on he could not tell. He was still in the same place, and still his master lay beside him dead. The mountains had not crumbled nor the earth fallen into ruin."

He first bolsters his motivation to carry on alone by reminding himself of the devastating consequences, should Sauron regain his Ring ("And that's the end of all of us, of Lórien, and Rivendell, and the Shire and all. And there's no time to lose, or it'll be the end anyway"; ibid) which leaves him with only two choices: "it's sit here till they come and kill me over master's body, and gets It: or take It and go" (Tolkien 1991:759-60, IV.10). The stark phrasing of alternatives points to an obvious conclusion, yet Sam's parting words to Frodo reveal that his resolve is also based on a changed personal perspective:

> 'Good-bye, master, my dear!' he murmured. 'Forgive your Sam. He'll come back to this spot when the job's done – if he manages it. And then he'll not leave you again. Rest you quiet till I come; and may no foul creature come anigh you! And if the Lady could hear me and give me one wish, I would wish to come back and find you again. Good-bye!'
> (Tolkien 1991:760, IV.10)

Although Sam's 'one wish' tacitly assumes suicide, or willed death,[58] upon his return, death is now envisioned as a 'quiet rest' that Sam can eventually share with Frodo, and a reunion that affirms an irrevocable bond. This re-interpretation of death takes the shape of a wish, replacing the earlier 'black despair'. Emotionally, Sam overcomes death as loss and terminal separation. But his wish also manifests an intuitive comprehension of Frodo's true state, contradicting surface appearances. His thoughts already refer to Frodo as though he was alive, and instead of debating with himself, Sam now speaks to Frodo as if he could be heard.

---

[58] The draft version renders the suicidal element explicit: Sam "cannot drag himself away from Frodo. Turns back – resolved to lie down by Frodo till death comes" (*HoME* 8, Tolkien 1997a:190).

As he approaches the pass, Sam is still reluctant to step into a future within which he is the sole remaining survivor and Ring-bearer, whereas Frodo is irrevocably lost:

> For a moment, motionless in intolerable doubt, he looked back [...] he thought he could see or guess where Frodo lay. He fancied there was a glimmer on the ground down there, or perhaps it was some trick of his tears, as he peered out at that high stony place where all his life had fallen in ruin. 'If only I could have my wish, my one wish,' he sighed, 'to go back and find him!' Then at last he turned to the road in front and took a few steps: the heaviest and the most reluctant he had ever taken.
> (Tolkien 1991:761, IV.10)

As uncertain as the "glimmer on the ground" may be, a reflection of combined grief and hope, it also translates a new insight into external reality, first glimpsed by the light of the Phial when Sam took his leave: "for a moment he lifted up the Phial and looked down at his master, and the light burned gently now with the soft radiance of the evening-star in summer, and in that light Frodo's face was fair of hue again, pale but beautiful with an elvish beauty, as of one who has long passed the shadows" (Tolkien 1991:760, IV.10).[59] This ambiguous perception of Frodo transcends the stark opposition of life and death, and, perhaps more significantly, extends to a previously unimaginable future: a point in time when Frodo's passage through the shadows of Cirith Ungol, through apparent death and the trials of the Quest, will have slipped into the remote past.

---

[59] This impression is already present in the earliest sketch, written before Tolkien completed 'Farewell to Lórien': "It lit Frodo's face and it looked now pale but beautiful, fair with [an] elvish beauty as of one long past the shadows" (*HoME* 7, Tolkien 1993:331; repeated word-for-word in the much later draft: *HoME* 8, Tolkien 1997a:185).

I have commented on this crucial section of the text in so much detail to demonstrate how Sam's responses and observations ultimately chart a path between the radical antipoles that mark the boundary of Mordor. The clash of light and darkness, the forking paths that lead to either death or survival, at first result in a paradoxical co-existence of opposites. While Frodo becomes physically trapped in a state of living death, the paradox filters into Sam's awareness, generating an equally conflicted choice of his future course. He chooses without having truly chosen and decides to go forward while his wish draws him backward. But the wish he speaks, invoking Galadriel's powers, is inherently connected to the Phial's light that illuminates a different reality, indeed a place in the future when Frodo will be removed from the mortal world. By transcending the limited perspective of linear temporality, Sam achieves a transition into 'Other Time' that secures a future for Frodo and himself.

In the folktale quoted at the beginning of this section, twilight marks the liminal space that extends between full light and darkness.[60] At Cirith Ungol, the Phial that reflects the light of Eärendil, which reflects the mingled light of the Two Trees, heralds the unexpected alternative, or third term, between rigid binary opposites. Sam's trials do not end when he consciously realizes that Frodo is alive, as he must still find a way to reach and rescue Frodo, but his orientation is clear as soon as the orcs approach Frodo's body: "He flung the Quest and all his decisions away, and fear and doubt with them. He knew now where his place was and had been: at his master's side" (Tolkien 1991:762, IV.10). While this certainty, on the subjective level, arises from Sam's love for Frodo, it also underlines that the 'impossible thing' Frodo anticipated on the Stairs can only be achieved between the two of them. It is Sam who overcomes the boundary of death, thereby returning Frodo to life as well.

---

[60] On the concept of 'liminality' and 'rites of passage' as reflected within literature cf. Turner (1981).

While Frodo is suspended in a liminal space, the opening field of temporal observation that marks Sam's inner progress draws more specific connotations to light. The Phial's radiance and Sam's perception of Frodo's 'elvish beauty' reinforce a theme first formulated in Rivendell and reiterated in Ithilien, where Sam notices the light that shines within Frodo:

> The early daylight was only just creeping down into the shadows under the trees, but he saw his master's face very clearly, and his hands, too, lying at rest on the ground beside him. He was reminded suddenly of Frodo as he had lain, asleep in the house of Elrond, after his deadly wound. Then as he had kept watch Sam had noticed that at times a light seemed to be shining faintly within; but now the light was even clearer and stronger. Frodo's face was peaceful, the marks of fear and care had left it; but it looked old, old and beautiful, as if the chiselling of the shaping years was now revealed in many fine lines that had before been hidden, though the identity of the face was not changed. (Tolkien 1991:678, IV.4)

Sam's perception reveals Frodo's essential, unchanged self – marked however by the 'shaping years' that the Ring's imposed youthfulness merely disguises – and at the same time confirms the transformation Gandalf foresaw. The vision of Frodo's elvish beauty at Cirith Ungol adds a future dimension and, with the reference to long-past shadows, also locates him outside mortal time. It seems, then, that Frodo has indeed stepped through a 'door', and the temporal displacement caused by Shelob is complemented by a glimpse of 'Other Time', framed by not only one but three different shadings of light in which Sam sees Frodo.

When Sam first voices his belief that Frodo is dead, "it seemed to him that the hue of the face grew livid green" (Tolkien 1991:758, IV.10). Set against this shade of death and decay (reminiscent, too, of the 'corpse-light' of Minas Morgul), is the scarlet light of the chamber in the tower that falls on Frodo's naked skin, so that "it looked to Sam as if he was clothed in flame" (Tolkien 1991:945, VI.1). The intermediate state between death and vividly depicted life is illuminated by the Phial's white starlight, suggesting timelessness and thereby prefiguring Frodo's future in the Undying Lands. That Frodo's cry to Eärendil is voiced in Quenya, developed by the Calaquendi who journeyed to Valinor during the time of the Two Trees, points in the same direction. Yet timelessness also recurs in Sam's song which first challenges the overbearing presence of darkness and death with a determined vision of spring and ultimately invokes eternal light ("above all shadows rides the Sun | and Stars for ever dwell"; Tolkien 1991:943, VI.1). Quite literally, this song propels Sam past a final dead end, opens the last door, and brings about a reversal from death to life.

At this point, the similarity with another improbable passage in one of Tolkien's central stories must be noted: Beren's entry into the hidden realm of Doriath.[61] Unknowingly, Beren breaches the boundary after passing through the wilderness of Dungortheb where "spiders of the fell race of Ungoliant abode, spinning their unseen webs in which all living things were snared" (*Silmarillion*, Tolkien 1979:197). The journey through this veritable land of death[62] leaves Beren "grey and bowed as with many years of woe" (ibid). This description of a prematurely aged Beren subtly hints that the spiders have affected his experience of time. They govern a space of "horror and madness", and Beren never speaks

---

[61] Beren is the first mortal to enter Doriath which is protected by the Girdle of Melian, an impenetrable boundary, described as "an unseen wall of shadow and bewilderment" (*Silmarillion*, Tolkien 1979:114). While Melian foresaw that Beren's 'doom' would take him to Doriath, "none know how he found the way, and so came by paths that no Man or Elf else ever dared to tread to the borders of Doriath. And he passed through the mazes that Melian wove about the kingdom of Thingol, even as she had foretold; for a great doom lay upon him" (*Silmarillion*, Tolkien 1979:197).

[62] *Silmarillion* (Tolkien 1979:197): "No food for Elves or Men was there in that haunted land, but death only."

of this particular journey, "lest the horror return into his mind" (ibid). And yet, another paradoxical development ensues: By passing through a region of unspeakable 'madness', Beren gains entry into Doriath, and his horror is soon superseded by blissful enchantment when he discovers Lúthien and beholds the "shining light" in her face (*Silmarillion*, Tolkien 1979:198). Indeed, it seems that Beren's passage through a liminal space that threatens life and sanity forms the condition for his access to the guarded realm, and only this most perilous and improbable route can lead to the encounter with Lúthien.

An equally unexpected reversal is, of course, present at the resolution of the Cirith Ungol episode. Sam's 'one wish' is granted more completely than he could have hoped. Cradling Frodo, he feels "that he could sit like that in endless happiness" (Tolkien 1991:944, VI.1). Under the most adverse and improbable circumstances, surrounded by the hideous evidence of senseless slaughter, Frodo and Sam share a moment's happiness and release from the burdens of the Quest. Indeed, their reunion in the tower of Cirith Ungol can be described as a liminal space of the Quest itself, since the Ring's influence is – almost miraculously – suspended or eclipsed during these moments (see section 6).

Sam's achievement and his entry into the topmost chamber of the tower must bring further similarities with the tale of Beren and Lúthien to mind.[63] Having set out to rescue Beren from Sauron's pits, Lúthien locates her beloved by means of a song: "In that hour Lúthien [...] sang a song that no walls of stone could hinder. Beren heard, and he thought that he dreamed; for the stars shone above him and in the trees nightin-

---

[63] The parallels between the Beren and Lúthien story and Frodo and Sam's part of the Quest are numerous: Most notable, beside the quoted scene, is their rescue by the eagles (cf. *Silmarillion*, Tolkien 1979:219). After Aragorn's introduction at Weathertop, Beren's quest is explicitly linked to Frodo's several times (twice by Sam; cf. Tolkien 1991:739, IV.8, and 986-87, VI.4). In the 'Epilogue', this is complemented by Sam's reference to the "choice of Lúthien" ('The Epilogue' B; *HoME* 9, Tolkien 2002c:125). Further on these similarities and their implications for Tolkien's concept of 'love' cf. Patrick Brückner's essay in this volume.

gales were singing" (*Silmarillion*, Tolkien 1979:209). All the defining elements of this description are echoed in the tower scene of *The Return of the King*. While Sam's song invokes stars and trees ("Or there maybe 'tis cloudless night | and swaying beeches bear | the Elven-stars as jewels white | amid their branching hair"; Tolkien 1991:943, VI.1), Frodo believes that he is dreaming when Sam appears at his side ("'Am I still dreaming?' he muttered. 'But the other dreams were horrible'"; Tolkien 1991:944, VI.1). In both stories, one protagonist challenges certain death to rescue the imprisoned other, a pattern reminiscent of Orpheus' journey to Hades to bring Eurydice back from the dead. With these particular parallels, Tolkien seems to emphasize not only the theme of confronting and overcoming death. Equally crucial is the participation of two protagonists in the unfolding and dénouement of the crisis, epitomized in the dialogue through song. Just as Beren responds to Lúthien's singing, so does Frodo to Sam's. Some important differences between the two narratives, however, hinge on the question of time.

As mortals, Frodo and Sam are bound to linear time, and their perception of the future at first reflects these limitations. This particular theme is explicitly introduced on the Stairs of Cirith Ungol, where Sam discovers and defines a far-flung historical context for their current situation, not least by drawing on Beren's quest for the Silmaril.[64] The Phial creates a connection that allows Sam to see Frodo and himself as part of the 'same tale'. In addition, he envisions their quest as a recorded story in later days and imagines a future when others will read and discuss this book. However, this imagined future skips across the dilemma that

---

[64] Tolkien (1991:739, IV.8): "Beren now, he never thought he was going to get that Silmaril from the Iron Crown in Thangorodrim, and yet he did, and that was a worse place and a blacker danger than ours. But that's a long tale, of course, and goes on past the happiness and into grief and beyond it – and the Silmaril went on and came to Eärendil. And why, sir, I never thought of that before! We've got – you've got some of the light of it in that star-glass that the Lady gave you! Why, to think of it, we're in the same tale still! It's going on. Don't the great tales never end?"

Frodo stresses when he says: "that's the way of a real tale [...]. You may know, or guess, what kind of a tale it is, happy-ending or sad-ending, but the people in it don't know" (Tolkien 1991:739, IV.8). The completed tale implies a spectator whose temporal field of observation extends beyond Sam and Frodo's view, albeit retrospectively. But the hobbits themselves are, as Frodo points out, "still stuck in the worst places of the story" (Tolkien 1991:740, IV.8), and they are equally trapped in not knowing how it will end. Their subsequent premonitions about approaching the border may contain elements of foresight, but the diverging responses of hope and fear also highlight their fragmentary character. If the future 'forks' at the pass, then everything depends on combining the apparently irreconcilable. The Cirith Ungol sequence as a whole explores how this is achieved with regards to the individual's perception of time.

Overcoming the boundary marked by death hence implies not only a re-interpretation that moves from death-as-separation to death-as-reunion, and an accompanying emotional progression that can embrace hope beyond fear. On the level of temporal perception, this dangerous passage involves a shift from anticipating an unknowable future within a linear continuum to the dawning awareness of a timeless present.

This is invoked at two crucial junctions: first when Sam prepares to leave Frodo and sees him transformed in the Phial's light, and again when Sam's song paves the way for their reunion. Significantly, this shift to another level of perceiving time resembles Sam's leap of imagination on the Stairs, when he envisions the present situation as part of a completed book. Yet in the two instances named above, it is Sam who (without consciously realizing it) occupies the position of an observer overlooking a widened field of time. Within this wider view, Frodo's apparent death is transcended and translated into a future that cannot be conceptualized within linear time. As 'one who has long passed the shadows' Frodo is neither dead – for the future of the corpse could only be envisioned as disintegration – nor self-aware and thus fully alive.

Sam's perception at this moment also answers Frodo's earlier implicit question about the ending of their tale: Neither happy nor sad, this view does not portend an ending at all, but its transcendence. This consequence is, in fact, adumbrated in the scene on the Stairs when Sam says about the Beren and Lúthien story that it "goes on past the happiness and into grief and beyond it" (Tolkien 1991:739, IV.8). As a reference to Beren and Lúthien's improbable reunion "beyond the Western Sea" (*Silmarillion*, Tolkien 1979:225), this description also preludes the hobbits' parting at the Grey Havens and their separate journeys to Aman.[65] Finally, attention must be drawn to another structurally significant element: the position of an observer and one who is observed and located within time – or beyond it. That Sam sees Frodo into the future is as significant as Frodo's own state of suspension.

6 FRODO'S HIDDEN PATH:
'A LIGHT IN THE DARKNESS OF HIS MIND'

Although the themes explored in the last section may seem to move away from the questions raised at the beginning of this article, they constitute the proper context for the 'trauma' caused by the events of Cirith Ungol. While Sam rather than Frodo becomes the chief protagonist in a drama concerning the transcendence of death and finite linear time, their respective positions as observer and observed are interdependent and equally essential for Tolkien's narrative about Frodo's

---

[65] That Sam eventually leaves Middle-earth to be reunited with Frodo is disclosed in the entry for the year 1482 in Appendix B (Tolkien 1991:1134). When Sam reveals his 'secret' to Elanor in the second version of the 'Epilogue' to *The Lord of the Rings*, he not only anticipates a reunion with Frodo but also remarks that he has learned to adopt the Elves' attitude towards time: "Before he went Mr. Frodo said that my time maybe would come. I can wait. I think maybe we haven't said farewell for good. But I can wait. I have learned that much from the Elves at any rate. They are not so troubled about time." (*HoME* 9, Tolkien 2002c:125).

transformation. Another quote from the 'Shelob's Lair' drafts can illuminate how this interdependence manifested in the writing process itself.

In an early version of the chapter, Frodo first makes use of the Phial without prompting from Sam (cf. *HoME* 8, Tolkien 1997a:193). But from the next draft onward, it is Sam who suddenly sees "a light in the darkness of his mind" (*HoME* 8, Tolkien 1997a:209). In the published version, Frodo's courageous attack of Shelob depends on Sam's memory of Galadriel's gift:

> Then as he stood, darkness about him and a blackness of despair and anger in his heart, it seemed to him that he saw a light: a light in his mind, almost unbearably bright at first, as a sun-ray to the eyes of one long hidden in a windowless pit. Then the light became colour: green, gold, silver, white.
> (Tolkien 1991:746-47, IV.9)

One of the reasons why this shift from Frodo to Sam occurred may be that it is Sam's part to recognize the light that becomes visible in Frodo himself. The published description certainly evokes an immediate connection between the Phial's light and Frodo's inner state:

> [A]s its power waxed, and hope grew in Frodo's mind, it began to burn, and kindled to a silver flame, a minute heart of dazzling light, as though Eärendil had himself come down from the high sunset paths with the last Silmaril upon his brow. The darkness receded from it until it seemed to shine in the centre of a globe of airy crystal, and the hand that held it sparkled with white fire. (Tolkien 1991:747, IV.9)

The light welling through Frodo's hand[66] appears as an externalized counterpart to the light that Sam perceives as he watches Frodo sleep in Ithilien and which, as Gandalf predicted, is revealed only "for eyes to see that can" (Tolkien 1991:239, II.1).

The variations of this theme outline a process by which Frodo is irrevocably changed and which finally takes him to the Undying Lands. As Tolkien summarized in a letter written after he had completed the last chapters of *The Two Towers*: "Frodo will naturally become too ennobled and rarefied by the achievement of the great Quest, and will pass West with all the great figures" (to Christopher Tolkien, 24 December 1944; *Letters*, Tolkien 1995:105). In concurrence with this general conception, my quintessential argument is that the encounter with Shelob, rather like the confrontation with the Ringwraiths at Weathertop, is linked to this process that begins with a mere 'hint of transparency'. In both episodes, the wounding by enemies of supernatural powers is ultimately shown to have unexpected – and certainly unintended – effects. Two questions remain to be considered: First, what precisely defines the Cirith Ungol stage in Frodo's transformation? Secondly, what are the implications of the March 13th episode in 'The Grey Havens', and why does the text emphasize the theme of injury and illness rather than 'ennoblement' and 'rarefication'?

The Cirith Ungol crisis unfolds the theme of an improbable passage through death, set against the backdrop of an ongoing tale that

---

[66] Tolkien (1991:735, IV.8): "the clear light [...] welling through his fingers." But it is noteworthy, too, that an equally direct connection between Sam and the Phial emerges later in the text, for instance when he fights Shelob: "As if his indomitable spirit had set its potency in motion, the glass blazed suddenly like a white torch in his hand. It flamed like a star that leaping from the firmament sears the dark air with intolerable light" (Tolkien 1991:757, IV.10). Similarly as the hobbits escape from the tower (Tolkien 1991:949, VI.1): "Sam drew out the elven-glass of Galadriel again. As if to do honour to his hardihood, and to grace with splendour his faithful brown hobbit-hand that had done such deeds, the phial blazed forth suddenly, so that all the shadowy court was lit with a dazzling radiance like lightning; but it remained steady and did not pass."

traces the history of time across an unbroken continuum of light. This fundamental juxtaposition of termination and continuity is resolved, as I have argued in the last section, when a third alternative emerges: Frodo's suspension between life and death, or temporal displacement, ultimately transcends endings within linear time and points to a timeless present which in turn foreshadows Frodo's journey to the Immortal Realm.

In this context, some of the more mystifying details can now be re-examined. The 'door' or 'path' of the draft version, which Frodo perceives in a state of 'madness', appears to be connected to this future passage into the West. Indeed, this perception would seem to explain the puzzling distortion in Tolkien's map of the Lair as well (see illustration 3). That north and south retain their usual positions, whereas the eastern end of the Lair (which opens onto the border) occupies the customary place of west, shows that the confusion stems from an impossible overlap of east and west. This overlap can however be described as a consequence of layered time: East, within the mortal continuum of Middle-earth, is here overlaid by the 'true' or 'far West' (Valinor) because Frodo moves on a path towards a state of timelessness.

This implicit disconnection of 'ordinary' west from the far West can be directly derived from the world's history in *The Silmarillion*. As essential dimensions of the created world, West and East exist independently of mortal time and precede the shaping of celestial bodies that define these directions. East and west, as Frodo and Sam know them, are identified by the rising and setting of the sun which was created only after the destruction of the Two Trees. However, the awakening of mortals in Middle-earth, and thus the beginning of mortal time, was marked by a first sunrise out of the West:

> At the first rising of the Sun the Younger Children of Ilúvatar awoke in the land of Hildórien in the eastward regions of Middle-earth; but the first Sun arose in the West, and the opening eyes of Men were turned

> towards it, and their feet as they wandered over the
> Earth for the most part strayed that way.
> (*Silmarillion*, Tolkien 1979:122)

The dawn of mortal time and the Halls of Mandos through which mortals are said to pass after death (*Silmarillion*, Tolkien 1979:124) are both situated in the far West – a concurrence which can be related to Frodo and Sam's conflicting perceptions of the pass, the gate, the path ahead of them: It may lead beyond the origins of mortal time, or it may lead towards death, but both lie in the West. While these underlying intimations are not immediately visible in the Cirith Ungol chapters, a variation of the same theme that appears much later in *The Return of the King* suggests the same connection.

In the Woody End, on the road to the Havens, Frodo sings Bilbo's old walking-song with changed words: "A day will come at last when I | Shall take the hidden paths that run | West of the Moon, East of the Sun" (Tolkien 1991:1066, VI.9).[67] This verse implies Frodo's ability to discover 'hidden paths' that lead beyond the dimensions of the mortal world, and his foretelling of his own future is at once answered by the Elves' singing.[68] This final reiteration of the 'hymn to Elbereth' also points back to the dialogue through song that may pass through walls or open locked doors. While the 'door' that Frodo perceived on the bound-

---

[67] Cf. Tolkien (1991:91, I.3): "Bilbo Baggins had made the words, to a tune that was as old as the hills, and taught it to Frodo as they walked in the lanes of the Water-valley and talked about Adventure. 'Still round the corner there may wait | A new road or a secret gate, | And though we pass them by today, | Tomorrow we may come this way | And take the hidden paths that run | Towards the Moon or to the Sun.'" The change of the speaking subject – from 'we' to 'I' – and, more importantly, the altered reference to Moon and Sun (now indicating a journey beyond the dimensions of mortal time in which east and west are defined by the rising and setting of the sun), document Frodo's changed awareness of himself and his future.

[68] Tolkien (1991:1066, VI.9): "And as if in answer, from down below, coming up the road out of the valley, voices sang: '*A! Elbereth Gilthoniel! | silivren penna miriel | o menel aglar elenath, | Gilthoniel, A! Elbereth! | We still remember, we who dwell | In this far land beneath the trees | The starlight on the Western Seas.*'"

ary of Mordor in Tolkien's draft is no longer manifest in the published text, a coherent semantic framework pervades the account of his journey and transformation. In retrospect, it becomes clear that the tunnels and passageways of Cirith Ungol shape a hidden path by which Frodo can travel into a future that takes him beyond mortal time.

But before Frodo indeed embarks on this journey, he is 'ill' on the anniversaries of his encounter with Shelob in 1420 and 1421, and these episodes warrant closer examination. What precisely is it that Frodo relives on every 13th of March? The drafts for the 'Grey Havens' chapter demonstrate that Tolkien was not altogether certain and apparently struggled to define the nature of these troubling aftereffects. His first draft (A) contains no reference to Frodo's March illness whatsoever (cf. *HoME* 9, Tolkien 2002c:108). The description that emerged as an addition to the second draft (B) still differs from the published version in vital respects:

> Sam was away on his forestry work in March, and Frodo was glad, for he had been feeling ill, and it would have been difficult to conceal from Sam. On the twelfth of March he was in pain and weighed down with a great sense of darkness, and could do little more than walk about clasping the jewel of Queen Arwen. But after a while the fit passed.
> (*HoME* 9, Tolkien 2002c:110)

This description features no element that could be read as an allusion to the Ring. Although the impact of remembered darkness forms the centre of this episode, its effect is physically less debilitating than the published version indicates. In *The Return of the King*, Farmer Cotton finds Frodo "lying on his bed", yet even in this account Frodo is not unconscious, and his state does not imply that he is thrust back fully into the suspension between life and death. That he seems "half in a dream" suggests a connection with the period immediately after waking from paralysis: In the tower of Cirith Ungol, Frodo at first finds it difficult to distinguish waking reality from dreams. While the published description yields only an external view of Frodo's condition, the draft adds "a great sense of darkness", which Frodo tries to counter by "walking about" and clasping Arwen's jewel. The latter element is still present in the published version as well, where Frodo is found "clutching a white gem that hung on a chain about his neck" (Tolkien 1991:1062, VI.9). The only direct expression of his subjective experience is contained in the two sentences he speaks: "'It is gone for ever,' he said, 'and now all is dark and empty.'" (ibid).

Any interpretation of these lines must take into account Frodo's waking in the tower, as the moment most directly related to his illness. It would be very tempting to identify "it is gone for ever" with Frodo's immediate response at Cirith Ungol, when he regains consciousness and notices the Ring's absence. However, the tower scene eloquently shows that this identification would be incorrect. After resting content in Sam's embrace ("he lay back in Sam's gentle arms, closing his eyes, like a child at rest when night-fears are driven away by some loved voice or hand"; Tolkien 1991:944, VI.1), Frodo becomes fully aware of himself and the circumstances, and recounts his experience to Sam without ever mentioning the Ring. His description features two significant elements in particular: the impression of 'stretched' time ("It seems weeks"; Tolkien 1991:945, VI.1) and the 'dark' dream-state ("I fell into darkness and foul dreams, and woke and found that waking was worse"; ibid). After this exchange, Frodo walks about, "his spirits rising a little", and remembers the fighting that occurred among the orcs. Only when Sam begins to plan their further journey into Mordor and alludes to Frodo's missing clothes, does Frodo finally realize that the Ring has been taken from him. If the line "it is gone for ever" is read as lingering desire for the Ring, we might expect an immediate expression of such a longing at this point. Yet Frodo's reaction is quite different and not at all self-centred:

> He cowered on the floor again with bowed head, as his own words brought home to him the fullness of the disaster, and despair overwhelmed him. 'The quest has failed, Sam. Even if we get out of here, we can't escape. Only Elves can escape. Away, away out of Middle-earth, far away over the Sea. If even that is wide enough to keep the Shadow out.'
> (Tolkien 1991:945-46, VI.1)

By an entirely unexpected turn of events, the Ring-bearer finds himself without the Ring. Tolkien uses this opportunity for a nuanced portrayal, demonstrating first that Frodo's thoughts and feelings are by no means governed by the Ring at all times. As he belatedly remembers the Ring, Frodo does not long for possession of it either and instead laments the apparent failure of the Quest.[69] That he expresses satisfaction and relief rather than regret – let alone a continued craving – when the Ring is destroyed, follows logically from these responses.

In the tower, Frodo despairs at the prospect of Sauron's triumph, and when he tries to envision an 'escape', his thoughts turn immediately to the passage across the sea. In the context discussed here, this instant association is very revealing and directly linked to the theme of a path into the West. It is this path that allows escape from the darkness and

---

[69] His attitude changes only when Sam tells him that he has kept the Ring safe. While Frodo's renewed awareness of the Ring affects his perceptions (from the 'strange' change of his tone to his "hideous vision" of Sam as an orc), it does so only temporarily. Immediately afterwards, Frodo explains: "It is the horrible power of the Ring. I wish it had never, never, been found. But don't mind me, Sam. I must carry the burden to the end. It can't be altered. You can't come between me and this doom" (Tolkien 1991:946, VI.1). The language employed here ('horrible power', 'burden', 'doom') and Frodo's wish that the Ring had never been found document that he is fully able to separate his personal desires from his appointed task and the Ring's influence.

emptiness experienced in Shelob's Lair, from the Shadow that Sauron may cast across all of Middle-earth. Indeed, this element is equally present during Frodo's March illness (but not on October 6th), now represented by Arwen's gift. The white gem is an explicit token of his opportunity to sail into the West: "when the time comes, and if you then desire it" (Tolkien 1991:1011-12, VI.6).[70] Meanwhile, as Arwen also tells him, it will aid Frodo against memories of fear and darkness. During the March 13th episode, Frodo is therefore "clutching" not only an antidote that brings relief but also the prospect of travelling beyond Middle-earth. It is this connection that defines the missing reference in his "it is gone for ever": 'it' then refers to the westward path that Frodo perceived before he was overtaken by Shelob, to the future revealed in the Phial's light, and the 'escape' he thought was for ever out of reach when he discovered the Ring's absence in the tower.

As a crucial stage in Frodo's transformation, the Shelob-encounter brings about the first manifestation of Frodo's future in the Immortal Realm. In Rivendell, Gandalf merely speculates about the nature and direction of this process, the ultimate result of which is not yet apparent. Its *destination*, a place outside the mortal continuum, emerges only from the crucible of Cirith Ungol. In the final chapter of *The Lord of the Rings*, Frodo then affirms his ability to divine the hidden path into the future that opens up for him. The subtle interweaving of different aspects of temporality in the Cirith Ungol episode, the confrontation of continuity and termination, and the theme of death transcended, all point to this conclusion.

---

[70] Tolkien (1991:1011-12, VI.6): "But in my stead you shall go, Ring-bearer, when the time comes, and if you then desire it. If your hurts grieve you still and the memory of your burden is heavy, then you may pass into the West, until all your wounds and weariness are healed [...]. When the memory of the fear and the darkness troubles you, [...] this will bring you aid."

Yet the sharply profiled elements of grief, loss, and choice emphasize that such a path is fraught with conflict and struggle. It is hardly surprising that Frodo, who hoped to resume his life in the Shire, is seen to be haunted by his memories rather than rejoicing in his 'ennoblement'. Arwen's gift confirms a potential foreshadowed by the crossing into Mordor and explicitly offers Frodo a future in Aman, yet her addition "if you then desire it" also underscores that the choice must be his own: a choice, apparently, that Frodo cannot make lightly or quickly. The grace bestowed on him is no easy gift, nor is it portrayed as a pleasant escape from the burdens of mortality. That Tolkien wished to stress this particular point is beyond question, not least from his remarks on the subject of 'escape' in his lecture *On Fairy-Stories*.[71]

After his return from the Quest, Frodo certainly does not consider himself 'rarefied', or equal to the company of a more 'noble kind', as his final confrontation with Saruman demonstrates.[72] Yet Frodo himself no longer 'fits' into ordinary Shire-life: His eventual withdrawal from community affairs, his efforts to conceal his illness in March 1421, and the 'strangeness' Sam notices in him on October 6th, 1420,[73] indicate

---

[71] See esp. Tolkien (1997:153): "And lastly there is the oldest, and deepest desire, the Great Escape: the Escape from Death. Fairy stories supply many examples and modes of this – which might be called the genuine *escapist*, or (I would say) *fugitive* spirit. But so do other stories (notably those of scientific inspiration), and so do other studies [...]. But the 'consolation' of fairy-tales has another aspect than the imaginative satisfaction of ancient desires. Far more important is the Consolation of the Happy Ending [...]. The consolation of fairy-stories, the joy of the happy ending: or more correctly of the good catastrophe, the sudden joyous 'turn' (for there is no true end to any fairy-tale): this joy which is one of the things which fairy-stories can produce supremely well, is not essentially 'escapist', nor 'fugitive'." For the 'joyous turn', evidenced too by Frodo's and Sam's reunion in the tower, Tolkien coins the term 'eucatastrophe'.

[72] Tolkien (1991:1057, VI.8): "'No, Sam!' said Frodo. 'Do not kill him even now [...]. He was great once, of a noble kind that we should not dare to raise our hands against. He is fallen, and his cure is beyond us; but I would still spare him, in the hope that he may find it.'"

[73] Tolkien (1991:1063, VI.9): "One evening Sam came into the study and found his master looking very strange. He was very pale and his eyes seemed to see things far away."

this fundamental state of displacement and unease. Finally, the only protagonist to ever formulate a concept of transformation is Gandalf. Neither Frodo nor Sam, let alone the society into which they return, possess a framework of knowledge that could render the changes in Frodo intellegible, or cast them in a hopeful light. All of these conditions account for the semantics of illness and injury that prevail in the final two chapters of *The Return of the King*.

In *Splintered Light: Logos and Language in Tolkien's World*, Verlyn Flieger gives a rather bleak description of the book's conclusion:

> Just as the Ring is un-made, so Frodo is un-made, broken down so that he may be transformed. But that transformation is withheld, for Tokien's story ends before it can be shown. We know what *may* happen to Frodo, but we are given no guarantee that it *will* happen, any more than we know what will happen to us. Hope without guarantees is all we have.
> (Flieger 2002:160)

The choice of analogies seems unfortunate, since it suggests an interdependence, if not an inherent resemblance, of the Ring's destruction and Frodo's transformation. While the two are inseparably interlinked, the change in Frodo by no means involves disintegration or total loss of identity. Nor is Frodo's transformation a process that sets in *after* the Ring is destroyed: it is adumbrated quite early by Frodo's prophetic dreams,[74] traced across various stages during the Quest, and outlined most prominently in Sam's 'visionary' perceptions of Frodo.[75] In many re-

---

[74] Most notably, his dream of the journey to Valinor in Tom Bombadil's house (Tolkien 1991:150, I.8).

[75] Compare, for instance, Sam's view of Frodo with 'other vision' in the Emyn Muil (Tolkien 1991:643, IV.1) or on the slopes of Mount Doom (Tolkien 1991:979, VI.3).

spects, Tolkien's text is thus more definite and explicit than Flieger's description posits.

At the final stage of Frodo's journey, we are indeed left without the assurance of a happy ending. But rather than concluding on a note of 'hope without guarantees', the text confronts two contrasting perspectives. Frodo's first glimpse of Aman[76] is immediately followed by Sam's perception of "a shadow on the waters that was soon lost in the West, while the sigh and murmur of the waves on the shores of Middle-earth [...] sank deep into his heart" (Tolkien 1991:1069, VI.9). These lines relate the perspective of the mortal who remains behind with the promise that his "time may come" (Tolkien 1991:1067, VI.9), while Sam's assimilation of the sea's voice suggests a connection with Frodo's early dreams.[77] Moreover, the final reference to the Phial's light – "the light of the glass of Galadriel that Frodo bore glimmered and was lost" (Tolkien 1991:1069, VI.9) – alludes to the crisis of Cirith Ungol and the "glimmer on the ground" that Sam could see at the very moment of parting. There may be no guarantees, but the remaining hope is not, as Flieger proposes, a vague, universal hope that all mortals share. It is, quite specifically, tied to Sam's wish at Cirith Ungol and his ability to reinterpret ultimate separation as a hope for reunion.[78] At the very last, we are reminded that Sam's apparently impossible 'one wish' did come true.

---

[76] Tolkien (1991:1068-69, VI.9): "And the ship went out into the High Sea and passed on into the West, until at last on a night of rain Frodo smelled a sweet fragrance on the air and heard the sound of singing that came over the water. And then it seemed to him that as in his dream in the house of Bombadil, the grey rain-curtain turned all to silver glass and was rolled back, and he beheld white shores and beyond them a far green country under a swift sunrise."

[77] Cf. Frodo's dream (Tolkien 1991:123, I.5): "Then he knew that it was not leaves, but the sound of the Sea far-off; a sound he had never heard in waking life, though it had often troubled his dreams."

[78] Far from being an expression of simple optimism, the complex nature of Sam's hope at various points during the Quest would certainly warrant closer examination as well.

JUDITH KLINGER Ph.D. is lecturer for German Medieval Studies at the University of Potsdam (Germany). Her dissertation deals with concepts of identity in the *Prosa-Lancelot*. She is currently working on a project in Gender Studies.
Homepage: http://www.uni-potsdam.de/u/germanistik/mediaevistik/1_anfang.htm

Bibliography

Carpenter, Humphrey, 2002, *J.R.R. Tolkien. A Biography*, (paperback edition, first edition 1977), London: Harper Collins.

Curry, Patrick, 1997, *Defending Middle-Earth. Tolkien: Myth and Modernity*, New York: St. Martin's Press.

Flieger, Verlyn, 1997, *A Question of Time. J.R.R. Tolkien's Road to Faërie*, London & Kent, Ohio: The Kent State University Press.

---, 2002, *Splintered Light. Logos and Language in Tolkien's World*, (second edition, first edition 1983), London & Kent, Ohio: The Kent State University Press.

---, 2005, *Interrupted Music. The Making of Tolkien's Mythology*, London & Kent, Ohio: The Kent State University Press.

Fonstad, Karen Wynn, 1991, *The Atlas of Middle-earth* (revised edition), Boston & New York: Houghton Mifflin.

Gaignebet, Claude and Jean-Dominique Lajoux, 1985, *Art profane et religion populaire au Moyen Age*, Paris: Presses Universitaires de France.

Garth, John, 2003, *Tolkien and the Great War. The Threshold of Middle-Earth*, Boston & New York: Houghton Mifflin.

Grimm, Jacob, 1981, *Deutsche Mythologie* Vol. I, (reprint, first edition 1835), Frankfurt a.M. & Berlin, Wien: Ullstein Verlag.

Laplanche, Jean and Jean-Bertrand Pontalis, 1983, *The Language of Psycho-analysis*, London: Hogarth Press.

Panofsky, Erwin, 1955, 'Titian's *Allegory of Prudence*: A Postscript', in *Meaning in the Visual Arts,* Garden City: Doubleday & Company, pp. 146-168.

Shippey, Tom, 2002, *J.R.R. Tolkien. Author of the Century*, (paperback edition, first edition 2000), New York & Boston: Houghton Mifflin.

Strachey, Barbara, 1984, *Journeys of Frodo. An Atlas of J.R.R. Tolkien's 'The Lord of the Rings'*, (reprint, first edition 1981), London: Unwin Paperbacks.

Tolkien, J.R.R., 1979, *The Silmarillion*, (edited by Christopher Tolkien), (first paperback edition, first edition 1977), London: Unwin Paperbacks.

---, 1991, *The Lord of the Rings: The Fellowship of the Ring. The Two Towers. The Return of the King*, (first edition 1954/1955, second edition 1966), London: Harper Collins.

---, 1993, *The History of Middle-earth* Vol. 7: *The Treason of Isengard*, (edited by Christopher Tolkien), (paperback edition, first edition 1989), London: Harper Collins. [abbr. HoME 7]

---, 1995, *The Letters of J.R.R. Tolkien*. A Selection edited by Humphrey Carpenter with the assistance of Christopher Tolkien, (paperback edition, first edition 1981), London: Houghton Mifflin.

---, 1997a, *The History of Middle-earth* Vol. 8: *The War of the Ring*, (edited by Christopher Tolkien), (paperback edition, first edition 1990), London: Harper Collins. [abbr. HoME 8]

---, 1997b, *The History of Middle-earth* Vol. 12: *The Peoples of Middle-earth*, (edited by Christopher Tolkien), (paperback edition, first edition 1996), London: Harper Collins. [abbr. HoME 12]

---, 1997c, 'On Fairy-Stories', in *The Monsters and the Critics and Other Essays*, (edited by Christopher Tolkien), (paperback edition, first edition 1983), London: Harper Collins, pp. 109-161.

---, 1998, *Unfinished Tales of Númenor and Middle-earth*, (edited by Christopher Tolkien), (paperback edition, first edition 1980), London: Harper Collins.

---, 2002a, *The History of Middle-earth* Vol. 1: *The Book of Lost Tales* (Part One), (edited by Christopher Tolkien), (paperback edition, first edition 1983), London: Harper Collins. [abbr. HoME 1]

---, 2002b, *The History of Middle-earth* Vol. 3: *The Lays of Beleriand*, (edited by Christopher Tolkien), (paperback edition, first edition 1985), London: Harper Collins. [abbr. HoME 3]

---, 2002c, *The History of Middle-earth* Vol. 9: *Sauron Defeated*, (edited by Christopher Tolkien), (paperback edition, first edition 1992), London: Harper Collins. [abbr. HoME 9]

---, 2002d, *The History of Middle-earth* Vol. 10: *Morgoth's Ring* (The Later *Silmarillion* Part One. The Legends of Aman), (edited by Christopher Tolkien), (paperback edition, first edition 1993), London: Harper Collins. [abbr. HoME 10]

Turner, Victor, 1981, 'Social Dramas and Stories about them', in W.J.T. Mitchell (ed.), 1981, *On Narrative*, Chicago: University of Chicago Press, pp. 137-164.

The Passing of the Elves and the Arrival of Modernity: Tolkien's 'Mythical Method'

THOMAS HONEGGER

Abstract

Tolkien's relationship with modernity – and in particular with literary modernism – is ambiguous and contradictory. As critics have noticed, Tolkien's work shares many of the formal characteristics of modernist literature while simultaneously rejecting most of its central 'ideological' tenets. Furthermore, the years between 1913 and 1920, which saw, among other things, the cataclysm of the First World War, proved not only formative for many modernist writers, but provided also the background against which Tolkien's mythology took shape. Authors such as T.S. Eliot or James Joyce, whose *The Waste Land* (1922) and *Ulysses* (1922), respectively, are considered to be the most important and accomplished examples of modernist writing, use the 'mythical method' to express the modern world's disillusionment and rupture with the past. Their references to mythical matter are often allusive, ironic and playful and demonstrate the inadequacy of traditional 'mythic' narratives and high diction to imbue modern life with coherence and meaning. Tolkien, too, employs a 'mythical method' to come to terms with the challenges of modernity, yet his use of 'mythical matter' aims at smoothing the break without glossing over the feeling of loss and sorrow. Tolkien endeavours to come to terms with 'modernity' by means of providing the lost context(s) to the fragments of modern existence so that he – and his readers – arrive in modernity not via ironic disenchantment but by commemorating of what has been lost.

INTRODUCTION

Paris, France, 1921. James Joyce is busy correcting the proofs for his *Ulysses*, which is scheduled for publication in February 1922 and will establish itself quickly as one of the most influential books of high modernism – and as one of the most important books of twentieth-century high literature.

Lausanne, Switzerland, 1921. Thomas Stearns Eliot, during his three-month convalescence leave, completes the drafting of *The Waste Land*. He shows it to Ezra Pound and together they revise it and cut more than half its length. The poem will be published in the States in *The Dial* and, in England, in *The Criterion* in 1922. It has, from the 1930s onward, often been considered to be 'the poem of the century' (Brooker and Bentley 1990:3).

Leeds, England, 1921. John Ronald Reuel Tolkien, Reader in English Language at the University of Leeds, is compiling his glossary to be used with Kenneth Sisam's *Fourteenth Century Verse & Prose*. The new edition of Sisam's book, now including Tolkien's contribution, will be published the following year. The glossary is a labour of love, gratefully accepted by generations of students but having no impact on the world of letters. It would have been all but forgotten had not its compiler achieved celebrity status later in life. At about the same time, and more to the topic, Tolkien must have entertained himself, his colleagues and students with some poems. One is in English, in spite of its Old English title (*Tha Eadigan Saelidan*; with the subtitle *The Happy Mariners*), but the two riddles (*Enigmata Saxonica Nuper Inventa Duo*) are written entirely in Anglo Saxon. They, together with the slightly comical *Why the Man in the Moon Came Down Too Soon*, are published in *A Northern Venture* (Leeds: Swan Press, 1923) in an edition of 170 copies (Hammond 1993:283). These early poems, of course, did not attract much attention and little did the readers of *A Northern Venture* know that the author of these moody and playful lines would, one day, be dubbed 'author of the century' (Shippey 2000). Nor would they necessarily connect 'mythical' references in *Tha Eadigan Saelidan*, such as "Western shores" (Tolkien 1923a:15, line 21), "Night's dragon-headed doors" (ibid., line 23) or "Ye follow Earendel through the West" (ibid., line 33) with anything but half-remembered classical and medieval legends and tales. A small number of colleagues and friends may have been aware that Tolkien's 'Western shores' do not necessarily refer to the known (e.g. Celtic)[1] concepts of the paradisiacal (is)land(s) in the west, and that 'Earendel', a name to be found in the Old English poem *Christ* in *The Exeter Book* and usually identified with the Morning Star (i.e. Venus), is also linked to Tolkien's *Legendarium*.

ALLUSIONS

Modern Tolkien scholars, from 1977 onwards, have had access to many of Tolkien's mythological-legendary writings and drafts in the form of *The Silmarillion* and the twelve volumes of *The History of Middle-earth*. They are therefore better equipped to unravel and appreciate the specifically Tolkienian dimensions of these allusions than a contemporary audience of 1921 that must have missed these peculiar implications. Yet the lack of specific information relating to Tolkien's private mythology is not jeopardising the understanding and appreciation of the poem as a work of art. Even a modern reader unfamiliar with Tolkien's work is able to read, understand, value, and enjoy the poem. S/he may miss some of the deeper and more private levels of meaning that are necessarily connected with the poem's mythical backdrop to be found only in the *Legendarium*, but Tolkien's re-definition of terms and concepts (e.g. that of 'fairy') does not preclude an 'uninformed' reading of the poem. The first person narrator tells the reader about a white tower that overlooks the sea, of fairy boats laden with treasure that sail away into the west, and of (fairy) mariners chanting on their way towards Western shores, from which only a wind returns to the lonely watcher in the tower. The general mood of the rather short poem (two stanzas with 19 lines each) is one of peaceful melancholy and nostalgia. The effect is

---

[1] Cf. the Imram tradition. Tolkien published an Imram poem in the periodical *Time and Tide* (3 December 1955; reprinted in *Sauron Defeated* [Tolkien 1993:296-299]).

achieved by mixing familiar literary *topoi* and concepts (the West, fairy boats passing by, snatches of chant rising to the onlooker) with a few unexplained allusions and obscure references that contribute to the general atmosphere of mystery and ask for an intuitive rather than an analytic reading of the poem. Notes, such as the ones that have become an integral part of all editions of *The Waste Land* ever since they were added for its publication in book form in 1922, would be completely out of place with Tolkien's poem. This seemingly minor detail highlights a crucial contrast between Tolkien's and Eliot's – and to some extent also Joyce's – use of allusions in their works. Eliot, in *The Waste Land*, in general refers to and quotes from published and, in theory, generally accessible works of literature. Yet the effect he creates for a 'general' reader is one of bewilderment and confusion.[2] Tolkien, by contrast, alludes to his private mythology that is known only to a handful of close friends and relatives; however, he makes use of such elements sparingly and embeds them within a context that provides the reader with sufficient information to grasp their general meaning.[3]

LOSS, COLLAPSE, AND THE MYTHICAL METHOD

It is thus the way the poets apply these allusions and not so much their theoretical 'accessibility' (references to published literature vs. private mythology) that is responsible for the overall effect – which could be hardly more diverse, though the underlying message may be very similar.

---

[2] The *literati* would, of course, recognize most of the allusions and quotations and be in a better position to unravel the dense web of the poem. Gish (1988:107) writes: "The poem [i.e. *The Waste Land*] can be read, and it will have an emotional impact, on its own, but much of it would be either blank or frustrating without a recognition of the allusions." Longenbach (1994:177) points out that much of modernist poetry is addressed to "highly trained connoisseur[s]".

[3] This observation also holds true for Tolkien's longer works of fiction, such as *The Lord of the Rings*, which contains numerous (often unexplained) allusions to the *Legendarium*.

Eliot, a highly educated and widely read *literatus*, creates a poetic collage that has become the most prominent literary example of twentieth-century disillusionment and rupture with the tradition in the wake of the Great War.[4] W.B. Yeats, almost at the same time, expresses a similar dread in his poem *The Second Coming* (1921; Allison et al. 1983:883, lines 1-3):

> Turning and turning in the widening gyre
> The falcon cannot hear the falconer;
> Things fall apart; the centre cannot hold;

In *The Waste Land*, this 'centre' that no longer holds could be identified as the literary canon or tradition – and with it European[5] cultural self-confidence and traditional values. This centre has fallen apart and its pieces are cluttering the poem in a seemingly random way. Whatever the meaning(s) of the poem, one clear message given, and perceived by most readers, is that of loss of structure and orientation. Sharratt (1994:225) characterises it succinctly as

> a complaint that the great tradition of European culture had dwindled to a few disconnected fragments, a case of battered books, which would not cohere any more than the poem itself would.

Eliot, although he makes numerous references to myths, and in particular to fertility myths as discussed in Jessie L. Weston's *From Ritual to Romance* (1920),[6] does not use them to structure *The Waste Land* in an

---

[4] Sharratt (1994:225) characterises *The Waste Land* as "a complaint that the great tradition of European culture had dwindled to a few disconnected fragments, a case of battered books, which would not cohere any more than the poem itself would."

[5] Eliot is, of course, an American by birth. Yet he spent formative years in Europe and became as much, if not primarily, a 'European' poet.

[6] Social realists such as Philip Larkin would react sharply to this and reject the idea of a 'common myth-kitty' (quoted in Rosebury 2003:148). See Armstrong (2005) for a concise overview of the development of myths through the ages.

obvious way and attempts by later scholars to see it as an illustration of the 'mythical method' have failed.[7] Eliot's poem is an illustration of modern people's loss of touch with "the mythical underpinning of their culture[.] Instead of understanding the inner coherence of their tradition, they know 'only a heap of broken images'" (Armstrong 2005:137). It is thus the other masterpiece of modernism that we have to turn to in order to see the mythical method at work: James Joyce's *Ulysses* (1922).

Eliot had read part of Joyce's work before its publication as a book in 1922 and was thus well acquainted with it. In a short article entitled 'Ulysses, Order, and Myth', which first appeared in *The Dial* (November 1923; reprinted in Eliot 1975:175-178), he argues that, firstly, *Ulysses* is "the most important expression which the present age has found" (Eliot 1975:175) and, secondly, that it is not, as a former critic had claimed, "an invitation to chaos" (Eliot 1975:176). Eliot discusses the latter point in some detail and he praises Joyce's structural use of myth as "a simple way of controlling, of ordering, of giving a shape and a significance to the immense panorama of futility and anarchy which is contemporary history" (Eliot 1975:177). He talks, of course, about the famous "mythical method" (Eliot 1975:178) – a term coined by Eliot in this very article. Joyce makes overtly use of *The Odyssey* as the foil against which the action of his 'epic' unfolds; yet it is equally clear that we cannot establish a linear one-to-one correspondence between the two works.[8] Leopold Bloom, whose journey through Dublin on 16 June 1904 provides the main plot structure, is no classical hero. Joyce has deliberately chosen Ulysses as the foil, because he is one of the most 'modern'

---

[7] Sharratt (1994:228) points out that "once the accommodating structure [i.e. Weston's book as well as the Grail legend itself] is itself registered as only another quotation a dizzying instability threatens."

[8] *Ulysses* has spawned an almost endless number of critical article and books. The parallels between *The Odyssey* and *Ulysses* are presented succinctly by Kenner (1955:226-227).

protagonists of the Trojan war.[9] Joyce may use the mythical method to give significance to an otherwise unremarkable and trivial account of 'a day in the life of L. Bloom'.[10] At the same time, the constant references to the 'mythical backdrop' cause an ironic distancing. The actions of the modern protagonists are fractured and distorted reflections of their classic prototypes and although parallels to *The Odyssey* are obvious, the events are no longer embedded in a meaningful context. Modern man may follow in the footsteps of Ulysses, but the structure is no longer able to create meaning. The works of Samuel Beckett, another Irishman, could be seen as the logical continuation of this development – with him even the structural pattern disappears and 'the immense panorama of futility and anarchy' and, one may add, absurdity, presents itself in unmitigated form.

THE FALL OF GONDOLIN – TOLKIEN'S MYTHICAL METHOD?

The great bulk of Tolkien's writings of that period were published only posthumously and the critical assessment, especially of the *History of Middle-earth* volumes, is yet in its infancy.

The Fall of Gondolin, one of the early tales of the *Legendarium*, was written 1916-17 during Tolkien's convalescence from trench fever and revised several times at later dates (*Book of Lost Tales* 2, Tolkien 1992b:146-149). It narrates the fate of the hidden Elven city of Gondolin, its betrayal to the armies of Morgoth, its fall, and the escape of some of its inhabitants, most notably Tuor, Idril and their son Eärendel. Alex Lewis and Elizabeth Currie, in their *The Forsaken Realm of Tolkien. J.R.R. Tolkien and the Medieval Tradition* (2005), argue at

---

[9] His unwillingness to join the Greek forces by feigning madness is not found in Homer, but reported by Apollodorus (*Epitome* 3.7) and Hyginus (*Fabulae* 95).

[10] I am not taking into account the stylistic and formal aspects of *Ulysses*, which contribute considerably to the interest and meaning of the book.

great length that Tolkien was patterning his tale after the medieval (and not the classic Homeric) accounts of the siege and fall of Troy. They point out that many of Tolkien's fellow officers and soldiers would perceive – at least initially – the war in terms of the epic struggle between the Greeks and the Trojans and that *The Iliad* was one of the favourite books among the officers (see Garth 2003:42). *The Iliad* provided thus the foil against which the modern conflict would be seen – with the effect that the glaring discrepancies between classic heroic battle and mechanised modern warfare soon led to a deep-reaching disillusionment. An entire generation of war-poets began to realise that the 'classical centre cannot hold' and, in an attempt to come to terms with the horror of the trenches, turned towards new poetic modes. Tolkien, however, did not do so but, according to Lewis and Currie, recast his traumatic war experiences in the 'classical' form of an epic struggle.

Lewis and Currie's argument has some validity, and the rather obvious parallels between early metallic, fire-breathing dragons and WWI tanks and flame-throwers cannot be denied. Yet to argue that Tolkien consciously modelled his tale on several of the medieval versions of the fall of Troy seems to me to overtax parallels that are likely to occur in any medieval account of a siege. Tolkien may have taken his inspiration from the medieval tales on the fall of Troy, but he went beyond the immediate models and established the (for later times mythical) proto- or archetype of which the legend of Troy is but yet another incarnation. His reaction to the seeming failure of the classic model was thus not the pointed abandonment of the inherited canon and an invitation to chaos, but the re-stating of the basic pattern – a pattern that goes beyond the heroic struggle before the walls of Troy. This way he re-invigorated and, simultaneously, transcended the tradition while his contemporaries believed it no longer possible to find in canonical literature the necessary poetic means to express their ideas and emotions. In *The Waste Land*, for example, the canonical structure has collapsed and the reader may no longer find consolation and meaning in poetry – the chaos of the modern world has not only afflicted moral issues, but it has caught up with literature, too. This is all the more grievous because, as Armstrong (2005:142) argues, literature has often taken over the functions of myths in modern societies. Tolkien, by contrast, still creates meaningful narratives and there is no hint of moral defeatism or lack of moral conviction. On the contrary: the battle for Gondolin is even more a fight between good and evil than the one between Trojans and Greeks, who may not be so easily categorised.[11]

If Tolkien had indeed modelled *The Fall of Gondolin* on the fall of Troy, then he must have taken great care to avoid (or, better, remove) all explicit references to the latter. The published drafts and texts do not provide any evidence for post-facto revisions aiming at removing 'Trojan elements'. It is, however, possible that Tolkien worked along the lines of a submerged 'Trojan pattern'[12] and, consciously or not, avoided all direct references right from the start.[13] We will, for the sake of the development of the argument, assume such a connection, even though it cannot be proven.

It is obvious that Tolkien, in contrast to Joyce, does not use the mythic pattern to control or order his narrative; nor does he need it to convey meaning. The motivation to make use of the Trojan 'myth' would be on another level. As a medievalist, Tolkien was familiar with the widespread belief that leading centres of European culture – be this Rome (Aeneas), France (Antenor), Britain (named 'Bruttenes lond' after Felix Brutus), or New Troy (aka London) – were founded by Trojan

---

[11] Classic and medieval accounts of the Trojan war often differ considerably in their attribution of blame and virtue and thus illustrate the ambiguity of both Greeks and Trojans.

[12] It is therefore, in my opinion, of little use to search for close parallels and detailed comparisons, as Lewis and Currie (2005) do.

[13] Cf. his avoidance and conscious omission of matters religious in *The Lord of the Rings*.

refugees and/or their descendants. The Middle Ages thus looked upon Troy, and not Greece, as the 'mother' of European civilisation[14] and every self-respecting European nation would try and establish such a 'Trojan connection'.[15] As a consequence, the Trojan myth in its medieval form became the 'foundation myth' for most European countries. *The Fall of Gondolin* may have been intended to take up a similar place within the overall structure of the *Legendarium*, and it is from the descendants of Tuor and Idril, via Eärendil and Elwing, that the 'mannish' high culture of Númenor (Elros and descendants), and thus of Gondor and Arnor, derives.[16]

THE MAN IN THE MOON – FROM NONSENSE TO MYTH[17]

Tolkien, in March 1915, wrote the first version of a poem about the Man in the Moon and his ill-fated visit to Norwich. It was published in *A Northern Venture* in 1923[18] and later collected, in a much-changed form, in *The Adventures of Tom Bombadil* (1962), where it appears as poem No. 6. It takes the popular nonsensical nursery rhyme about the Man in the Moon as its starting point:

> The man in the moon
> Came down too soon,
> And asked his way to Norwich;
> He went by the south,

---

[14] The Middle English poem *Sir Gawain and the Green Knight* (c. 1380), edited by Tolkien and Gordon in 1925, recapitulates the 'Trojan foundation myth' succinctly in its first stanza.

[15] See Beaune (1991:226-244), Eley (1991), and Albu (2001).

[16] Tolkien would later combine the 'Trojan model' of the spreading of culture with the 'Atlantis model'.

[17] See Honegger (2005) for an in-depth discussion of the 'Man in the Moon' tradition both in our world and in Tolkien's work.

[18] See also the early version of the poem published by Christopher Tolkien in *The Book of Lost Tales 1* (Tolkien 1994:204-206).

> And burnt his mouth
> With supping cold plum porridge.
> (Opie 1997:346)

Tolkien's poem, then, strives to show that the surviving lines are the sorry and garbled survivals of "an ancient story of earthly disillusionment" (Shippey 2003:37) and he re-creates the original events from the nonsensical rhyme. His technique is similar to that of the nineteenth-century philologists who tried to reconstruct the original states of languages, even cultures, on the basis of the surviving linguistic and literary evidence.[19] Tolkien had also an even more direct model in the short tale 'Puss-Cat Mew' by E.H. Knatchbull-Hugessen (first published 1869, reprinted in Anderson 2003:47-86), which gives the story behind the nursery rhyme

> Puss-cat Mew jumped over a coal;
> In her best petticoat burnt a great hole;
> Puss-cat Mew shan't have any milk
> Till her best petticoat's mended with silk.
> (Anderson 2003:47)[20]

Tolkien knew the tale since, in a letter to Roger Lancelyn Green (Carpenter 2000:407), he writes that he was (i.e. before 1900) "very fond of [a story] called 'Puss Cat Mew'." These aetiological tales are 'mythic' in so far as they 'explain' the nursery rhymes.

Tolkien's Man in the Moon, though certainly not one of the central characters of his works, develops together with and as part of the *Legendarium*. The earliest versions (c. 1915) are making use of real-world geographic references ("Ocean of Almain" (line 40) = the German

---

[19] See Shippey (2003:28-54) for an excellent discussion of this aspect of Tolkien's work.

[20] Opie (1997:425) gives a slightly different version: "Pussy cat Mole jumped over a coal / And in her best petticoat burnt a great hole. / Poor pussy's weeping, she'll have no more milk / Until her best petticoat's mended with silk."

Sea; "a Yarmouth boat" (line 43), "Anglian Norwich" (line 69) etc.), which are, in the later versions, either omitted or replaced by Middle-earth names ("windy Bay of Bel" (line 48) in the 1962 version published in *Adventures*). But the Man in the Moon is not transferred to Middle-earth as a simple after-thought. We find him, complete with his "palid minaret" or "little white turret" at the very inception of Tolkien's universe (c. 1916-17) – as a stowaway on the celestial Ship of the Moon in *The Tale of the Sun and the Moon* (*Lost Tales* 1, Tolkien 1994:174-206). He is described as

> an aged Elf with hoary locks [who ...] stepped upon the Moon unseen and hid him in the Rose, and there dwells he ever since [...]. [T]hat is Uolë Kúvion [...]. Some indeed have named him the Man in the Moon, [...]. (*Lost Tales* 1, Tolkien 1994:192-93)

Christopher Tolkien thinks him a misfit that "seems almost to have strayed in from another conception" (*Lost Tales* 1, Tolkien 1994:202), but Honegger (2005:48-54) has shown how the parallel and simultaneous existence of 'high' and 'low' mimetic elements fits Tolkien's overall vision of the *Legendarium*.

As the example of The Man in the Moon illustrates, Tolkien uses 'myth' on different levels. He, for instance, applies it to reconstruct a coherent background for the garbled and nonsensical pieces that have come down to us. In this, he shares Eliot's discontent with the fragmented nature of contemporary culture. Yet Tolkien takes 'low mimetic' matter as his starting point rather than canonical 'high literature'. His diverging and stylistically versatile renderings of the (basically) same matter illustrate the development and mutation of narratives. However, he does not share the 'romantic' idea of growth, flowering, decline and demise of narrative matters, but advocates a less 'organic' concept as expressed in his image of 'the cauldron of story' ('On Fairy-Stories', Tolkien 1997b:125). 'Low' and 'high' mimetic elements need not inhabit mutually exclusive spheres but may mix and mingle. We find thus no such juxtaposition of 'high mimetic' (*Odyssey*) against 'low mimetic' (a day in the life of L. Bloom) matter, like in Joyce's *Ulysses*, but rather a transitional interconnectedness of the different levels. The 'folksy' figure of the Man in the Moon may strike 'modern' readers as odd in the 'mythic' context of the Lost Tales, but this is due to the post-medieval conception of 'literary propriety' rather than to any inherent literary criteria.

Modernists such as Eliot may mourn the fact that 'high literature' has lost the power to provide meaning to modern life. Tolkien however, in the tradition of the nineteenth-century philologists, would look to the bedrock foundation on which the castles of 'high literature' have been erected: language and folk tales.

Tolkien is also not satisfied with providing merely 'a meaning' to the nonsensical fragments. He, in the case of 'The Man in the Moon', transcends the poem's 'allegorical' nature as a tale of 'earthly disillusionment' and endeavours to penetrate to the 'story behind the story'. This step would bring him inevitably into the realm of 'myth' – which may be defined as the creative attempt of coming to terms with human limitations by means of narrative techniques.[21] Yet Tolkien makes an important differentiation. The 'Man in the Moon' is, as *The Book of Lost Tales* shows, rather an 'Elf in the Moon'. The events described, although irrecoverable in human terms, are within living memory of the Elves (e.g. Galadriel) and not so much 'myth' as 'history'.[22] Tolkien, by

---

[21] See Armstrong (2005:6) who writes: "Mythology was [...] designed to help us to cope with the problematic human predicament. It helped people to find their place in the world and their true orientation."

[22] See Frodo's astonishment at Elrond's account of the Last Alliance: "'You remember?' said Frodo, speaking his thought aloud in his astonishment. [...] [Elrond answers]: "[...] my memory reaches back to the Elder Days. [...]"' ('The Council of Elrond', Tolkien 1992a:260).

means of the Elves and Elvish longevity, establishes direct links to the (human) pre-historic past.

ELVISH LEGENDS

> Gil-galad was an Elven-king.
> Of him the harpers sadly sing:
> the last whose realm was fair and free
> between the Mountains and the Sea.
> (Tolkien 1992a:202)

These lines, spoken by Sam on their way to Weathertop, are no nursery rhyme, but they are equally puzzling to all his companions with the exception of Strider. It is one of those instances of Tolkienian 'depth', i.e. allusions to legends and tales, that evokes the feeling that there are uncounted tales waiting to be told – if there were only time and space enough. We know that the evocation of depth is, in Tolkien's case, no mere bluff. The pre-*Silmarillion* reader may not be familiar with the story of Gil-galad,[23] but this does neither imperil the understanding of the main story nor convey a feeling of chaos. The reader, identifying mostly and predominantly with the 'hobbit narrators',[24] accepts it as part of the wider and as yet unknown world of Middle-earth. Also, and maybe most importantly, Middle-earth is still a basically heroic and pre-modern world that is pervaded, though almost imperceptibly, by Eru's divine will[25] and thus embedded into a larger, meaningful context. Sauron, in the case of *The Lord of the Rings*, is a grave danger to Middle-

---

[23] About sixty pages later, Elrond will provide some further information on Gil-galad and his death on the slopes of Orodruin ('The Council of Elrond', Tolkien 1992a:260), but these references do not constitute a proper narrative.

[24] See Thomas (2000) for a discussion of some of Tolkien's narrators.

[25] See Dickerson (2003) and the study by Honegger, Johnston, Schneidewind, and Weinreich (2005:19-24) for a discussion of free will and predestination in Arda.

earth, yet he does not constitute a threat to the moral or ethic foundations. The Free Peoples are faced with extinction, but not with finding their traditional values rendered useless in a 'modern' world.[26] Yet neither is it a world where God or the gods are still in direct communication with Elves or men. Many of the Elvish legends collected in *The Silmarillion* could be classified as myths of a pre-historic age, to use Armstrong's (2005) categories. They show Elves and 'gods' (Valar) in direct contact and the divine would pervade their daily lives. Things change with the 'fall' of the Elves – at least for those caught up in the consequences of the rape of the Silmarils and the kinslaying of Alqualondë. The Valar largely break off their contact with Middle-earth and it is only once that they, moved by Eärendil's plea, intervene directly and in person at the end of the First Age (War of Wrath). The final rupture, then, happens with the drowning of Númenor and the reshaping of the earth from disc to globe. The Third Age is very much an 'Axial Age'[27] in so far as the sacred seems remote, even alien, and the supreme reality (read 'Valinor') impossibly difficult to access. Also, it is an age during which people are, at least in the latter half, "acutely conscious of the suffering that seem[s] an inescapable part of the human [and, we may add, Elvish] condition" (Armstrong 2005:80-81). *The Lord of the Rings* is very much a myth that illustrates the key characteristics of such an Axial Age. Individual conscience and morality[28] take centre stage and rituals lose in importance. Tolkien's epic does indeed without any reference to organised religion or religious rituals and thus takes the development to its logical consequence.[29] It is, in this aspect, very much a work of a post-

---

[26] 'The New Shadow' (in *Peoples of Middle-earth*, Tolkien 1997c:409-421) may be considered the one tale that comes closest to depicting the 'modern malaise'.

[27] See Armstrong (2005:79-103) for a concise discussion of Karl Jasper's term.

[28] See Honegger, Johnston, Schneidewind and Weinreich (2005) for an in-depth discussion of ethics and morality in Tolkien.

[29] The only instance of a 'religious ritual' to be found in the main text of *The Lord of the Rings* is the Gondorian custom of 'facing west' before sitting down to a meal

axial age where literature has taken over many of the functions of myth. It straddles the ages by participating, on the one hand, in the mythic power of narrative. On the other hand, it acknowledges the transition from 'myth' to 'history' and 'literature' and, implicitly, the loss of the direct link with transcendence.

The Lord of the Rings is thus a literary myth, yet one that does not join the general development of modernist literature. Tolkien, instead of depicting and re-enacting the rupture with tradition and the alienation of modern man, turns to 'literary myth' to present the very same themes. This is not so much due to his 'Victorian' socialisation, as some critics have argued, but rather to his training as philologist and medievalist. As such he was keenly aware that the history of mankind and human culture has not been one of continuous progress, but that it meant more often than not 'fighting the long defeat' – a view that has found its supreme expression in the Ragnarök of northern mythology.[30] Tolkien incorporates this 'pessimistic view' also on a less obvious level, as Dirk Vanderbeke (2005) has illustrated by means of an analysis of Tolkien's valuation of 'knowledge' and 'lore'. 'Knowledge', i.e. information newly acquired by means of research, experiment or logical deduction, usually carries negative connotations and causes destruction, whereas 'lore', i.e. information handed down for generations, is seen positively and is used to heal and construct. Tolkien's perception of loss and encroaching chaos may not be that different from Eliot's or other modernist writers' vision.[31] Yet he is not surprised by the (seemingly

---

(Tolkien 1992a:702-703). The descriptions of Rohirrim burial customs, though they are most likely also part of a religious ritual, make no reference to matters transcendental.

[30] See Tolkien's comments on 'northern courage' (1997a:20-28).

[31] Brooker and Bentley (1990:13) point out that the crisis of the modern world was "related to the collapse of ways of knowing that had served the Western mind at least since the Renaissance and that had received canonical formulation in the seventeenth century of Newton and the philosophy of Descartes."

sudden) breakdown of traditional values. Tolkien does not show the *literati* of Middle-earth composing elegiac poems in the manner of *The Waste Land*, nor are his protagonists depicted as leading an alienated existence like Joyce's 'modern Ulysses' Leopold Bloom.

There are, of course, no exact equivalents to either of the two in *The Lord of the Rings*. The hobbits, as Shippey (2003:55-93) has argued persuasively, are the closest we get to 'modern man'. Yet even their attitudes, customs, and ideals are markedly pre- (and sometimes anti-) modern. This is also true for Bilbo who is the most prominent author/narrator-figure. He is a preserver rather than a creator and his 'poetic' achievement seems to consist mainly in collecting, editing, translating and adapting Elvish lore and 'literature'. In this, he resembles the nineteenth-century philologists rather than the twentieth-century poets. There is, however, one important difference between Bilbo on the one hand, and the nineteenth-century philologists, on the other, namely the differing nature of their access to the mythical. Jacob Grimm, for example, had to try and reconstruct the (largely) lost tradition of early Germanic myths and legends by means of the surviving fragments and allusions in literature and language. He published the results of his painstaking research in the three volumes of his *Teutonic Mythology* (*Deutsche Mythologie*) in 1835. The Elf-friend[32] Bilbo, by contrast, had still direct access to the mythic past via the Elves, who are living real-world relics of this (for humans) 'mythic' time. The Elves are, on the one hand, preservers of the mythic tradition and the leading figures of Rivendell and Lothlórien still remember the 'mythic times' of the Elder Days.[33] On the other hand, these Elvish leaders are also real-world incarnations of the mythic, who preserved direct access to the transcenden-

---

[32] See Flieger (2000) for a discussion of the topos of the Elf-friend.
[33] It is, however, necessary to differentiate between low mimetic elves (e.g. whose comical songs accompany the arrival of Thorin & Co. at Rivendell in *The Hobbit*) and high mimetic elves (e.g. Elrond himself).

tal.[34] As Gandalf points out, talking about Glorfindel, "those who have dwelt in the Blessed Realm live at once in both worlds" (Tolkien 1992a:239) and, as the narrator comments, "in Lórien the ancient things still lived on in the waking world" (Tolkien 1992a:368).

CONCLUSION

The quickening pace of a changing world increasingly endangers the Elvish tradition of memory and direct participation in the transcendence. The Passing of the Elves at the end of the Third Age signals the loss of the direct access to 'mythic dreamtime'. All that remains is to "keep alive the memory of the age that is gone" (Tolkien 1992a:1067).[35] And this is what Tolkien is doing in *The Lord of the Rings*, which has been written in a 'modern' age when even the *logos* (i.e. the theme of the post-axial age centring on logic and reason) has lost its power. It is, to some extent, a retreat to an earlier, axial age, and tries to re-cast its basic truth in a 'modern' form.

The Lord of the Rings is a fairy tale in Tolkien's sense of the word[36] in so far as the readers catch a glimpse of a fuller communion between the transcendence and our world – a communion that has been, in later times, seemingly replaced by the *logos* of the post-axial age, that, in turn, has caved in under the weight of 'modern' reality. Yet even though it may look as if 'things fall apart', we must not give up hope and, against all hope, trust in the final eucatastrophe in favour of mankind and the entire creation. This does not mean that we can expect this 'joyous turn' to occur in our own lifetime. We may have to spend our lives fighting the long defeat, but, if we accept Tolkien's message, it

---

[34] See Hiley (2004:844-45) who discusses this form of 'myth-realization'.
[35] The feeling of nostalgia is also prominent in modernist writing (cf. Barry 1995:83), yet it does not attain mythic power.
[36] See Tolkien (1997b).

is not a pointless battle. *The Lord of the Rings* does remind us of the basic (metaphysical) truths and patters[37] underlying human existence and thus provides "a way of controlling, of ordering, of giving a shape and a significance to the immense panorama of futility and anarchy which is contemporary history" (Eliot 1975:177).

THOMAS HONEGGER holds a Ph.D. from the University of Zurich and is the author of *From Phoenix to Chauntecleer: Medieval English Animal Poetry* (1996). He has co-written a study on the moral dimension in Tolkien's narrative work (*Eine Grammatik der Ethik* 2005) and edited numerous volumes on Tolkien and medieval language and literature. He has furthermore written about Chaucer, Shakespeare, and mediaeval romance and is currently involved in a large-scale project for a web-based interdisciplinary encyclopaedia of animals in medieval literature. He teaches, since 2002, as Professor for Mediaeval Studies at the Friedrich-Schiller-University Jena (Germany).
Homepage: http://www2.uni-jena.de/fsu/anglistik/homepage/Honegger3.htm

---

[37] Brooker and Bentley (1990:17) argue that the old Newtonian 'dispensation' which favoured 'causation' as the dominant principle, has been superseded, since Nils Bohr's discoveries, by 'chance'. Tolkien's point of view could be seen as an alternative to this new 'dispensation'.

Bibliography

Albu, Emily, 2001, *The Normans in Their Histories: Propaganda, Myth and Subversion*, Woodbridge: The Boydell Press.

Allison, Alexander W. et al. (eds.), 1983, *The Norton Anthology of Poetry*, (third edition), New York and London: Norton.

Anderson, Douglas A. (ed.), 2003, *Tales before Tolkien: The Roots of Modern Fantasy*, New York: Del Rey.

Armstrong, Karen, 2005, *A Short History of Myth*, Edinburgh: Canongate.

Barry, Peter, 1995, *Beginning Theory*, Manchester: Manchester University Press.

Beaune, Colette, 1991, *The Birth of an Ideology. Myths and Symbols of Nation in Late-Medieval France*, (translated by Susan Ross Huston, edited by Fredrich L. Cheyette; French original *Naissance de la nation France* published 1985), Berkeley, Los Angeles, Oxford: University of California Press.

Bell, Michael and Peter Poellner (eds.), 1998, *Myth and the Making of Modernity*, Amsterdam: Rodopi.

Brooker, Jewel Spears and Joseph Bentley, 1990, *Reading 'The Waste Land': Modernism and the Limits of Interpretation*, Amherst: The University of Massachusetts Press.

Carpenter, Humphrey, 1977, *J.R.R. Tolkien: A Biography*, London: Unwin Hyman.

---, (edited with the assistance of Christopher Tolkien), 2000, *The Letters of J.R.R. Tolkien*, (first published 1981), Boston and New York: Houghton Mifflin.

Davidson, Harriet, 1994, 'Improper Desire: Reading *The Waste Land*', in A. David Moody (ed.), 1994, *The Cambridge Companion to T.S. Eliot*, Cambridge: Cambridge University Press, pp. 121-131.

Dickerson, Matthew, 2003, *Following Gandalf. Epic Battles and Moral Victory in The Lord of the Rings*, Grand Rapids, MI: Brazos Press.

Eley, Penny, 1991, 'The Myth of the Trojan Descent', *Nottingham Medieval Studies* 35, 1991, pp. 27-40.

Eliot, Thomas S., 1974, *Collected Poems 1909-1962*, London: Faber & Faber.

---, 1975, *Selected Prose of T.S. Eliot*, (edited by Frank Kermode), London: Faber & Faber.

Emig, Rainer, 1998, 'Macro-myths and Micro-myths: Modernist Poetry and the Problem of Artistic Creation', in Michael Bell and Peter Poellner (eds.), 1998, *Myth and the Making of Modernity*, Amsterdam: Rodopi, pp. 181-196.

Flieger, Verlyn, 1997, *A Question of Time: J.R.R. Tolkien's Road to Faërie*, Kent, Ohio: The Kent State University Press.

---, 2000, 'The Footsteps of Aelfwine', in Verlyn Flieger and Carl F. Hostetter (eds.), 2000, *Tolkien's Legendarium. Essays on The History of Middle-earth*, Westport, Connecticut and London: Greenwood Press, pp. 183-198.

Garth, John, 2003, *Tolkien and the Great War. The Threshold of Middle-earth*, London: HarperCollins.

Gish, Nancy K., 1988, *The Waste Land: A Poem of Memory and Desire*, Boston: Twayne Publishers.

Grimm, Jacob, 1875-78, *Deutsche Mythologie*, (three volumes; fourth edition; first edition 1835; reprint 1992), Wiesbaden: Drei Lilien Verlag.

Hammond, Wayne G. (with the assistance of Douglas Anderson), 1993, *J.R.R. Tolkien: A Descriptive Bibliography*, Winchester: St Paul's Bibliographies.

Hiley, Margaret, 2004, 'Stolen Language, Cosmic Models: Myth and Mythology in Tolkien', in *Modern Fiction Studies* 50, 2004, pp. 838-860.

Honegger, Thomas, 2005, 'The Man in the Moon: Structural Depth in Tolkien', in Thomas Honegger (ed.), 2005, *Root & Branch: Approaches towards Understanding Tolkien*, (second edition; first edition 1999), Zurich and Berne: Walking Tree Publishers, pp. 9-70.

---, Andrew James Johnston, Friedhelm Schneidewind, Frank Weinreich, 2005, *Eine Grammatik der Ethik*, Saarbrücken: Edition Stein und Baum.

Joyce, James, 1992, *Ulysses*, (first editon 1922), London: Penguin.

Kenner, Hugh, 1955, *Dublin's Joyce*, London: Chatto and Windus.

Lewis, Alex and Elizabeth Currie, 2005, *The Forsaken Realm of Tolkien. J.R.R. Tolkien and the Medieval Tradition*, Oswestry: Medea Publishing.

Longenbach, James, 1994, '"Mature poets steal": Eliot's Allusive Practice', in A. David Moody (ed.), 1994, *The Cambridge Companion to T.S. Eliot*, Cambridge: Cambridge University Press, pp. 176-188.

Opie, Iona and Peter (eds.), 1997, *The Oxford Dictionary of Nursery Rhymes*, (second edition; first edition 1951), Oxford: At the Clarendon Press.

Rabaté, Jean-Michel, 1994, 'Tradition and T.S. Eliot', in A. David Moody (ed.), 1994, *The Cambridge Companion to T.S. Eliot*, Cambridge: Cambridge University Press, pp. 210-222.

Rosebury, Brian, 2003, *Tolkien: A Cultural Phenomenon*, (revised and enlarged edition; first published 1992), Houndmills: Palgrave Macmillan.

Sharratt, Bernard, 1994, 'Eliot: Modernism, Postmodernism, and After', in A. David Moody (ed.), 1994, *The Cambridge Companion to T.S. Eliot*, Cambridge: Cambridge University Press, pp. 223-235.

Shippey, Tom A., 2000, *J.R.R. Tolkien: Author of the Century*, London: HarperCollins.

---, 2003, *The Road to Middle-earth*, (third edition; first edition 1982; second edition 1992), New York: Houghton Mifflin.

Thomas, Paul Edmund, 2000, 'Some of Tolkien's Narrators', in George Clark and Daniel Timmons (eds.), 2000, *J.R.R. Tolkien and His Literary Resonances*, Westport, CT: Greenwood Press, pp. 161-181.

Tolkien, John Ronald Reuel, 1923a, 'Tha Eadigan Saelidan', in *A Northern Venture*, Leeds: Swan Press, pp. 15-16.

---, 1923b, 'Why the Man in the Moon Came Down Too Soon', In *A Northern Venture*, Leeds: Swan Press, pp. 17-19.

---, 1923c, 'Enigmata Saxonica Nuper Inventa Duo', in *A Northern Venture*, Leeds: Swan Press, p. 20.

--- and Eric V. Gordon (eds.), 1925, *Sir Gawain and the Green Knight*, Oxford: At the Clarendon Press.

---, 1992a, *The Lord of the Rings*, (one volume edition with the text of the second edition; first edition 1954-55; second edition 1966), London: HarperCollins.

---, 1992b, *The Book of Lost Tales 2*, (edited by Christopher Tolkien, *History of Middle-earth* volume 2; paperback edition; first edition 1984), London: HarperCollins.

---, 1993, *The Treason of Isengard*, (edited by Christopher Tolkien, *History of Middle-earth* volume 7; paperback edition; first edition 1989), London: HarperCollins.

---, 1994, *The Book of Lost Tales 1*, (edited by Christopher Tolkien, *History of Middle-earth* volume 1; paperback edition; first edition 1983), London: HarperCollins.

---, 1995, *The Adventures of Tom Bombadil*, (first edition 1962), London: HarperCollins.

---, 1997a, 'Beowulf: The Monsters and the Critics', (originally the Sir Israel Gollancz Memorial Lecture to the British Academy read on 25 November 1936; first published in 1939), in John Ronald Reuel Tolkien, 1997, *The Monster and the Critics and Other Essays*, (edited by Christopher Tolkien), London: HarperCollins, pp. 5-48.

---, 1997b, 'On Fairy-Stories', (originally Andrew Lang Lecture given on 8 March 1939; first published in 1947), in John Ronald Reuel Tolkien, 1997, *The Monster and the Critics and Other Essays*, (edited by Christopher Tolkien), London: HarperCollins, pp. 109-161.

---, 1997c, *The Peoples of Middle-earth*, (edited by Christopher Tolkien, *History of Middle-earth* volume 12; paperback edition; first edition 1996), London: HarperCollins.

Vanderbeke, Dirk, 2005, 'Language, Lore and Learning in *The Lord of the Rings*', in Thomas Honegger (ed.), 2005, *Reconsidering Tolkien*, (Cormarë Series 8), Zurich and Berne: Walking Tree Publishers, pp. 129-151.

The Shaping of 'Reality' in Tolkien's Works: An Aspect of Tolkien and Modernity

HEIDI KRUEGER

(translated by Heidi Steimel)

Abstract

One of the key terms in the history of literature from the beginning until today is 'reality'. The way reality is shaped and interpreted in a work is an important criterion for recognizing whether the author is working on contributing to the cultural task of his time or whether he refuses to do so. This essay places Tolkien, on the one hand, in the context of a broad literary current which opposes the conventional concept of modernity and partially overcomes it. On the other hand it investigates some of Tolkien's central literary means in order to position him in relation to the 'modern' interpretation of reality within this literary-cultural current. It remains to be seen that Tolkien's *way* to create reality not only follows progressive literary programmes of earlier authors but also leads to new territory by means of his narrative technique – despite a superficially conventional narrative approach. He thereby confronts our time with a concept of reality that requires further investigation.

1 INTRODUCTION TO THE QUESTION: WHAT IS MODERNITY?

The title of this book project is: *Tolkien and Modernity*. This can be understood in various respects. For example: "How does *Tolkien* judge the modern world?" Or: "How does *modernism* judge Tolkien?" Or: "What connection exists between Tolkien's *work* and modernity?"

I have chosen the third version, though I shall touch upon the others. Therefore I shall, among other things, answer the question: Can Tolkien's works be considered modern in any way, yes or no?

First of all two further questions must be answered: What is 'the Modern'? And: What establishes the modernity of a literary work? –

These are very difficult questions, and I would like to give some rather common answers first:

The Modern is usually understood as concerning the time since the Enlightenment, the beginning of industrialisation and the emancipation of the individual. Everything that is analyzed with critical reason is modern; everything that eludes it is not.

A literary work is felt to be modern when its *form* differs significantly from the accustomed literary works on the one hand, and when it concerns and reacts to modern social, political, cultural, intellectual or similar processes, on the other. Conversely, works are frequently considered *not* modern, but rather escapist or even reactionary if they are conventional in *form* on the one hand and do not face up to modern processes on the other, either because they offer only entertainment or because they – though in themselves of artistic worth – hold on to values that are considered antiquated and outdated. Cheap novels ('Heimatromane') are an example of the first type of literature; literary Romanticism, accused of falling back to a time before the Enlightenment, even before the Renaissance, and of attempting to invoke irrationalisms that have been combated and destroyed with so much effort and success, would be an example of the second type.

These commonplace conceptions are frequently used to judge the modernity of Tolkien's works – not only by critics, but often by the Tolkien community itself. The key word is 'escapism' ('flight from reality') – considered negative by the critics, though frequently positive by the community.

An in depth look into the discussion and research concerning the nature of modernity in aesthetic-literary works is necessary in order to get away from the conventional answers. At this point I would like to restrict my subject for the first time: This essay is not concerned with the connection between Tolkien and modernity in general, but with the *concept of reality* in modernity.

2 PLACING TOLKIEN'S WORK IN A GREATER LITERARY CONTEXT

Since the accusation of escapism (flight from reality) plays such an important role in the judgement of Tolkien's works, I would like to point out the fact that this accusation is shared with many other authors since the Enlightenment who did not serve the mainstream. There have always been undercurrents in literary history that do not see the 'ratio' as the only part of civilized man worth cultivating, but that deal intensively with the subconscious of man and humanity, with dreams, projections, delusions, and visions – and give these a literary place; specifically all that can be called 'unreal' or 'surreal'. The most prominent example is the previously mentioned literary Romanticism, which gained a hold in all of Europe. Dada as well, an influential though brief era, is also a part of this undercurrent, which was always present, though sometimes almost invisible and often disparaged.

For example, it is obvious that Tolkien's works belong to this undercurrent because both Dada and Tolkien intended to create new realities out of the sound of language,[1] that both the Romanticists and Tolkien wrote *art legends* and *art fairy stories* on the one hand, investigated what was enchanting and wondrous on the other: this above all else is interpreted as a flight from hard reality. But that does not claim that Tolkien's works are on a level with the aesthetic quality of the representatives of both above-named literary eras. However, it does open up the possibility of seeing Tolkien in the context of a wide cultural current in order to make the assessment of this phenomenon fruitful for the interpretation of Tolkien by research.

---

[1] Tolkien's often expressed thought that the *semantic* meaning of a word is not its primary meaning, but that the uncorrupted human makes his own inner image of things, which can be expressed adequately by sound rather than by meaning, is partially also the origin of Dada.

2.1 Literary Romanticism and Its Evaluation Regarding Modernity

2.1.1 The Previous Model

If we view the triumph of the natural sciences over humans and society as a criterion of modernity, then we can assign Romanticism a retrograde function in the three-part division of history – classical antiquity/Germanic period – Middle Ages – modern age (from the Renaissance or Enlightenment until today): with the Enlightenment the struggle of rationality against irrationalisms and all systems of rule began, whether the belief in irrational powers or natural spirits, or the voluntary and involuntary subordination under unlegitimized orders and authorities. In this model Romanticism is regressive, as it does not accept the Enlightenment with rationality's claim to power, but falls back on pre-Enlightenment thought patterns.

This increases if we decide to begin the modern age not with the Enlightenment but with the 20th century: the experience of two world wars, in which the appeal to the irrational nature of man dragged a whole part of the world into intellectual and spiritual ruin seems to require once again that human rationality triumphs, that all irrational efforts be combated with literary works too, because they carry pre- or post-fascist traits. As a matter of fact, both Romanticism as well as Tolkien are often associated subliminally with 'forbidden' views.

Now, cultural research has not stood still, and today we find ourselves – though this has apparently not yet entered the consciousness of the critics – in a complete re-orientation concerning the evaluation of Romanticism. I would like to deal with this more comprehensively here, as this also throws a decisively new light on Tolkien's work.

2.1.2 The New Model

Marianne Thalmann, who is well-known through her analysis of art fairy tales of the Romantic age, published her work *Das Märchen und die Moderne* (*The Fairy Tale and Modernity*) with the subtitle: *Zum Begriff der Surrealität im Märchen der Romantik* (*On the Concept of Surreality in Fairy Tales of the Romantic*) in 1961. I would like to quote two excerpts from two passages of this book:

> Today we are aware of the fact that Romanticism is closer to us than an unromantic post-war generation seems to consider plausible. In the Romantic age a young generation made an effort to distance itself from a classical model, and it attempted to push the limits of what is sayable further into the future. The fact that new horizons emerged no longer needs to be defended. It needs neither to be admired nor condemned. However, we must assess Romanticism as a first rebellion of the modern age, to which we today have an historic distance. (Thalmann 1966:5)

> The thrust of these forces, which takes place under the protection of fairy-tale fiction and is allowed to distort and deform, prepared the way for the birth of modernity. It is a beginning that will not die.
> (Thalmann 1966:109)

From these texts we can infer that Thalmann (already in 1961) makes an assessment of modernity in which Romanticism does not stand in opposition to it but rather establishes the *foundation* for it. Through Romanticism, potentialities were developed for the literary opening up of horizons that had remained unexplored till then; these crossings of borders prepare the way for new thinking by *revolting* against the fixed boundaries of the Enlightenment and Classicism. In this respect Romanticism's concern is *future oriented* and not – though it may appear to be so on the surface – looking backwards.

Dirk von Petersdorff, a prize-winning poet and literary scholar at the University of Saarbrücken, born in 1966, has also analyzed the significance of Romanticism for current modernity, almost forty years later and – at the point of time of writing – forty years younger than the Grande Dame of literary research. Here is a quote by Dirk von Petersdorff:

> Since the epochal year 1989 a renewed thinking about the conditions of modernity is taking place, because a system of life and faith disappeared with the decline of the last political religion. [...]
> For Romanticism is the first philosophic-aesthetic movement which reflects the conditions of modernity and has formulated answers to it that came alive again in the 19th and 20th centuries in various forms and under changed circumstances.
> (von Petersdorff 1999:80)

Similarly to Thalmann, von Petersdorff therefore sees an acute reason for dealing with the fundamentals of Romanticism in the respective concrete current situation, which requires a *new orientation*. Thalmann has recognized that this literature opens new horizons, that, in other words, the deadlocked conception of reality is widened by it. Dirk von Petersdorff looks more closely at the theoretic reflections of Romanticists, which reflect an alternative for the destroyed view of life of whole generations.

At that time Thalmann met with a lack of understanding in the academic world, for the most part. But forty years later this "world had changed". Dirk von Petersdorff is not at all, at the turn of the millennium, a lone voice that took up and deepened Thalmann's re-evaluation.

In 1996 an international congress took place in Hildesheim on the topic: *Ästhetische Moderne in Europa – Grundzüge und Problemzusammenhänge seit der Romantik (Aesthetic Modernity in Europe – Characteristics and Problem Connections since the Romantic Age)*.[2]

---

[2] Quoted here as ÄME

The conclusions that were won there and published in an extensive anthology in 1998 are absolutely amazing. The 're-evaluation' of Romanticism is taken on so radically, the criteria of modernity are so extended, specified, and newly established, that not only the intellectual-cultural development from antiquity to the present, not only the romanticist undercurrents, but implicitly Tolkien's works become perceptible in a completely different streamline and network.

2.2 Modernity in a New Light

The contributors see the beginning of European modernity not in the Enlightenment, not in the 20th century, but actually in early German Romanticism around 1800. That does not mean that they were not aware that the entire development is rooted in the collapse of classical antiquity (compare ÄME 3). But it would be the year 1800 that would have initiated something new which would still have a lasting effect today. What was first radically adopted as a programme by early Romanticism would finally have found its literary realization partially in the 20th century, and would partially yet to be realized. Actually, we would find ourselves only at the beginning of the entire development, into which a new consciousness would attempt to come through. Eras such as Rationalism or Naturalism – hitherto evaluated as mainstream, which would repeatedly have been foolishly undermined by irrationalisms such as Neoromanticism – are here seen as eras that interrupted the birth of modernity.

That is daring – it is really daring. Here two separate concepts of modernity stand opposite one another: *rationalistic* modernity and the *consciousness crisis* of modernity. Both are part of modernity in all of their strained tension and their struggle against each other. And both have their counterparts on the aesthetic level:

Rationalistic modernity, which owes its success among other things to the triumph of instrumental reason and is characterized by basic concepts such as progress, individuality, self-determination, and secularization, has its equivalent on an aesthetic level in literary norms such as unity in meaning, coherence, and closeness.

And the *consciousness crisis* of modernity, which accompanies the great tension in world history and has taken place through the breaking down and the fragility of rationalism, has its equivalent on an aesthetic level in concepts such as reflexivity, incoherence, fragmentalization, self-representation, experimentalism, etc. (compare ÄME 290).

With that an era covering approximately 200 years – as of 1800 – is focused on, into which we ourselves (including Tolkien) belong and which – despite or perhaps because of the inner contradictions – increasingly pursues an overall theme, whose emergence and development we can observe and describe, once it has been identified, though its end is still open.

Therefore if one agrees with this there can be no doubt that Tolkien is part of this complicated process. Whether he plays a large or merely small role there may be proved someday. The contributors to the Romanticism Symposium are aware of the fact that research on this new view of modernity is still in its beginnings. The same holds true for Tolkien research. It would be good if the investigation of Tolkien's works were simultaneously a brick in the answer to the question, what composes modernity specifically and what kind of modernity actually is supposed to be 'born' since the Renaissance, what with the labour pains lasting for centuries. The question is no longer: Can Tolkien's works be referred to as modern in any sense of the word, yes or no? But: Which contribution has Tolkien made to modernity?

3 WHICH CONTRIBUTION DOES TOLKIEN MAKE TO AESTHETIC MODERNITY?

First we must examine whether at least some of the criteria, which have hitherto been considered typical for the question of modernity, actually apply to Tolkien.

At this point I must again limit my theme: This essay is not primarily concerned with the changed conception of reality *per se*, but rather with that which is produced by aesthetic-fictional literature. Of course the two are connected: a changed consciousness of reality will have an effect on art. And a new artistic style will have a changed consciousness of reality underlying it. New artistic styles may even create a new consciousness. However, the method of literary research is, among other things, to uncover and describe changed literary reality – in comparison with other literary works – by way of analysis of artistic works.

I would like to supplement the new developments that have appeared on the horizon since Romanticism with a further quote from the foreword of the above-mentioned anthology, in order to establish a concrete basis for the treatment of this topic:

> This is the quintessence that we can note: Only since the Romantic age has that dialectic taken place which is constitutive for the modern age as a whole, according to Michel Foucault. Though Foucault also sees the unthought, later known as the dimension of the un- and preconscious, principally set with Descartes' reality principle of *cogito*, nevertheless the actual history of modernity can only begin when the firm foundation of absolutized reason begins to shake. In philosophical history, this happened after Kant, historically after the *terreur* of the French Revolution. Only here does the concrete dialectic of a specifically modern history of subjectivity begin, which rebuilds the whole of reality according to technical-economic progress in a planetary style on the one hand, but in-

> creasingly must plumb the uncertainty and bottomless depths of modern self-experience on the other. (ÄME 40-41)

This and the previous quotes show in all urgency that the breaking down and the fragility of rationalism, the destructiveness of the world view of natural sciences, the ever stronger and more threatening consciousness of *subjectivity*, the deep fear and panic-producing question, whether our Self is even what it appears to be, the growing dread of uncontrollable and inscrutable powers – that all of this can neither be adequately described nor resolved by works of art in their previous *realistic* forms. New ways must be sought in order to recognize both the "dimensions of being" which have become conscious and the "uncertainty and bottomlessness" *as reality*, to 'plumb' their depths and to shape them artistically.

From the abundance of possibilities I have chosen two central literary artistic methods, which were raised to be a program in the Romantic age, which were – consciously or unconsciously – decisively developed by Tolkien and were considered essential in further important works of modernity (or pre-modernity), though in a different fashion, in order to shape newly perceived phenomena as reality.

3.1 The Un- and Preconscious or:
Legend, Fairy Tale, Myth, and the Fantastic

3.1.1 Making Subreality Visible

With a sure instinct, Tolkien from the very beginning grasped a literary form that is able to focus the dimension of the 'un- and preconscious' as well as to make it visible in literary form. The yearning for a 'different and lost land' is expressed already in his early poems,[3] and the search for

---

[3] For example in the poems 'Come sing ye light fairy things', 1910, Carpenter (2002:71) and 'Eärendel sprang up from the Ocean's Cup', 1914, Carpenter (2002:101-102).

what was lost runs through his whole life's work, experiencing a broad range of expression. Earlier, Schiller speaks of the loss which mankind suffered when natural existence was given up – had to be given up –,[4] in order to develop further in his consciousness. The Romantics broadened that to include the lost *mythical* consciousness and so made a topic of the lack not only in the individual but also in a whole civilization. And they speak of the responsibility of poetry to find what was lost and to win it back again.[5] What Marianne Thalmann recognized as 'surreal' in romantic fairy tales – that which transcends reality – can also be described as subreality: what lies underneath reality and so achieves a psychological or collective-psychological component.

Modernity's problem is, however, the fact that this un- and preconsciousness can frequently only appear in the form of a devil, because it was repressed and 'devilized' for so long.

Precisely this problem was developed by Goethe in his *Faust*: Faust is magically attracted to Mephisto, actually a 'fantastic creature' like the ringwraiths: this devil's sphere of existence is a part of our western culture, as effective as every other reality. Thomas Mann, a contemporary of Tolkien's, referred to this layer as the 'demonic', which is latently present in our culture and can break through at any time.[6] Thomas Mann also needed 'fantastic' alienated figures for that: The strange wanderer and the false youth in *Der Tod in Venedig* (*Death in Venice*) run through the whole novel and show up in places where they – always as the same – normally could not do so geographically. Franz Kafka,[7] also a contemporary of Tolkien's, succeeds in visualizing the horror that comes from reality as well only through literary alienation. And Tolkien?

---

[4] Compare Schiller (e.g. 1972:5 and 22).
[5] Compare Fr. Schlegel, *Rede über die Mythologie*.
[6] See on this topic, above all, Thomas Mann, *Doktor Faustus*.
[7] The most important work of Franz Kafka in this context is probably *Der Prozess*.

3.1.2 Does Tolkien Make Sub-reality Visible?

The decisive question will be whether his whole fantastic arsenal is only 'show' – a playful skirmish with dragons and wizards, goblins and elven beings – or whether there is a genuinely existential statement behind it, born of our time and able to open our eyes concerning subliminal matters which occur in our time.

Even if a thorough answer to this question goes beyond my topic, I would at least like to suggest a way to explore this: There is a fairy tale by Ludwig Tieck, *Der Runenberg* (*The Rune Mountain*), published in 1804. The protagonist, a young, restless man – comparable to Eriol of *The Book of Lost Tales* – sees a gigantic supernatural female figure in the magical rune mountain on one of his wanderings. He is bewitched by her, but also fears her and sees her as a great danger. Even without much knowledge of literary history it is obvious that this woman is a relic of matriarchal paganism, which clearly endangers the simple, orderly, and content life, which appears to be the ideal. The fairy tale therefore expresses a conflict between competitive views of life and the world: the threat to self by past, yet not overcome dimensions of being.

In *The Lord of the Rings* we find two similarly opposing and structured interpretations of the world and life: the familiar, homey, well-protected Shire – and the dangerous strangeness that breaks into the well-defined daily life both as a threat and as a fascination.[8] Within the literary context, they stand opposite of that which is sheltered as something foreign, even alienated: Tieck's supernatural woman, Tolkien's living-dead ringwraith, Thomas Mann's strange wanderer, and Goethe's demonic being Mephisto. However, outside of the literary context they are – if they are genuine confrontations with modern times – part of the

---

[8] On this topic of both 'worlds' compare Krüger (2006), 'Der Autor als Chronist'.

human race, part of its history, its civilization, and its future; though they are in themselves disintegrated and hostile.

Whether genuine confrontations with modern times or modern people can be found in Tolkien's work will be easier to answer if we find the track of the mystery of this 'other-reality' (corresponding with the sub- or surreal), which is not possible here. For this does not only contain the ringwraiths and Sauron in Tolkien's works, but also lofty Elven beings and natural deities; and these are in no way clearly delineated from one another, but are linked to each other. This is already shown in *Faust*, where the Otherworld holds God and angels, sphinxes and kabirs and more besides Mephisto. It is also shown in Romanticism, where in *Der Goldene Topf* (*The Golden Pot*) by E.T.A. Hoffmann, for example, the wicked woman also takes on motherly characteristics, whereas the good spirit prince takes on demonic traits (similar to the *Zauberflöte/The Magic Flute*). The Subreal does not function causally, not dually, but ambivalently, like our dreams and our psyche. In Tolkien's works we see this interconnection, for example, in that Galadriel is experienced very differently by Boromir than by Frodo – in the eyes of many she is a dangerous woman. Only if the *ambivalence* of this subreal world, even first of all this mythical world as an opposite or supplementary world to the ordinary world, is seen and studied, can the question be answered, whether Tolkien grasped effective forces of our time or era.

It cannot be overlooked that all these fantastic figures and happenings are in a certain measure both remnants of our cultural past and present, as well as of our own psyche. They are partly our nightmares made visible, even when they appear filtered through the hobbits – for they are at first *their* nightmares, not ours.[9] I would like to add that there are not a few young people today who consider Tolkien's ring-

---

[9] On the forming of the narrative levels in *The Lord of the Rings* compare Krüger (2006).

wraiths *real* – undead who have been steering our world, the capital, and the decisions of governments for centuries. Such things result when artistically created realities cannot be distinguished from realities that *actually* exist; reason is flooded by subreality, so to speak, and submits to it.

3.1.3 The Relationship between Real and Subreal

In this context it is highly interesting that the 'other side' wins for Tieck. The protagonist is finally bewitched by the supernatural woman and appears – to the world – to have gone mad. Yet the storyteller leaves no doubt, that even the encounter with her is a disaster and that one should beware of such encounters, that is: raising the fence against these dangers.[10]

How different is this 150 years later in Tolkien's writing, where the demonic madness – seen in real history – has seized and shaken whole peoples: in all of his works, where the confrontation with the 'other side of reality' is a theme, there is no warning against this confrontation, but the opposite: it is recognized as absolutely necessary. Not those who flee are shown, not those bewitched by the demonic side, but those who face it. If we consider that the story of the Ring is not one of the genuine past, but a fairy story and legend, that makes subreal reality visible which is present here and now, then we can recognize one of the many opposites to Romanticism: there is no longer time to ignore the situation.

The Notion Club Papers describe the seriousness of this situation in all urgency: The 'other reality' makes itself noticeable in the ordinary reality – like it is for Thomas Mann, for Kafka, for the Romanticists, though in varying degrees. It 'calls'. In all of these works there are individuals who hear this call and must follow it. But who or what is calling?

---

[10] In *Der Goldene Topf*, however, the 'Other-Reality' wins in the positive sense of the word: The protagonist forsakes the normal reality and stays in Atlantis (the realm of poetry) forever.

And just what is the situation? The protagonists of *The Notion Club Papers* differentiate themselves from earlier poets in that they are not victims, but rather school their sensitivity consciously, in order to be able to stand up to the task.

The *Hobbit*-Bilbo is no longer a victim either. The entire work is based on the dangerous magic, which comes from the lofty aesthetics of beautiful shining jewels. The dwarves' deep-flowing singing, full of longing, in Bilbo's hole is a prelude to the danger that possesses Bilbo briefly. Faust experiences lasting change by Mephisto, and for him deed and force become one. Gustav Aschenbach[11] cannot separate beauty and desire and, as a result, he dies. But Bilbo frees himself of the 'dwarvish desire' with little literary effort – Tolkien needs no more than a brief casual sentence (*The Hobbit* p. 287) – in order to end a world battle in which so many are bewitched by the dragon magic. Again it is highly interesting that Tolkien refuses to use the classical solution of a well-constructed adventure story, incidentally: Bilbo's acquired inner independence is of absolutely no use in this world battle, his sacrifice does not end the battle. Instead he is taken out of the middle of the action and can go home. The actual adventure seems to take place elsewhere and is not a part of this story.

3.2 Fragment and Incoherence

> It is not necessary to provide an elaborate proof for the correctness of the thesis, that the aesthetic was always or almost always linked to the principle of uniformity, coherence and functional closeness in the western history of art and thought. (ÄME 179)

---

[11] Gustav Aschenbach is the main protagonist, an author, in *Der Tod in Venedig*.

This quote by Jürgen H. Petersen describes once more the ideal of humanistic-classicistic cultural understanding in contrast to aesthetic modernity, which attempts to find its way on a rubble heap of ideals and illusions. Even without taking into account the shock that a positive view of humanity experienced from unimaginably cruel torture and perversity, inflicted on humans by humans, the path which the history of thought has taken makes clear that the firm ground of self-security must break away beneath humanity some day. When Immanuel Kant (in 1781/87)[12] showed the limits of the intellect understandably and effectively for an era, namely that man does not see reality as it is with his intellect, but rather as it appears to be, that is: according to the inherent structure of the intellect; when in addition to that psychoanalysis emerges around 1900,[13] which proves that the intellect not only deceives itself about the outside world, but also that the self, for reasons of self-preservation, is frequently a *construction* of securities, which deceives itself so much as to its own real being and as to the real being of others, because it perceives itself mirrored everywhere and does not penetrate to reality: then there is real trouble. For then the so-called ordinary reality is a *false* reality, and the modern quest immediately is: Seek the *real* reality. And if an author wishes to shape the results of his search artistically, completely different forms emerge than previously: "Many works of the old ones have become fragments. Many works of the new ones are so from the very beginning" (Petersen quoting Friedrich Schlegel in ÄME 180).

And now Andrew James Johnston about Tolkien:

> The growing abundance of details and stories, that Tolkien [...] creates, leads not to a totality, but to a

---

[12] Kant, *Kritik der Reinen Vernunft*.
[13] Sigmund Freud, one of the most important founders of psychoanalysis, published the influential work *Die Traumdeutung* in 1899.

fragmentation – a fragmentation, that is possibly inherent in the mythological genre itself. After all, myths and legends tend to be transmitted in contradictory or fragmentary versions.
(Johnston 2005:92)

3.2.1 Fragment, Narrator and Self-Expansion

The modern self, which is on a quest and searching for a reality beyond the contrived false reality of ego and world, can encounter this reality only in fragments. Johnston is right, mythical reality especially is – as something that was lost for millennia – accessible to a serious searcher only in fragments, if at all. This modern search for authenticity finds its literary expression, for example, in the fact that the author of a story or a novel more frequently pays attention to the *perspective* under which he lets his narrator perceive facts and events – for objectivity was only illusion, it is not possible for humans to achieve it. Tolkien clearly accounts for that in *The Book of Lost Tales*, in that he makes the Eriol-character practically a first-person narrator. Though this is not formally a first-person narrative it is still one in hidden form. We hear about nothing that Eriol could not have written as a reminiscence.[14] Here we have the starting point from which the discovery begins – the subjective self, which attempts to obtain information that exceeds itself.

Let us now consider the two time travel novels, *The Lost Road* and *The Notion Club Papers*, which were relatively complete or sketched by Tolkien in their structural layout, and in which both the incoherency and the fragmentary nature are recognizably structural. Within them the channel, through which the mythical reality is threaded into the normal reality, is at first as thin as a needle. In no way do the 20th century pro-

---

[14] Naturally Eriol could not remember the long stories he was told, but since he later wrote them down or read up on them, the work can still be considered a hidden first-person narrative.

tagonists experience the 'Ainulindale' or the 'Silmarillion' directly, but only a few foreign word fragments, that become more over the decades, until they are joined together as a mini-grammar of a language unknown on earth. Finally sentence fragments, text fragments become known; and only when the academic protagonists fall from their ordinary reality into another plane of existence through an 'incoherent fracture' do they find themselves personally on the ground of mythic reality. But do they really do so? This is not certain in the time travel novels. However it is certain that Tolkien on the one hand used acausality in his narrative technique (and not only here) – for the piercing of the self-restriction undoes the laws of nature –, on the other hand he seeks to create in literature a dimension of existence that is not ordinary reality nor pure imagination, but a third thing, that has *one* characteristic of both: a distinct feeling of reality from the ordinary reality, an intellectual creation from the imagination, that allows an escape from time and space: but this level is all the more subjective, though to some extent 'intersubjective'.

In *The Book of Lost Tales* the way to the 'mythical truths' and the Book of Lost Tales was even simpler. One only had to sail the sea aimlessly for a few decades, and then one was, if one was called Eriol and a son of Eärendil's,[15] suddenly at Tol Eressëa with one's ship ...

Twenty, thirty years later Tolkien apparently could not let his protagonists arrive at this mythical reality so simply, they had to work hard for it, and they got only splinters at first. From Tolkien's sketches we know that a possible variation of the narrative concept was, that the time travellers – one of whom Ælfwine basically was, though he earned his money at the university in Oxford in the 20th century –, were also to view the Book of Tales on Tol Eressëa. Whether this was to be 'real', in

---

[15] "If a beam from Eärendel fall on a child new-born he becomes a 'child of Eärendel' and a wanderer." (*Book of Lost Tales 1* p. 24)

a dream, or in a death version, were possibilities of which Tolkien made scattered notes here and there. Even from that one can see that the 'other reality', which he sought was not clear to him in its substance. I personally believe that this was the deeper reason why he did not achieve a fully developed conception. He possibly did not himself recognize what he wanted to achieve. A little more on that in the chapter 'Dialectic Tension'.

3.2.2 The 'Reality' Produced by Means of the Narrative Concepts

I have left out the Silmarillion complex[16] in my considerations because there – in contrast to *The Book of Lost Tales* and the time travel novels – the narrative concept, in which the 'lost tales' were to be presented to the protagonists in their genuine reality, is not elaborated. In *The Lord of the Rings*, on the other hand, the concept is very clear again: in the Appendices and in the Prologue we find comprehensively carried out that almost all documents from which the chronicler drew, put together his novel and presented as reality are kept in the libraries of the Shire.[17] There we also find the 'Silmarillion', for Bilbo translated it in Rivendell and sent it to the Shire with Frodo. How then did it come to Rivendell? "That the story does not tell." However it is a fact that this is a part of a further narrative concept that differs from that of *The Book of Lost Tales* and the time travel novels, and that the concepts are similar in the breadth of their variation to the 'real' different mythical records which were spoken of earlier.

A further noticeable fact is that we find two very different textual presentations concerning the Númenor complex. On the one hand there

---

[16] I understand the term 'Silmarillion complex' to mean not *The Silmarillion* as published by Christopher Tolkien in 1977, but rather all of the remaining texts by Tolkien which – in the wider sense – are concerned with the planned 'Silmarillion' work.

[17] For further details on this topic see Krüger (2006).

are the time travel novels, in which Númenor and other mythical worlds are set foot on – by the training of consciousness – in places that arise from some deeps and which the reader only comes to know as much as the time travellers themselves: and there are finished reports about Númenor that are technically not integrated in the narrative and seem to be factual reports. In which relationship should we see these two forms as to the nature of their literary reality? Why does Tolkien write two versions of the same material, parallel to each other, so different in their narrative technique, which, if we see both stories as finished and ready for printing, start from completely different intentions? The narrative technique of the time travel novels comes from a modern consciousness, takes into account what was previously mentioned as typical for aesthetic modernity. The 'objective' report about an imaginary island, however, seems to be a relapse into times in which one still believed that the author knows what is happening in the whole world and how everything is linked in life and in the world.

My first answer: I suspect that Tolkien wanted to make the background for his novel clear for himself when he developed these reports on Númenor. This is a common method for actors and stage directors. We get to know Hamlet on the stage in only a few hours of his life. But the actor must imagine how Hamlet's whole life has gone, for he could not otherwise play those few days within this larger context. The actors of the castle guards must imagine the Castle Kronberg with its terrace in many details, otherwise the ghost Hamlet cannot encounter them 'in person'. And an author must imagine the whole of Númenor for his novel, before it is given to a man in Oxford drop by drop.

An additional answer could be that Tolkien later had embedded these single reports as 'legendary records' functionally in a narrative concept: as for example in *The Lost Road*, where the father tells his son the story of Sauron in order to move him to leave off with his fascination with Sauron. Incidentally, the tales told to Eriol every evening by the exiled Elves in *The Book of Lost Tales*, are functional too – the framing story in no way serves to give a more or less transparent occasion for 'objective narrations': the telling intends to bring about Eriol's arousing so that he will help them out of their misery, and the narratives are constructed accordingly. And according to outlines they were to have achieved their goal, Eriol was to become an Elf and fight for the liberation of the continental Elves side by side with the exiled Elves.

A further answer could be that Tolkien had built up an imaginary archive – similar to that of Rivendell, Gondor and later the Shire –, in which all these reports and narratives – collected, written down or invented at some time by unknown story-tellers and chroniclers – are stored as subjective accounts and, in all of their fragmentation and subjectivity, give testimony to interpretations of reality and explanations of the world in very different ways.

To emphasize this once again, the thought should always be taken into account that there is always a '*final* editor' of all these 'documents' in the structurally completed narrative projects, always also a medium that receives or has received information from a more or less known source. Even in the structurally incomplete Silmarillion complex Tolkien usually names the fictitious source or the fictitious author of the legends. That is: the chronicler is *part* of the structure. The literary reality is the reality to which he has access; he has received this and no other, for whatever reason.

This is also true of *The Lord of the Rings*. There we even have the case that Tolkien did not actually write all of those fragments but only fictitiously claimed their existence. The Appendices do hold some of those that were actually written, but they are only a fraction of the documents that the chronicler of *The Lord of the Rings* had as a basis for his narrative. These 'documents' are not transmitted with certainty, the chronicler writes, and in addition he chooses as he sees fit (though he does not write that) from among them, and finally he invents quite a bit additionally (which he most certainly does not admit).[18]

Of course a real author does all of this as well – in fact he writes fragmentarily, he throws spotlights into a dark void, and his imagination conjures up colourful scenes there, which he then writes down and later constructs as an interrelated story. But the decisive point is whether he wants to give the reader the illusion that the world is rounded and complete, of which he reports only partially, though he seems to understand clearly the purpose of the world affairs, or whether he delivers his construction principle to the reader: showing that he has no idea how the world functions, but is blowing soap bubbles profoundly, just like the motto of the Funny Person ('Lustige Person') in the prologue at the theatre in *Faust*:

> In colourful pictures little clarity,
> Much wrong and a grain of truth,
> Thus the best drink is brewed,
> Which refreshes and builds up the whole world.[19]

However, because Tolkien does not merely blow soap bubbles (or smoke clouds?), but always introduces the constructor as well, who personally makes connections between 'transmitted' fragments, he is modern. We cannot stay away from making poetry. Our imagination is constantly productive, and we have the drive to explain the world with it. But what if we have lost, deep in our soul, the coherent, consistent model of explanation of the world – what do we do then? Then we not only write, perhaps we also express our doubts concerning the correctness of what was written. Nowadays that is called self-reference or constructivism by many.

---

[18] Compare Krüger (2006).
[19] *Faust I*, 'Vorspiel auf dem Theater', lines 170-173.

Tolkien as a constructivist? One who plays with pure artifical forms? Well, not quite that. To find the basis for this phenomenon, that Tolkien's works superficially appear old-fashioned in their narrative tendency, but the structural analysis shows a modern author who mistrusts a simple narrative mode, setting everything in quotation marks, so to speak, I would like to make a brief excursion to Peter Szondi's *Theorie des modernen Dramas* (*Theory of the Modern Drama*). With that I also pick up a thought from before, that Tolkien's very own consciousness of mythical or literary reality was possibly never really clear to him – or that he refused to face it.

3.3   Dialectic Tension
3.3.1 Peter Szondi

Although Peter Szondi's very influential analysis of the modern drama does not naturally concern itself with the epic, it is important for the thoughts in this essay because Szondi developed a method for deciphering authorial works not mono-causally, but dialectically: that is, he sees at least two powers at work: one conscious and one unconscious, one dominant and one latent, which can contradict each other. His own concept is that of form and content – both are connected in tension, in a dialectic relationship. In the ideal case the form is manifested content, the content fulfilment of the form. Here one of his examples:

The classical drama after the Renaissance lives from its dialogue. This form of drama is fulfilled when its persons can actually express themselves through dialogue, when their medium is language. That presupposes a belief in an intact, reason-oriented interpersonal relationship. When people no longer have anything to say and no longer want to speak with each other, but the author still wants to use drama as his medium, he can only let his protagonists say what they would not say voluntarily, yet must under the pressure of the genre: that means, form and content are no longer identical: the persons speak on the stage because they are forced to do so, but they do not express themselves, otherwise they would have something to say. The content no longer fits the form, stands in opposition to it.

With that, Szondi has placed an instrument at our disposal with which we can examine every drama to see if it is hollowed out from the inside – through defective ability for dialogue in this case -, and to which degree it is so. At the same time a statement is made about the intactness of the interpersonal relationship.

According to Szondi some dramas express the *crisis* in these interpersonal relationships, while others attempt to conceal it by a strict usage of the formal laws, and yet others have already found a new form internally – having hollowed out the old one -, though they have not yet noticed it themselves. So August Strindberg did not create genuine togetherness in his early naturalistic dramas,[20] no more genuine dialogue, but only a dominating self, that, in a sort of diseased delusion, hears exactly what it fears from other persons: the self misuses the other for its – unintentional – projections. The partner does not express himself, but that which the diseased self has already expected. It is – subliminally for the author – an Other-Self.

On the one hand we recognize here the phenomenon of the consciousness crisis again, in which the ego is imprisoned within itself and colours the world of objects with itself. This fact not only causes the naturalistic drama to shake, but also the realistic novel. Strindberg later burst open these dramatic forms – recognizing the underlying intentions – and placed a large number of strange figures on the stage that are all self-projections, practically tearing the self apart. With that a form was created (the expressionistic) which corresponds with the content.[21]

---

[20] Especially *Fadren* belongs to this.
[21] E.g. in *Till Damaskus*.

On the other hand we can see that these instruments, which were described by Szondi, can also be applied to the epic and especially to Tolkien.

3.3.2 Tolkien

My thesis is that in Tolkien's works as well no identity of content and form can be found – either the adequate form for the content was not fully found or both are in contradiction with one another, and that he belongs to those who, according to Szondi, have already found a new form inwardly, without facing the consequences of it.

Take for example *The Book of Lost Tales*: Originally Tol Eressëa was to be located in the middle of the sea and later be pulled in the direction of the Great Lands, where it was then to be renamed England. In this version Eriol originally came from Helgoland. Tolkien then set out a further version: England was always in its place, and Tol Eressëa also always existed. There everything looked like England, with the difference that Elves (who could also speak English) lived there. And the Helgoland native Eriol became the Englishman Ælfwine.

Neither idea – that Tol Eressëa was pulled into the position of England and that Tol Eressëa was an elven mirror of England – was carried out by Tolkien: they possibly blocked each other. But what he perhaps did not see was that the statement in both versions is the same, both are literary translations for the same basic feeling: the real England is based on a mythical-elven reality. There is a human and an elvish side, and the elvish is forgotten and must be brought to awareness again somehow. Tolkien seemingly did not understand that clearly for himself, but stayed caught in the story itself, not being able to get enough distance to it as Tieck or Thomas Mann or Goethe, who distinctly formed that genuinely present subreality, clad in images and action, as an invasion of irreality. Instead, Tolkien got caught up in purely material contradictions and – possibly – did not come to the knowledge that they could have been formally shaped *as* contradictions. It is possible that he did not have a distinct consciousness of theory and did not care much about aesthetic theories of his or previous times, and therefore, almost unprofessionally, called the reality which he sought and attempted to create, Faërie. This is, however, a concept from (popular) poetry, not one of literary theory, not even psychological or philosophical. The Celtic 'Otherworld' is certainly preciser and expresses through the word that there is a connection, however it may be, between 'this' and the 'other' world: both have the option of being two sides of the same thing and related to each other in tension. Tolkien did not use this term often, but – perhaps – thought of it.

He felt instinctively that the way to Faërie could not be shaped without a break; he knew this of his own accord. For he saw in the fairy tales which he read and analysed that the forming of the 'genuine myth' was lost, and he perceived also in his own literary production that his various narrative concepts blocked each other. That this contradiction, incoherency, and fragmentation in mythical experiences could be left as it is, because the modern man – if he lives from a genuine depth and not from constructions of convictions – is able to discover authentic reality only in fragments: this he certainly let the club members in *The Notion Club Papers* discuss thoroughly, but he found no well thought-out narrative concept for it. Beginnings were there, especially in *The Notion Club Papers*: the alien mythical element drips successively into the thinking and feeling of the club members, changes them and lets them make border experiences that show exactly this state of ambivalence of which I spoke earlier and which Tolkien made the subject of *On Fairy-Stories*: a third state, which is neither ordinary reality nor pure imagination, but *reality* created through imagination (e.g. in *On Fairy-Stories* p. 52).

We see similar things in the above-mentioned Ælfwine events from *The Book of Lost Tales*, which find their echo in the fact that the Oxford lecturer Lowdham, whose first name was actually Ælfwine, was incarnated as just that mythical Ælfwine during his time travels to find the Book of Stories, which he actually knew as just the same mythical Ælfwine. Lowdham found these fragments, which he received psychically, strangely familiar occasionally. Did Tolkien himself realize that, on at least one level of interpretation, it was about the self-discovery of his literary frame characters? About a self-expansion on a large scale? About the expansion of the self, which is bound to time and space, to include its mythical counterpart, which existed beyond time and space, but was lost or not even actually existent? That the boundaries of reason, shown by means of Kant's theory of cognition – marked by the captivity in space, time, and causality – could be broken: initially by way of artistic imagination?

He must have been aware of this in *The Notion Club Papers*, for he composed the Ælfwine motive skilfully and approached the Leitmotiv technique of Thomas Mann and Richard Wagner in doing so – although this mirroring of the real and the mythical self in *The Notion Club Papers* fades into vagueness and imprecision; the forming is missing, which could have worked out this confrontation of temporal and intemporal self. The many continuation sketches which Tolkien left behind, which gave material rather than formal information,[22] cause me to suspect that Tolkien was caught up too much in the *material* whole and therefore should have, as Johnston wrote above, stayed fragmentary, but, I would add, did not raise the fragmentary element to his form.

3.3.3 Result and Transition

From Szondi we learned that the content of a work can stand in contradiction to its form, but that the seed of a new form can be enclosed, though possibly unrecognized. By use of individual examples I have at-

---

[22] However, it must be considered that we do not find all of Tolkien's notes in *The History of Middle-earth* and that above all the reflective-theoretic ones were not published.

tempted to show why I think this is the case with Tolkien. Therefore I see his complete work – though underlying and noticeable as an inner form, yet not consciously constructed – as heading toward the goal that I would like – somewhat 'tollkühn', i.e. recklessly – to call a 'renewal of the ancient epic thought'.

My explanation of this constitutes the conclusion of my essay. This too can take place only in a very fragmentary fashion, as signposts. This last chapter is necessary because the treatment of my theme – 'The Shaping of 'Reality' in Tolkien's Works' – only achieves the desired precision by means of a description of this presumed objective. For literary reality is also that which is recognizably existent as a structure, even when it has not matured to a fully worked-out narrative concept.

4 ON THE WAY TO AN EPOS

4.1 Novel

The question, to which genre Tolkien's works belong, has caused some headaches in the past.

The modern novel as a genre was developed approximately at the time of the Enlightenment, when the self was considered able to achieve free reason and humanity. Goethe's *Wilhelm Meister*, the prototype of this novel, shows progressively how the protagonist Wilhelm must work to his development through the years of apprenticeship and mastership in his life, in order to finally find his place and purpose in this world.

It is fairly obvious at first sight that Tolkien does not play in this league. One could be tempted to read Bilbo or Frodo as characters of a novel of development or education ('Bildungsroman'), but in my opinion this misses the mark concerning the construction of *The Hobbit* and *The Lord of the Rings*. It is true that these characters develop, but the events around them were not invented by the author exclusively to *enable* the characters to develop. Those critics who complain that

Tolkien's figures do not have enough complexity, do not actually experience character changes, should ask themselves whether they have the wrong ruler in their hand. Can I complain about a lyrical drama because it does not have the characteristics of a mystery? About a short story, because it has too little epic fullness? About an epos, because it does not show the traits of a psychological novel?

4.2 The Ancient Epos

Georg Lukácz writes in his famous *Theorie des Romans* (*Theory of the Novel*) in 1914/15:

> Therefore the question, to which the epos is the shaping answer, is: How can life become essential?
> (Lukácz 1965:23)

> The hero of the epos is, strictly speaking, never an individual. For a long time the characteristic of an epos has been defined in that its object is not a personal fate, but that of a community.
> (Lukácz 1965:64)

This – related to Tolkien – already sounds much more like familiar ground. Tolkien's literary work has – in its objective – passed by the whole realistic-psychological novel tradition[23] and has turned to other forms of expression in its conceptional forming from the very beginning. That the Romantic age was an exception is because it made a daring design for the novel, which was not bound to a genre and was able to find a late realization, for example, in 1970 in Arno Schmidt's *Zettels Traum* (*Zettel's [i.e. Bottom's] Dream*)[24] (a title that would suit Tolkien's entire work extraordinarily well!).

---

[23] However, Tolkien learned much from realism for his style.
[24] The title is a quote from the German translation of Shakespeare's *A Midsummernight's Dream*, at the end of Act IV, Scene II.

That Tolkien as well did not bind himself to a genre can be seen in that the 'Silmarillion', had it ever been completed, would presumably have consisted of long poems, chronicles, narrative reports, novellas, dialogues, novel-like constructions, etc.[25] However, this alone does not constitute an epos, even when it breaks up the usual novel form.

According to Lukácz the epos is identified by two criteria: First, it is not about a personal individual fate, but about the fate of all of humanity or the world, merely expressed in individuals. "The fate of the world is the content-giving element of the events." (Lukácz 1965:66). Second, the earth is part of the cosmos and is home. "The world is wide and yet one's own house, for the fire that burns in the soul is of the same nature as the stars." (Lukácz 1965:22)

4.2.1 Is an Ancient Epos at all Possible Today?

Both named facts were, according to Lukácz, completely lost in the time after classical antiquity, for since the awaking of rational interpretation, the world has been divided into subject and object, and the object has drifted ever further away from the subject. The subject can – I would add – no longer recognize its own inner light in the bright neon light above it, and especially not the divine light. Applied to Tolkien: It cannot recognize in an orc the own self and the immeasurable beauty of the starry sky. Orcs must be killed. They are not felt to be a part of the divine universe, not considered 'star brothers'.

Here the gaping wound is distinctly visible that runs through our culture and becomes vivid especially in the romantic currents: Whole parts of the pre- and unconscious are 'devilized', rejected, and destroyed. Precisely this has distanced us from the epos and let us create literature in which this 'night side' is either ignored and the belief in reason, which would enlighten and drive away the darkness, is cultivated – or where this

---

[25] On this topic see also Noad, 'On the Construction of 'The Silmarillion''.

night side was no longer ignored: either because acute real horrors forced them to this, or because the dark side began to fascinate as demonic.

I have shown above that since the Romantic age, at the latest, this gaping wound has been laid open through the literary means of the fantastic and that Tolkien continued on this path. How then should an epos (in the strict sense) be possible here, an epos that makes obvious to us, to pick out only the second criterion, that all of the barbarian wars and acts of madness of the centuries in which we live only mirror the wandering stars in the end?

4.2.2 Pros and Cons

To explain that I would like to mention the following points once more and deepen them:

First, Tolkien used a kind of trick in order to keep himself out of the concrete history of the world: He used fantastic characters, placed them in a fantastic country. If it is right – as I alleged above (3.1.2) – that his whole fantastic arsenal is not "only show – a playful skirmish with dragons and wizards, goblins and Elven beings", but that "there is a genuinely existential statement behind it, born of our time and able to open our eyes concerning subliminal matters which occur in our time": then this whole fantastic realm which is spread out before our eyes is a reflection of our own – broken, mirrored, distorted – consciousness of the world.

Second, we therefore find no *ex-cathedra* statements about the meaning of our 20th-century battle slaughter there, nor any *ex-cathedra* judgements about the correctness or falseness of the various religions in this realistic world of ours. Tolkien's literary starting point is a seeking person, who will (or must) explore a different reality than the one in time and space and causality. This reality is not objective, but the material for the search originates in his own self. This person begins his quest, to judge by the time travel novels, with his dreams and visions. In them he encounters realities that are at first difficult to grasp, which he seeks to firm and then develops to literature, until they can be tread upon, that is: until the confrontation with the area of the unconscious and preconscious is distinct and clear. With other narrative concepts but similar intentions this also happens in other works, as I have written above. The immense mythical world of images that, as I interpret Tolkien's narrative concept, should open up ever wider, like a funnel, to the seeker, is never detached from the subject or subjects that experience all of this. They are *their* inner distorted and puzzling images, *their* interpretation of the world. The exploration of the solid ground of reality alone no longer offers solutions for all of the many dead ends of our times, whereas

> Themistokles, when devastation threatened Athens, moved the Athenians, to leave it completely and to found a new Athens on the sea, on a different element. (Marx 1966:108)

4.3 A Modern Epos

No, an ancient epos is no longer possible today (for we do not feel ourselves pushed around world history by faulty gods), but perhaps a renewal of the epos idea nevertheless. It must be founded on new ground, and this ground can – according to all theory of dialectic change – only arise where the core of the evil lies: in the self without steadiness and bottom:

> I've got a very Briny Notion
> To drink myself to sleep.
> Bring me my bowl, my magic potion!
> Tonight I'm diving deep
> down! down! down!
> Down where the dreamfish go.
> (*The Notion Club Papers* p. 224)

This is what the Oxford lecturer Lowdham sings in a strange mood on one club evening, a few months before he finds himself in other realities and boards a ship to Númenor.

The new focal and pivotal point is therefore the abyss within man himself. Eyes are no longer closed at this abyss, it is not denied or forbidden, but is explored. The modern quest, the modern odyssey goes right through it. Here or nowhere can the alternative to our destructive model of the world be found.

4.3.1 The Shaping of Characters Out of the Fate of the World
In a modern novel the characters are alienated from the whole world or society, their fate must assert itself against the demands from outside: subject and object are split and usually hostile to each other. The epos however, according to Lukácz, does not shape purely personal destinies that are outside the fate of the world or humanity on the whole.

Exactly this is true, as in the epos, almost continuously and conspicuously, for Tolkien's characters! A *basic problem* is related that has grown out of the division between Melkor and Eru, both of whom cannot understand themselves as necessary poles and parts of a higher unity. All of Tolkien's other main characters do nothing else in the end than to attempt to cope with the results of this basic problem somehow; their own problems are not distinguished from it. Elrond, Galadriel, Gandalf, Saruman, Frodo, Túrin, Aragorn, Arwen etc. – they are all part of the great task, which they solve one way or another; but it is always transparent to the reader how their tasks, destinies and difficulties have arisen from the whole history. Fëanor already carries his temperament in his name; his fate – and the ensuing terrible tragedies – arise from the fact that not only he desires the enclosed 'divine light', but Melkor as well. They too stand opposite an object that is basically part of their 'being', but was alienated from or denied them.

With this, Lukász' so important criterion – the epos is the shaping answer to the question, how life can become *essential* – applies to Tolkien.

4.3.2 Subject – Object Dualism

When we take a *literary* myth as what it is: not as an historical past, but as a – marked – subliminal yet always 'feelable' state of being, which would like to be understood and recognized, then this basic conflict between Eru and Melkor describes a part of the subreal in our whole culture, with which we obviously must urgently come to terms. Therefore we can understand this epos, which emerges in contours, as a broadly planned development of the above-named basic difficulty, with all facets of attempts to escape or overcome this basic evil.

At this point, where the entire outline is in view, it becomes clear that the rift which goes through Tolkien's created world is the same that goes through our world. We are shown this fact, but it is not explained by Tolkien. Tolkien does not explain the world to us, but shows us how we explain it ourselves. (And thereby makes it possible for us – consciously or unconsciously – to recognize the cause of the rift from the outside.)

4.3.3 Acausality, Self-Reference

Unlike the attempted totality of the ancient epos, which assumed a unity of world view in which everything goes back to cosmic harmony in the end, a modern work of literature arises from a disaster – the sharp division between object and subject -, and must, if it would - in epic proportions - lead out of this almost unbridgeable gap, do this according to the current state of consciousness. Tolkien does this. He is at the height of his time.

As Verlyn Flieger states, Tolkien occupied himself intensively with the theory of relativity and other physical research about acausal time references,[26] and he picks up the thought of self-reference again[27] (which was already contained in the Romantic age as well as in Shakespeare's works), that is actually able to cause new connections on 'new ground':

When Heinrich von Ofterdingen[28] discovers a book in which precisely what he is doing at that time is written, when Sam recognizes himself as part of a story which does not yet exist, when Galadriel says that the future can be caused by attempting to prevent it, then we see before our very eyes an 'acausal reality'; then persons and events are connected to each other in a way that is depicted in a literary work as 'mythical', but which means a simultaneous occurrence of opposites in subreality. Tolkien's works are full of that. The realm *beyond* the *ratio* no longer divides like the *ratio*: completely different, more or less unexplored laws are valid there, subject and object are not separated. Even psychology remains in the forecourt most of the time, investigating the realistic self. Tolkien, however, 'dived deep' to see upon which mythical basis our messed-up world swims.

4.3.4 Home

Many of Tolkien's creatures do not feel at home on earth. The Elves were torn from their roots early, and because they got to know the light of Aman, they are no longer able to feel at home in their hereditary homeland. They are torn, one way or the other. Figures of the frame stories who are on a quest and long to hear or read the stories that could give them insight into the cause of all of this misery, are often torn as well. Still: Never did one of his figures manage to bring the book of stories into the human world. Or did one?

---

[26] On this topic compare, above all, Flieger, *A Question of Time*.
[27] On this see e.g. Flieger, *Interrupted Music* pp. 72-73.
[28] The main protagonist in Novalis' *Heinrich von Ofterdingen*.

Ernst Bloch, who wrote his major works at the same time as Tolkien, explains again and again that myth does not merely point the way to a lost past, but above all to a not yet developed future:

> Man still lives in prehistory everywhere, yes, anything and everything still stands prior to the creation of the world, as a right one. The real Genesis is not at the beginning, but at the end, and it begins to begin when society and existence become radical, that is to seize itself at the roots. The root of history is the man who is working, creating, reshaping and exceeding circumstances. When he has grasped himself and based what is his own in real democracy without relinquishment and alienation, then something is created that shines into everyone's childhood and in which no one yet was: home.
> (Bloch 1979 (3):1628)

We must only remember how central imagination, fantasy and literary creation was for Tolkien, in order to understand the similarity to Bloch. Imagination creates reality – that is one of the main statements of *The Notion Club Papers*, and the same phenomenon can be proved in *The Lord of the Rings* when one compares the sources given by the chronicler to the story itself: it became *real* because it was told. That is why it is so important to Tolkien that it be told *rightly*. Home lies ahead of us, not behind us. It is created with the help of imagination. Consciousness and being are not so very different as Karl Marx still believed.

One can read Tolkien so that everything declines, everything that is beautiful leaves the world and leaves us behind alone. Yet the literary myth shows no historical past, but acquired subreal mechanisms including the yearning – and ability – to break through those, and with that the inlying seeds for the future. Naturally Gandalf and Elrond have left Middle-earth – in the story. Actually, they only just arrived on our earth: about 50 years ago.

5 CONCLUSION AND OUTLOOK

We have come a long way. Starting with the cautious question whether Tolkien can even be counted among those who have worked strongly on the development of our culture, we now see him at the front, where concepts of reality are being developed, that will or are able to form a firm foundation for the near or farther future. The key words for this are *time, space, causality*. The understanding of 'reality' depends upon our understanding of these concepts, and at the time they are all changing in a way that cannot yet be estimated. They were and are being examined in many disciplines in the 20th and 21st centuries, in linguistic studies as well as in modern physics and by means of art, and Tolkien is right in the middle of this many-voiced concert. Unfortunately I could only give fragmental glimpses, could only set up road signs to show where the quest can lead. I did not intend to give finished answers here; my aim was to prove that Tolkien's life's work is to be found active in the centre of modernity, and not, at which conclusions he arrived. Those would be new tasks.

> The solution to the mystery of life in time and space lies *outside* of time and space. (Not the problems of natural science are to be solved here.)
> (Wittgenstein 1921, *Tractatus* 6.4312)

It is as though Tolkien had taken Einstein's $E=mc^2$ and reshaped it to his own use.
  (Verlyn Flieger 2000,
  A Question of Time p. 171)

HEIDI KRUEGER, born 1944 in Potsdam, studied Philosophy and German Philology in Tubingen and Zurich. She worked as lecturer at Växjö University (Sweden) and taught numerous seminars on literature and philosophy. Next to her philological and philosophical education, she also underwent a training as director for theatre and opera and has translated operas and dramas from Norwegian and Finnish. Since 2003 she has been increasingly specialising in Tolkien and the research of his works as an aesthetical phenomenon and has, to date, published two essays on this topic.

Bibliography

Ästhetische Moderne in Europa [ÄME], 1998, (edited by Silvio Vietta and Dirk Kemper), Munich: Wilhelm Fink.

Bloch, Ernst, 1979, *Das Prinzip Hoffnung, Bände 1-3*, (first edition 1959), Frankfurt: Suhrkamp.

Carpenter, Humphrey, 2002, *J.R.R. Tolkien: A Biography*, (first edition 1977), London: HarperCollins.

Flieger, Verlyn, 1997, *A Question of Time*, Kent, Ohio: The Kent University Press.

---, *Interrupted Music*, 2005, Kent, Ohio: The Kent University Press.

Freud, Sigmund, 1991, *Die Traumdeutung*, (first edition 1899), Frankfurt: Fischer.

Goethe, Johann Wolfgang von, 1982, *Wilhelm Meisters Wanderjahre,* (first edition 1821), Ditzingen: Reclam.

---, 1986, *Faust. Der Tragödie erster Teil,* (first edition 1808), Ditzingen: Reclam.

---, 1986, *Faust. Der Tragödie zweiter Teil*, (first edition 1833), Ditzingen: Reclam.

---, 1986, *Wilhelm Meisters Lehrjahre*, (first edition 1798), Ditzingen: Reclam.

Hoffmann, E.T.A., 1976, *Der Goldene Topf*, (first edition 1814), Ditzingen: Reclam.

Johnston, Andrew James, 2005, 'Ästhetische Strategien und ethische Vielfalt', in Thomas Honegger, Andrew James Johnston, Friedhelm Schneidewind and Frank Weinreich, 2005, *Eine Grammatik der Ethik*, Saarbrücken: Edition Stein und Baum, pp. 89-109.

Kafka, Franz, 1995, *Der Prozess*, (first edition 1925), Ditzingen: Reclam.

Kant, Immanuel, 1986, *Kritik der Reinen Vernunft*, (first edition 1781, second extensively expanded edition 1787), Ditzingen: Reclam.

Krüger, Heidi, 2006, 'Der Autor als Chronist', in Thomas Le Blanc and Bettina Twrsnick (eds.), 2006, *Das Dritte Zeitalter*, Wetzlar: Phantastische Bibliothek Wetzlar, pp. 68-96.

Lukácz, Georg, 1965, *Die Theorie des Romans*, (first edition 1920), Neuwied: Luchterhand.

Mann, Thomas, 1992, *Tod in Venedig,* (first edition 1912), Frankfurt: Fischer.

---, 1990, *Doktor Faustus*, (first edition 1947), Frankfurt: Fischer.

Marx, Karl, 1966, 'Hefte zur epikureischen, stoischen und skeptischen Philosophie – Sechstes Heft', (first edition 1840), in Karl Marx, *Texte zu Methode und Praxis I. Jugendschriften 1835-1841*, (edited by Günther Hillmann), Reinbek: Rowohlt, pp. 54-126.

Mozart, Wolfgang Amadeus and Emanuel Schikaneder, 1986, *Die Zauberflöte*, (world premiere 1791), Ditzingen: Reclam.

Noad, Charles E., 2000, 'On the Construction of 'The Silmarillion'', in Verlyn Flieger and Carl F. Hostetter (eds.), *Tolkien's Legendarium. Essays on The History of Middle-earth*, Westport, Connecticut, and London: Greenwood Press, pp. 31-68.

Novalis, 1965, *Heinrich von Ofterdingen*, (first edition 1802), Stuttgart: Reclam.

Petersdorff, Dirk von, 1999, 'Ein Knabe saß im Kahne, fuhr an die Grenzen der Romantik. Clemens Brentanos Roman *Godwi*', *Aktualität der Romantik, Text + Kritik* 143 (1999), pp. 80-94.

Schiller, Friedrich von, 1972, *Über naive und sentimentalische Dichtung*, (first edition 1795), Stuttgart: Reclam.

Schlegel, Friedrich, 1969, 'Gespräch über die Poesie (I): Rede über die Mythologie', *Athenäum. Eine Zeitschrift 1798-1800* (II), (edited by Curt Grützmacher), Hamburg: Rowohlt, pp. 174-180.

Schmidt, Arno, 2004, *Zettels Traum*, (first edition 1970), Frankfurt: Fischer.

Shakespeare, William, 1965, *Ein Sommernachtstraum*, (translated by August Wilhelm von Schlegel, first English edition 1600), Stuttgart: Reclam.

Strindberg, August, 1957, 'Fadren' (The Father), (first edition 1887), in *Skrifter av August Strindberg XII Samtidsdramer*, Stockholm: Bonniers.

---, 1962, 'Till Damaskus' (The Way to Damaskus), (first edition 1898-1902), in *Skrifter av August Strindberg XI Lyriska Dramer*, Stockholm: Bonniers.

Szondi, Peter, 1966, *Theorie des modernen Dramas*, (first edition 1959, second edition 1966), Frankfurt: Edition Suhrkamp.

Thalmann, Marianne, 1966, *Das Märchen und die Moderne. Zum Begriff der Surrealität im Märchen der Romantik*, (first edition 1961), Stuttgart: Kohlhammer, Urban.

Tieck, Ludwig, 2004, 'Der Runenberg', (first edition 1804), in Ludwig Tieck, *Der blonde Eckbert/Der Runenberg*, Ditzingen: Reclam.

Tolkien, John Ronald Reuel, 1965, *The Lord of the Rings*, (first edition 1954/55), New York: Ballantine.

---, 2001, 'On Fairy-Stories' in *Tree and Leaf*, (first edition 1964), London: HarperCollins, pp. 1-81.

---, 2002, *The Book of Lost Tales 1*, (The History of Middle-earth vol. 1, first edition 1983; edited by Christopher Tolkien), London: HarperCollins.

---, 2002, *The Book of Lost Tales 2*, (The History of Middle-earth vol. 2, first edition 1984; edited by Christopher Tolkien), London: HarperCollins.

---, 2002, 'The Lost Road', in *The Lost Road*, (The History of Middle-earth vol. 5, first edition 1987; edited by Christopher Tolkien), London: HarperCollins, pp. 36-108.

---, 2002, 'The Notion Club Papers', in *Sauron Defeated*, (The History of Middle-earth vol. 9, first edition 1992; edited by Christopher Tolkien), London: HarperCollins, pp. 145-327.

---, 2003, *The Annotated Hobbit*, (edited by Douglas A. Anderson), (first edition 1988), London: HarperCollins.

Wittgenstein, Ludwig, 1969, *Tractatus logico-philosophicus. Logisch-philosophische Abhandlung*, (first edition 1921), Frankfurt: Edition Suhrkamp.

Index

A

Adams, Robert A., 126
Adorno, Theodor, 55, 56, 57, 58, 60, 62, 68
adventure novel
  British 19th century, 87
Aelfwine, 250, 257, 259
Akers-Jordan, A. Cathy, 22
Aragorn
  and Frye's theory of modes, 79
  as a novelistic, romance, and epic character, 90
  as epic and romance hero, 105
  as epic hero, 101
  as novelistic character in Bree, 82
  as novelistic hero, 104
  as romance hero, 93, 108
  as Strider, 81
  contrasted with Boromir, 92
Aragorn vs. Boromir
  parallels to Hector vs. Achilles, 95
Armstrong, Karen, 219, 225
Arwen and Aragorn, 22
  as variation of Beren and Lúthien, 2, 23
Aschenbach, Gustav
  main protagonist in Thomas Mann's *Der Tod in Venedig*, 247
Auden, W.H., 134
Axial Age, 225

B

Barthes, Roland, 12
beauty
  of Lúthien, 6
Beckett, Samuel, 217
Benoit de St. Maure
  Le Roman de Troie, 95
Beowulf, 101, 115
Bettelheim, Bruno, 119, 120
  The Uses of Enchantment, 119
Bildungsroman, 260
Bloch, Ernst
  Das Prinzip Hoffnung, 268
Book of Lost Tales, 250
Book of Tales, 250
Brittnacher, Hans Richard, 18
Brook, Rupert
  Peace, 116
Butler, Judith, 21

C

Campbell, Joseph, 119
Carlyle, Thomas, 120

Chanson de Roland, 75
Chrétien de Troyes, 124
Christ
   in *The Exeter Book*, 213
chronotope, 80
Classicism, 237
Curry, Patrick
   Defending Middle-earth, 54, 71

D

Dada, 235
de Paco, Albert, 92
decline, 66
Descartes, René, 241
Dickens, Charles
   The Pickwick Papers, 81
      parallels to the hobbits' arrival in Bree, 81
disenchantment, 139
Douie, Charles, 139

E

Edith and John Tolkien
   as variation of Beren and Lúthien, 3, 49
Edith Tolkien
   as Lúthien, 48
Einstein, Albert, 144
Eliot, T.S., 70, 76, 216, 223, 226

The Waste Land, 68, 212, 214, 215, 218, 227
elves
   and time, 177
Enlightenment, 234, 235, 236, 237, 239
epos
   Tolkien's work as epos, 261, 264
Eriol, 244, 249, 257
Erll, Astrid, 47
escape, 205
escapism, 234, 235
eucatastrophe, 120, 122, 228

F

Faërie, 258
fairy stories, 235
fairy tales, 236, 243
Faust, 247
Flieger, Verlyn, 89, 178, 179, 266
   A Question of Time, 54, 144, 177
   Splintered Light, 206
Fonstad, Karen Wynn
   The Atlas of Middle-earth, 150
Foucault, Michel, 16, 47, 241
friendship
   contrasted with love, 2
Frye, Northrop, 76, 79
   theory of modes, 76

G

Garth, John, 118
Goethe, Johann Wolfgang von, 243
   Faust, 243, 254
   Wilhelm Meister, 260
Gollum
   his role in the relationship between Sam and Frodo, 37
Grimm, Jacob, 227
   Teutonic Mythology (Deutsche Mythologie), 227
Grimm, Jacob and Wilhelm, 119

H

Halperin, David, 46
Hamlet, 252
hero
   Aragorn, 131
   Beren, 124
   Beren (and Lúthien), 124
   Bilbo Baggins, 129
   Frodo, 135
   modern, 122
   Sam, 137
   Túrin, 126
heterotopia, 7, 16, 18, 36, 37, 39, 42, 45, 47
   and music, 21
high mimetic, 223

high modernism, 211
Hoffmann, E.T.A.
   Der Goldene Topf, 245
Holle
   also Holda, Hulda, 186
Homer, 118
   The Illiad, 115, 116, 218
   The Odyssey, 75, 216
Hourihan, Margery
   Deconstructing the Hero, 119
Hughes-Hallett, Lucy, 120
husband-father economy, 20. see also love: husband-father economy
Huxley, Aldous, 123

I

Iglesia, Toda, 87
Inklings, 122
intertraditional dialogue, 77, 110
   and Aragorn, 79
   and modernism, 110
irony
   and modernism, 78

J

Jerome, Jerome K., 104
Johnston, Andrew James, 248
Joyce, James, 70, 216, 217, 219
   Ulysses, 78, 211, 216
Jung, Carl Gustav, 119

K

Kafka, Franz, 243
Kant, Immanuel, 241, 248
kleos, 120, 121, 137
Knatchbull-Hugessen, E.H.
  Puss-Cat Mew, 221
knowledge
  vs. lore, 226

L

late style, 55, 58
  and Modernism, 57, 63, 70
  and the editor-persona, 63
  and *The Lord of the Rings*, 58
Layamon, 115
  Brut, 132
Le Chanson de Roland, 94
Lewis, Alex and Elizabeth Currie, 12, 30
  The Forsaken Realm of Tolkien. J.R.R. Tolkien and the Medieval Tradition, 217
Lewis, C.S., 119, 131
  Surprised by Joy, 122
  The Chronicles of Narnia, 122
  The Cosmic Trilogy, 122
lore
  vs. knowledge, 226
love
  and sexuality, 46, 47
  Aragorn's love for Arwen as social climbing strategy, 24
  as a literary phenomenon, 45
  husband-father economy, 9, 17, 24
  identity, 9
  political vs. private spheres, 9, 17, 21, 26, 27
  romantic love, 21
low mimetic, 223
Lubkoll, Christine, 37
Luhmann, Niklas, 3, 4, 5, 14, 19, 20, 23, 26, 45, 47
Lukácz, Georg, 262, 265
  Theorie des Romans, 261

M

Malory, Thomas
  Le Mort D'Arthur, 75
Man in the Moon, 221, 222, 223
Mann, Thomas, 243, 259
  Der Tod in Venedig, 243
Marie de France, 124
marriage
  and love, 1
Marx, Karl, 268
melancholy, 66
Miller, Dean, 83, 106
Milton, John
  Paradise Lost, 116

Index 277

Paradise Regained, 121, 136
modernism, 233
modernity, 233, 234, 237, 239
   consciousness crisis, 240
   rationalistic modernity, 240
mortality, 66
Mortimer, Patchen, 66
Mozart, Wolfgang Amadeus
   Die Zauberflöte, 245
music
   and heterotopia, 21
   and love, 21
Music of the Ainur
   and time, 175
myth, 225
   Germanic, 227
   of the Fall of Troy, 219
   The Lord of the Rings as literary myth, 226
   vs. allegory, 223
   vs. history and literature, 226
mythic dreamtime, 228
mythical method, 216
mythology
   for England, 66

N

narrative zone, 80
Naturalism, 239
northern mythology, 226

novel, the modern, 260

O

Orwell, George, 54
Other Space, 144
Other Time, 144, 180, 185, 190
Otherworld, Celtic, 258
Owen, Wilfried, 117, 118, 119
   Strange Meeting, 117

P

Petersen, Jürgen H., 248
Phial of Galadriel, 159, 194
post-axial age, 228
Pound, Ezra, 212
primary vs. secondary world, 64, 66, 69, 70, 115
Propp, Vladimir, 119
Proust, Marcel, 70

R

Ragnarök, 226
Rationalism, 239
Romantic age, 263
Romanticism, 236, 237, 238, 239, 241, 245
   literary, 234, 235, 236
Romanticism, German, 239
Rose Cotton

as vehicle to transmit the genealogy of Sam and Frodo, 43
Rosebury, Brian, 70
Rowbotham, Sheila, 20

S

Said, Edward, 55, 57, 58, 65, 69, 71
Sale, Robert
   Modern Heroism, 124
Sam
   emulating Arwen's choice, 33
Sam and Frodo
   as loving couple, 30
   as variation of Beren and Lúthien, 2
   emulating Beren and Lúthien, 36, 40
Sassoon, Siegfried, 118, 119
   Songbooks of the War, 117
   The Hero, 117
Schiller, Friedrich von, 243
Schlegel, Friedrich, 248
Schmidt, Arno
   Zettels Traum, 261
Senior, W.A., 59
sexuality
   and love, 46, 47
Sharratt, Bernard, 215
Shippey, Tom, 227
   J.R.R. Tolkien. Author of the Century, 54, 70
Sisam, Kenneth

Fourteenth Century Verse & Prose, 212
sophrosyne, 120, 121, 123, 137
Spenser, Edmund, 124
   The Faërie Queene, 121
Strachey, Barbara
   Journeys of Frodo, 151
Strindberg, August, 256
style
   modern characteristics of Tolkien's style, 55
sub-creation, 65, 77
Subreal, The, 245
Szondi, Peter, 255, 256, 257, 259
   Theorie des modernen Dramas, 255

T

Thalmann, Marianne, 236, 238, 243
   Das Märchen und die Moderne, 236
The Watchers
   of Cirith Ungol, 164
Theweleit, Klaus, 9, 23, 25, 45
Thomas, Edward, 76
Tieck, Ludwig
   Der Runenberg, 244
time
   and elves, 177
Tol Eressëa, 250, 257
   and England, 257
Tolkien and Modernism, 70

Tolkien, Edith, 47
Tolkien, J.R.R.
   On Fairy-Stories, 68, 120, 205, 258
   The Book of Lost Tales, 244, 249, 250, 251, 253, 257
   The Lost Road, 249, 252
   The Notion Club Papers, 246, 249, 258, 268
Trojan 'myth', 219
Troy
   as model for Gondolin, 218

U

Ungoliant, 158

V

van Beethoven, Ludwig, 56, 62
   as example of late style, 55
Vanderbeke, Dirk, 226
Veugen, Connie, 79
Virgil, 118
   The Aeneid, 115, 116

von Matt, Peter, 36, 47
von Petersdorff, Dirk, 237, 238
Vonnegut, Kurt, 54

W

Wace, 115
Wagner, Richard, 259
West, true or far, 199
Weston, Jessie L.
   From Ritual to Romance, 215
Williams, Charles
   The Greater Trumps, 122
   War In Heaven, 122
World War I, 76, 116, 118, 124, 131, 138, 215

Y

Yeats, W.B., 65, 70
   Sailing to Byzantium, 58, 63
   The Lover, 63
   The Second Coming, 215

Walking Tree Publishers was founded in 1997 as a forum for publication of material (books, videos, CDs, etc.) related to Tolkien and Middle-earth studies. Manuscripts and project proposals can be submitted to the board of editors (please include an SAE):

Walking Tree Publishers
CH-3052 Zollikofen
Switzerland
e-mail: walkingtree@go.to
http://go.to/walkingtree

Cormarë Series

News from the Shire and Beyond. Studies on Tolkien.
    Edited by Peter Buchs and Thomas Honegger. Zurich and Berne 2004. Reprint. 1st edition 1997. (Cormarë Series 1)

Root and Branch. Approaches Towards Understanding Tolkien.
    Edited by Thomas Honegger. Zurich and Berne 2005. Reprint. 1st edition 1999. (Cormarë Series 2)

Richard Sturch. *Four Christian Fantasists. A Study of the Fantastic Writings of George MacDonald, Charles Williams, C. S. Lewis and J.R.R. Tolkien.* Zurich and Berne 2001. (Cormarë Series 3)

Tolkien in Translation.
    Edited by Thomas Honegger. Zurich and Berne 2003. (Cormarë Series 4)

Mark T. Hooker. *Tolkien Through Russian Eyes.* Zurich and Berne 2003. (Cormarë Series 5)

Translating Tolkien: Text and Film.
    Edited by Thomas Honegger. Zurich and Berne 2004. (Cormarë Series 6)

Christopher Garbowski. *Recovery and Transcendence for the Contemporary Mythmaker: The Spiritual Dimension in the Works of J.R.R. Tolkien.*
    Zurich and Berne 2004. Reprint. 1st edition by Marie Curie Sklodowska University Press, Lublin 2000. (Cormarë Series 7)

Reconsidering Tolkien.
    Edited by Thomas Honegger. Zurich and Berne 2005. (Cormarë Series 8)

Tolkien and Modernity 1.
    Edited by Frank Weinreich & Thomas Honegger. Zurich and Berne 2006. (Cormarë Series 9)

www.ingramcontent.com/pod-product-compliance
Lightning Source LLC
Chambersburg PA
CBHW070725160426
43192CB00009B/1321